1985

University of St. Francis
GEN 071.3 C339
Casey
The press in perspective

3 0301 00008216 0

☜ W9-CLF-835

071.3
C339   37995

071.3   37995
C339
Casey,Ralph D.
The Press in Perspective

DATE DUE	BORROWER'S NAME	RECD
MAY 17 '73		451
APR 15 '82		921

LIBRARY
College of St. Francis
JOLIET, ILL.

5, 27

THE PRESS
IN
PERSPECTIVE

Marquis Childs
Thomas L. Stokes
James B. Reston
Reinhold Niebuhr
Elmer Davis
Alan Barth
Eric Sevareid
George V. Ferguson
Henry S. Commager
Herbert L. Block
Doris Fleeson
Gerald W. Johnson
Louis M. Lyons
Joseph W. Alsop, Jr.
Pierre Salinger and James Hagerty
John Fischer

THE PRESS
IN
PERSPECTIVE

edited by
RALPH D. CASEY

LIBRARY
College of St. Francis
JOLIET, ILL.

LOUISIANA STATE UNIVERSITY PRESS · BATON ROUGE

Copyright 1963 by
Louisiana State University Press
Manufactured in the United States of America by
Vail-Ballou Press, Inc., Binghamton, N.Y.
Library of Congress Catalogue Card Number 63-16657
Designed by E. S. Diman

071.3
C339

Contents

v

37995

Introduction

If professional men are to play their part in preserving the freedom and improving the character of American democracy, a continuing assessment of their roles by leaders within their own ranks is a primary obligation of their craft. Every profession finds itself compelled to make continuing adjustments to meet social change.

In their own forums, journalists traditionally subject their endeavors to the scrutiny of their group membership. They feel required, as do those in other callings, to talk among themselves about their institutional performance. But they need to talk oftener to public groups or to assemblies in which craftsmen and members of the public look together at the ways of the press. "Playback" of audiences can be helpful to journalists. Interchanges between speaker and audience can be fruitful, too, in giving laymen a basis for understanding the complexities faced by the communications media.

Through the past sixteen years, both the professional journalists and members of the public talked together about press problems at a forum on the University of Minnesota campus. What was said by experts of the press and by qualified laymen now appears in this volume of collected addresses.

Established through a grant from the Newspaper Guild of the Twin Cities, the forum has brought to the university a succession of distinguished professionals from journalism, as well as speakers from the fields of public affairs and education.

From the beginning, the lecture series won the attention of communications personnel, journalism teachers and students, and interested laymen. Words spoken from the lecture platform, I think it is fair to say, have contributed importantly to serious thinking on the role of the press.

The lectures were inspired by the desire of the Twin Cities guildsmen to pay tribute to members of their organization who had lost their lives in war service. Three guildsmen were casualties: Carroll Bon, Minneapolis *Tribune,* killed at the Anzio beachhead in Italy; Lawrence Cragg, Minneapolis *Star,* lost when his transport was sunk off North Africa; and Riley McKoy, also a *Star* newspaperman, who died after forty-one months of overseas service.

The guild voted an annual appropriation for a memorial. The memorial committeemen at first agreed to provide an annual scholarship at the University of Minnesota School of Journalism; and I, as the journalism school's director, welcomed the suggestion. During our discussions, however, it occurred to me to submit an alternative proposal that might be considered appropriate for memorializing the guild servicemen. Since both the guild and the school of journalism were dedicated to improving ways to prepare young men and women for careers in an exacting profession, why not consider bringing to the campus active journalists in a series of public lectures on problems of the press?

Annual lectures would stimulate a desirable interplay among guildsmen, journalism teachers and students, laymen, and the visiting "pros" of the press. Speakers would be men recognized by their peers as leading thinkers on the social goals of newspapers and other media. Although journalists are hard pressed in their daily endeavors, we believed we might count on their willingness to take time off from their responsibilities to analyze the techniques and obligations of the press in the relative calm of an academic setting.

The guild committee thought over the suggestions and agreed to try the plan.* As a result lectures have been presented annually since 1947 under the joint auspices of the guild and journalism school. A committee from both groups selects the speakers. The director of the school of journalism serves as general chairman.

* The Guild Memorial Committee consisted of the following members: Eugene T. Newhall, chairman, Harold Chucker, Angelo Cohn, and Wendell Weed. William Hendrickson was president of the Twin Cities Newspaper Guild at the time. Special thanks are due the guild committee that cooperated with the Louisiana State University Press in publication of this book.

Once the program was set up, criteria for the nomination of speakers were pretty much taken for granted by the lecture committee. All of us sought outstanding journalists of broad experience who had demonstrated a willingness to bring candor, as well as understanding, to a discussion of the role of the press. Nonjournalists invited to appear were personages possessing an insightful knowledge into the responsible goals and outcome of journalistic practice. In short, the committee wanted men of conviction and independent mind who had risen to high standing in their respective callings, men who had something to say and would say it.

Over the years, the lectureship sponsors found that its nominees, for the most part, came with all the "virtues" we had outlined so ambitiously at the beginning. Early fears that we might find difficulty in persuading our invited guests to grace the platform turned out to be groundless.

Readers of this volume will find few, if any, eulogies so characteristic of the conventional banquet hall and no trifling handbookish accounts of the routine duties of reporters, deskmen, editors, and broadcasters. Fundamentally, lecturers examined the functions that are fulfilled by the press, its obligations, and the part it is playing in modern life.

Speakers stressed, within a social context, the great importance of the press's obligation to present accurate, coherent, and continuous accounts of community and national life. The relation of the press to public affairs was heavily emphasized as the lecture program developed, a recognition by the visiting professionals that the crucial decisions made by society are political decisions. But techniques in gathering, writing, and illuminating events and current trends were not undervalued. An accent on the obligation of the press and its practitioners to live up to a high standard of public service in their professional conduct and action has recurred through the guild addresses.

The man on the street may not conceptualize "obligation" and "responsibility" as the journalist sees them, although the so-called intellectual "elite" will not hesitate to suggest definitions. The average consumer of communicated symbols will be thinking in terms of "editorial policy," "news policy," and "broadcasting policy" in the case of a given newspaper or electronic medium.

Certainly, the upper cultural level of persons in our society asks: Is the editorial policy of many of the mass media socially and politically backward? Does news policy fail to make what seem to be necessary adjustments to satisfy changing reader and viewer needs and desires? Or in another context, does policy change as the professional journalist—the expert technician—thinks it should change? These are matters that concerned guild speakers, as we shall see.

Warren Breed gives us an acceptable definition of newspaper policy.[1] He sees it as "the more or less consistent orientation shown by a paper, not only in its editorials but in its news columns and headlines concerning selected issues and events." He adds that although the owner or representative of ownership has the nominal right to set the paper's policy and to see that staff activities are coordinated so that policy is enforced, "conformity is *not* automatic."

It is not automatic because in today's institutionalized operation, editorial and news workers exert a degree of influence that is, in a very real sense, a significant shared responsibility with top management. Their professional norms, or working principles, are both technical and, to use Breed's terminology, ethical.

Herbert Ellison, one-time editor of the Washington *Post,* explained in 1949 to an Ohio audience that to assume the publisher is responsible for all policy decisions on a newspaper is to fail to envision the number of professionals who combine up and down the institutional ladder, to produce its news-editorial content. In the case of editorial page policy, the publisher makes his contribution, as do all the editorial writers, and suggestions flow into the editorial sanctum from all departments. Policy, of course, is made in the news pages as well, Ellison adds.[2]

Several guild speakers thought predominantly of responsibility at the news level: the power of initiative in putting subjects on the daily news agenda, the power of exclusion of news, and the power of presentation of news tidings.

They revealed professional dissatisfaction with the bonds of old, time-worn news traditions and practices restricting them in giving the best service to the public. They were critical of failures of the press to adjust or adapt its behavior to meet new or changing demands. They stressed the leadership function of the newspaper.

"The ingredient of leadership," observed Dean Fred S. Siebert of Michigan State University in a Don R. Mellett memorial address recently, "is the obligation to expose, to pass judgment, to call for remedies for abuses in the community. This is a newspaper function a newspaper cannot avoid if it is to serve a free society." [3]

In reading this volume from front cover to back, one can see shadowed as on a screen, many significant occurrences and changes in postwar America. The impression gained, I think, is that of viewing a kind of continuum of critical events, loosely linked, it is true, but nonetheless revealed by intermittent lightning flashes in what seems to be an unending political and social storm. The lecturers were not posing as social and political historians, yet they portrayed the press within this turbulent modern-day environment.

The postwar world was taking shape when Marquis Childs, Thomas L. Stokes, Jr., and James B. Reston—the first three lecturers—came to speak under the umbrella of the guild and the school of journalism.

The rift then developing among former war allies; indecision in foreign policy; the "frightening inquisitions" launched by Congressional committees fearful of real or fancied subversive activities at home; the continuation and expansion of federal controls over news sources—these were a few of the tendencies in American and international life speakers took into account.

An underlying thesis seems to me to run through the first three addresses. The press was not truly *communicative* in early postwar years. It put before the reader a confusing welter of facts from the varied life of the nation and the world. Because of faulty news techniques or the lack of editorial will, vital issues were not interrelated and interpreted in understandable form for the reader.

If a great many newspapers were guilty in the late 1940's of attachment to outworn conventions in organizing and presenting the news, their "social lag" in failing to reorient their policies and techniques was clearly demonstrated in the early fifties.

This turbulent period was characterized by attacks on freedom of thought and expression and by the invasion of individual rights. The fires of controversy, fanned by irresponsibles in and out of Congress, created an atmosphere of tension and misunderstanding on the part of the public. A crisis in public confidence developed.

Struggles over the Bill of Rights and related constitutional questions and the demagogic excesses of Senator Joseph R. McCarthy and his followers imposed a heavy responsibility upon the mass media to help right the balance by a wise and careful handling of the news. A sizable segment of the press seemed incapable, however, of adjusting traditional news "folkways" to this grave new situation.

What was required from editors and newsmen was a thorough reexamination of traditional formulae in the handling of the news. Parenthetically, the emotionally charged controversies demanded a searching reorientation of many a bland and debilitated editorial page. Timely and forceful measures were needed to combat the forces of intolerance and ignorance which were threatening to play havoc with traditional American liberties. But editorial page delinquency on the part of many journals is perhaps another story.

On the news side, there was insufficient self-analysis of performance by editors and newsgatherers. Their failure lay in their not fully questioning news techniques and editorial policies or in not readapting them to confront the explosive situation in the national capital and in other communities at home and abroad.

Critics within the press did arise, however, who rebelled against the disheartening and frustrating news conventions that prevented them from telling readers and radio listeners the central truths of what was happening at vital news centers.

Elmer Davis and Eric Sevareid, two former daily newspapermen turned news broadcasters, brilliantly analyzed the problem in their addresses. Both journalists challenged the "straight news" or "literal" kind of reporting that went on, for example, at Congressional hearings, and analyzed the dangers of what Sevareid has termed "the flat, one-dimensional handling of the news." The extra-judicial investigations in Washington were pungently described by Davis as "the new doctrine of Congressional jurisprudence called 'perpetual jeopardy.' "

When he appeared as a guild lecturer, Henry Steele Commager turned the attention of his audience to the far-reaching control of ideas, speech, association, and the press by governmental agencies and Congressional action. Commager's address on the "Leviathan State" and some of its procedures is a veritable *tour de force* in recounting instances of the violation of civil liberties. It might well be required reading for every public official, and if it were possible to influence the vigilantes and the confused "super patriots" in our society, their scanning of Commager's discourse would be socially useful, too.

Commager protested that journalists had failed to foresee the danger to their own calling of highly federalized governmental authority and had neglected to guard adequately against its controls, an observation that may not be accepted by those leaders in the press who have led the fight for "the people's right to know." The sting of Commager's criticism was perhaps softened by his singling out J. Russell Wiggins, the executive editor of the Washington *Post,* as one "who has done more to vindicate freedom of the press than any other journalist."

Implicit in Commager's discourse, it seems to me, is the belief that only as the press aids in helping to preserve all the constitutional guarantees can it really assure itself of remaining free. One of the first institutions to feel the pressure of extremists is the press itself. To report and interpret information and ideas that may be regarded on occasion as "inconvenient" to those at some levels of the social scale, will arouse pressure from dissident groups. Those who feel themselves capable of exerting organized power will seek to muffle or silence the voice of the press.

In a lecture on the press and foreign affairs, George V. Ferguson, a leading Canadian editor, described the "technology" of modern journalism as an influence over the press. His remarks seem relevant to what was said or implied by other speakers—by Davis and Sevareid, for example. Ferguson observed:

> Technology lays every emphasis upon speed and upon the immediate impact of the presentation of facts or opinions upon readers and listeners. When it has achieved this, technology has accomplished its main function. What happened the day before, or what is likely to happen tomorrow takes very much of a back seat. . . . The sense of continuity, of the steady, implacable flow of history from the past into the immediate present is largely forgotten. . . . The result is a kind of breathlessness, a panting sense of excitement, which we build up almost subconsciously because that is the way, and the only way, in which we have been taught to play our roles.

The foregoing, I confess, was something of an aside to Ferguson's major theme. More compelling, I think, was what he said so effectively on the phenomenon of public opinion—the stimulus to public opinion generated by the press. He dwelt importantly as well on the relationship of the fabric of the news to the type of constitutional national state within which it originates.

Both Ferguson and Alan Barth, who was the sixth lecturer in the series, have won wide recognition as editorial analysts of the political and social developments in their respective sovereignties. International affairs has been one of Ferguson's preoccupations. Barth is an expert on party politics, civil liberties, and the press.

Joseph W. Alsop, Jr., and Doris Fleeson observe and report on the Washington scene. Neither hesitates to go after news in state capitols when the developments there seem to require the knowledge and skills of a trained journalist specializing in public affairs. Alsop takes off on journalistic missions abroad when important diplomatic, political, and military events are brewing overseas.

Distinction as a trenchant editorial cartoonist has not prevented Herbert "Herblock" Block from escaping from his drawing board to compose for print his criteria for an independent press.

Only a careful reading of Reinhold Niebuhr's remarks will fully convey his cautions on the reporting of foreign news and his injunction on the moral obligations of the press in all news categories.

In the belief of Louis Lyons, no other institution has been subject to so little professional criticism as the press. Over the years, Lyons has worked for improvement of the standards of journalism. It has seemed to him unfortunate that American newspapermen are not joined in a common bond of professional association, "independent alike of management and union." Lyons, in his address, called upon the schools of journalism to exert a greater influence in helping to set standards for the press.

Gerald W. Johnson's address on "Personality in Journalism," a subtle but rewarding venture into an area not often attempted by those who depict the press, was a sharp departure from the content of the other lectures.

Press secretaries of American presidents occupy sensitive roles in government. Laymen are not usually aware of the extent of their influence in assisting the press corps to obtain news from the White House. What is the extent of responsibility in serving as a news channel from the office of the nation's chief magistrate? What additional function does he have, if any, as a public relations counselor throughout the government in Washington? The lecture committee invited Pierre Salinger and James Hagerty to throw light on these questions.

John Fischer who was the first guild speaker from the magazine field drew parallels and contrasts between the daily newspaper and periodicals.

Recurring throughout the addresses are two themes: an insistence that the press give greater attention to the interpretation and meaning of the news, and that in a more general sense it constantly seek to upgrade its performance as a trustee of the public interest.

The problem of press responsibility is very much in the air.[4] Among sections of the public the feeling prevails that many newspapers have fallen behind in reorienting editorial outlooks in keeping with the times and have failed to adapt pragmatic techniques in the newsroom to changing needs and new demands of readers.

Allan Nevins, a distinguished historian and former newspaperman, in a public address at the University of California, Berkeley, based a significant comment on the fact that while the number of press organs has greatly diminished in recent years, the population has greatly increased. The "tragedy of the situation," to use his words, lies in this: ". . . the variety and individuality of press service and press opinion have fallen at the very time that the intellectual and cultural heterogeneity of the American people has risen; so that the portion of the population which stands fairly well above the line of low average taste and capacity is left without facilities which it needs."

"It is not the suppression of competition *per se,* as Oswald Garrison Villard used to allege," Nevins continued. "It is the effect of this suppression in destroying the differentiation between reading publics of high and low standards, and in the thrusting many newspapers to a choice of low-standard clientele, leaving the better readers stranded."

Other critics who are readers of so-called monopoly newspapers argue that what they miss is a clash of competitive editorial viewpoints in their communities. Opposing community viewpoints, they say, do not get adequate representation in one-publisher situations.

Whatever may be the reasons for complaints, there is no dearth of suggestions looking toward improvement in the quality and performance of the press.

Some members of the laity, for example, declare their support for the creation of a press council or court of honor fashioned after the agencies operating in a few democratic countries abroad. Those who sponsor the proposal have confidence that once in operation, council reports, admonishing those who offend a code of journalistic practice, would have a salutary effect in raising standards of communications behavior.

Without going into the merit of such organizations, I think it is safe to say that our own journalists, by and large, see no necessity of a press council or any other similar body. Certainly, were a council given power to exert sanctions against journalists, publishers, editors, and broadcast station owners would stoutly resist them. Moreover, there is every reason to believe that the public could not be persuaded to support any enforcement procedure.

Those spokesmen for the press who in the 1940's were severely critical of the report of the Commission on Freedom of the Press, a document that contained no suggestion of the use of sanctions, have long since recovered from their initial shell shock. Today's editors, many of them, find recommendations of which they approve.

But journalists are skeptical of proposals for another commission. They see no necessity for such an agency; they feel any external, independent agency, empowered to review or criticize the press, is likely to misunderstand the terms under which the newspaper operates.

An editor friend of mine once remarked: "There is a sense in which the first responsibility of the press is to be read. Public taste and the level of public education and interest determine what will or will not be read

—within limits. The operative phrase here, from the point of view of press responsibility is the last: 'within limits.' "

In essence, the foregoing comment makes the valid point that social factors condition the press. In a pluralistic society, the press is subject to pressures, economic, political, racial, and so on. But intellectual, moral, and ideological concepts that govern any individual communications medium cannot be ruled out as tests of its behavior.

The individual publisher, editor, and newsman in his daily performance does have a choice of options and alternatives, within limiting social pressures, which he accepts or rejects, in determining his policy.

What then are the remedies for shortcomings of the press? What are the measures that will improve its performance and upgrade its standards?

The first response among leaders in journalism is summed up in the belief that there presently exists a sufficient agitation within the profession to encourage self-analysis, self-criticism, and self-improvement to meet their obligation to society.

Erwin D. Canham, editor of the *Christian Science Monitor,* in addressing an audience from the American Society of Newspaper Editors and the International Press Institute a few years ago, said this:

> The American press is very fully organized, at many levels. These organizations have a continuous and often profound bearing on the better performance of the American press. Their efforts constitute self-control in the very real sense of self-improvement. Indeed, they are the very essence of self-control in terms of evoking a very deep, earnest, and fundamental acceptance of professional responsibility. And they often bring to bear the most powerful of disciplinary influences, which is the sense of pride in professional achievement, and shame at doing less well than we can.[5]

No doubt there is a good deal of support for Canham's concept—the encouraging of a better performance of the American press through organized groups of journalists. But if we accept the view of a former president of the American Society of Newspaper Editors, "no one can speak for the American press except individuals speaking individually. . . . Our members are united on only one object: their dedication in whatever their consciences dictate." [6] That would seem to negate expressions by organized societies of professionals on matters of press performance. We know that professional newsmen's groups shy away from condemnation of the errant journalistic practice of an individual member. We have a feeling journalists would find disenchanting the creation of a press council, citizens' council, or board of review.

In the end, the influence that public opinion brings to bear on the mass media, and the professional standards those in the craft evolve would appear to be the prevailing determinants that will continue to govern press performance. Professional "standards" would seem to imply a continuing adaptation of the press to the current public needs.

But there is no denying that many segments of the press are encrusted with deeply rooted traditions and conventions that no longer serve a viable journalism. The creative journalist who demands necessary innovations and variations in the press, and a reanimation of its values within a democracy, needs to play a more positive role in his own craft; that is to say, if the present rigidity and complacency too prevalent within journalism are to make way for an advance along the frontier of editorial practice.

RALPH D. CASEY

THE PRESS
IN
PERSPECTIVE

Which Direction

for America?

The Mississippi Valley is in more ways than one the center of the nation. It is the great center of our productivity.* Not so many years ago this region was the source of one of our greatest forms of natural wealth. Vast stands of timber covered millions of acres. The tradition of the time was to consider these stands of timber inexhaustible. But in less than a century—actually in fifty years—this supposedly inexhaustible source of wealth disappeared. One of our greatest shortages today is lumber to build houses for millions who have never known a proper home.

So rapid and so complete has been our exploitation of the great natural wealth of this country that it is difficult to realize that we did have a choice more than a hundred years ago. Nothing like it had ever happened before in history—no such movement of peoples and no such development of the resources of a vast continent.

There was a choice more than a century ago. Or, rather, there seemed to be a choice. It coincided with the beginning of the administration of one of the most remarkable men who have been presidents of the United States. That was John Quincy Adams, the sixth president, who was inaugurated in 1825. The son of the second president, he was a member

---

* This lecture was delivered May 23, 1947.

of one of the great families that have come up in our political life, a family of great individualists.

Old John Quincy Adams was an intellectual and a moralist, if you will. He owed a great deal to his New England heritage. On taking office as president, he was intensely aware of the great expanse of natural wealth in the as yet undeveloped continent. In the White House he sat down to write a memorandum, very careful and scientific and thorough, on how our natural resources should be developed. This neglected document is one of the most remarkable in our political history.

In the belief of John Quincy Adams, this development should be carried out under the supervision of the federal government. He believed, in fact, that the federal government should participate directly in the exploitation of our resources as an active working partner. But while John Quincy Adams was a thinker and in a sense a scientist, he was not, in the ordinary use of the word, a politician. He had very little understanding of the temper of the country. Consequently, he was shocked and disillusioned when the recommendations contained in his memorandum were ignored by the Congress and the people.

His successor was a man of entirely different temperament. Andrew Jackson was an astute politician who understood the tremendous forces that were even then beginning to move out into the country. The great westward movement was under way, and the American people were not to be deterred by any scientific or intellectual prescriptions. They believed that the inexhaustible natural wealth of the continent was their heritage and their right, and they set out to exploit it with all the vigor and the confidence of a pioneering people. That was the decision. It is doubtful that in actuality there was a choice.

Through all its history the Adams family has produced individualists who were not afraid to speak what they believed to be the truth. John Quincy's son was Charles Francis Adams, one of the greatest American diplomats, who was minister to England during the difficult and trying years of the Civil War. Charles Francis' sons were two of America's great philosophers and historians. Henry Adams, the esthete, philosopher, and historian, is well known. His brother, Brooks Adams, is less well known. Brooks Adams was one of those prophets not without honor save in his own land.

In his historical writing, Brooks Adams showed how profoundly he was aware of the choice that his grandfather believed lay before the people of this country in 1825. But Brooks Adams looked ahead too. He understood the choice that we would face in our time. Brooks Adams published in 1900 a very remarkable book which almost no one read and almost no one understood. It was called *America's Economic Supremacy*.[1]

Brooks Adams had developed earlier the theory that the trade of the world moved inevitably from East to West, with the dominant center of trade determined by this movement in accord with the speed of technological change. Thus the focus of world trade moved from the ancient centers of the East to Constantinople, and thence to Venice, Amsterdam, and finally to London. Brooks Adams foresaw in searching detail the decay of Great Britain, the culmination of which we are witnessing in our time. He understood that our own country, the United States, would be the greatest center of economic and technological power in the world's history. In *America's Economic Supremacy* he foresaw the time when there would be only two great powers in the world, Russia and the United States.

In short, he foresaw the moment of historical crisis in which we are now living. I am sure that it seems to many of you, and particularly to those of you who are still young, that we have lived constantly in a time of turmoil and crisis. But I believe that we are now approaching what will be an even greater test of the system under which we live: a test that will determine for a very long time the future of that system.

It is particularly the duty of those of us who are newspapermen to try to examine the nature of the test that lies before us. It is our special obligation to the generation that went out into the far corners of the earth to fight the war that ended two years ago. It is our special obligation to those who did not come back. It is, above all, our obligation to those whom we honor here—to Carroll Bon, Lawrence Cragg, and Riley McKoy. It is our particular obligation to them because they gave their lives in the belief that truth would survive in this world.

There are those who look with dark pessimism at our future. They believe that we have passed the zenith. They believe that we are moving down the course to slow decay. Sometimes this has been expressed as the poet Robinson Jeffers expressed it with a kind of majesty in his poem "Shine Perishing Republic." He said:

While this America settles in the mould of its vulgarity, heavily thickening to empire,
And protest, only a bubble in the molten mass, pops and sighs out, and the mass hardens.[2]

There are those of course who would like to believe that protest is only a bubble, as intangible and inconsequential as the poet would have us believe. But it is our function to protest, to try to examine the facts of our time as we see them.

In moments of pride we say that our press is the greatest in the world. By many standards that is true today. Certainly it is true by the standard of technical proficiency. It is true in the absence of restrictions on the freedom of expression, although it is well to remember that this is a negative criterion.

But even as we make our boast, we must be conscious of the inadequacies of our channels of information, the press and the radio. We must realize that mass circulation is too often dependent on shock and sensation, with the important elements of the news reduced to this same formula or treated as merely incidental to entertainment and diversion. We are aware of the way in which the means of mass expression have been increasingly concentrated and we know that this inevitably makes for an increasingly narrow range of expression and opinion. We must be aware of the timidity of opinion and the unrelenting pressures for conformity.

Concentration of control, which finds expression in organized management and in organized labor, contributes to this conformity. It tends to stifle opportunity and therefore also to stifle the kind of creative imagination that we need above all else at this moment. We need a creative imagination and the free expression of opinion if we are to understand the meaning of the recent changes that have taken place in our world. Without these qualities we shall fail to comprehend that we do have a choice if we will only have the courage to understand what that choice is.

The nature of the crisis that we face here in this country is twofold. First of all, it is concerned with the concentration of economic control that has been enormously accelerated by two wars and particularly by World War II. Second, it is concerned with the fact that at the same time the powers of government are those devised for a community of planters and farmers who lived on a fringe of the continent on the eastern seaboard. In the headlong rush of developing the natural wealth of this continent, we have scarcely stopped to consider the instrument of government. We have almost wholly ignored the tremendous technological changes that have utterly altered the position of man on this planet.

When the founding fathers met at Philadelphia to draft the charter of our government, the instruments of power available to mankind were not essentially different from those available to human beings at the time of Alexander the Great. They were the human back, the wheel, the horse, and a low explosive.

I flew out to Minneapolis in a DC-6 with four motors, each of them generating more than 3,000 horsepower. We flew from Washington to Chicago in three hours. By next year new stratocruisers will be in service on the European routes that will make London eleven to twelve hours away from New York. This is one obvious measure of the contraction of our planet.

Such revolutionary technological changes always make for centralization of power. They make for greater and greater concentration of economic power. There can be no doubt that this concentration has been enormously accelerated in recent years. A study just completed by the Federal Trade Commission shows that in the past five years (1942–47), 1,800 companies have been merged with larger companies, and most of these mergers have taken place in the past two or three years. The important point is that these 1,800 companies represent 5 per cent of the total value of all manufacturing corporations.

In the late 1930's the Temporary National Economic Committee named by Congress did an exhaustive study, now contained in many volumes,[3] showing how swiftly the process of concentration occurred after 1900. In 275 categories of manufactures the Census of Manufacturers for 1925 showed there were 54 in which the four largest firms produced more than two-thirds, by value, of the total supply. The massive volumes of the TNEC report show in innumerable ways how this concentration has taken place.

The leading figure in directing the TNEC study was Senator Joseph C. O'Mahoney, of Wyoming, one of the ablest members in Congress today. In speech after speech on the floor of the Senate and before audiences all over the country, Senator O'Mahoney has been trying to warn his fellow-countrymen. He believes that unless the present trend is checked we shall come inevitably to the end of the free enterprise system. This will come about not because any group of individuals wills it but because of the working of these great economic forces which seem to move quite beyond our control.

Senator O'Mahoney has put together some extremely interesting figures. He shows that a dozen of our giant corporations have greater revenues and greater economic power than all but a few of our states. He speaks of these giant corporations as "private socialism." Being an astute politician, he knows that private socialism will not very long remain private socialism under our democracy. It will become public socialism, or perhaps, national socialism.

We saw how this happened in Italy and in Germany. We saw the rise of the corporate state with a business monopoly, and a labor monopoly, both completely under the domination of a dictatorial state. We know from our own experience the evils of monopoly and concentration. By eliminating competition we eliminate opportunity, enterprise, and imagination. We saw in 1933 how government, faced with a fearful economic crisis, resorted to something very like the corporate state. Fortunately it was rejected by both the courts and the people.

The Senate has been debating ways of ending what they are fond of calling a "labor monopoly." We know in our own profession that there are hazards in a labor monopoly. It attempts to impose arbitrary standards that may work grave hardships in individual instances since they may fit one community while they do not fit another community. But if there is a labor monopoly, it has come into being in response to monopoly, or near monopoly, in industry.

On the economic side, the effect of monopoly is all too plain. We hear a great deal in these times about high prices. Prices have become a political issue. We are told that, if they do not go down, we shall have not a "corrective recession" but perhaps a major depression. When Associate Justice Robert Jackson was in the Department of Justice, he made a very penetrating study of monopoly and prices; and he had this to say:

> If rigid prices meant stability of employment in industry, we would find price control more tolerable. But generally the more rigid and inflexible the price of a product during the depression, the more calamitous was the decline in its labor payroll. . . . Payrolls for the iron and steel industries declined about 75 per cent, while the wholesale price of ingots declined only 16 per cent. The depression prices of cast iron pipe declined 7 per cent and the payrolls declined 74 per cent. While agricultural implements declined 14 per cent in price, the industry payrolls took a price decline of 83 per cent. Virgin aluminum went down 21 per cent in price, and payrolls of aluminum manufacturers declined about 70 per cent. Cement declined 13 per cent, and its payrolls 72 per cent.

This was in sharp contrast with industries in which competition was still an important factor. Senator O'Mahoney has proposed a cure. He proposes federal incorporation for our large corporations. This, he argues, would make them responsible to government. He argues that their power today transcends state boundaries and state authority and that is fairly obvious to anyone who looks at the facts.

Whether this is a cure no one can say. But it is certain that we must try to find a cure. The rapid drift into private socialism and thence into public socialism will bring an end to the values which we prize most highly in our America.

This, then, is one phase of the nature of the crisis that is just ahead of us.

The second phase is directly related to it. It poses, above all, the question of whether in our age of enormously centralized power we can govern under our system of checks and balances. That system, as has been well said, tends to be all checks and no balances.

It was intended to be a government of extremely limited powers. It has been on the whole a government that has confirmed economic decisions which were taken by the men who controlled and directed our economic life. This may have been of small moment when we were an insular power shielded by the supremacy of Great Britain in Europe. Whether we now have the capacity to reach sure and fairly rapid decisions is a question that vitally affects not alone 135 million Americans. Today it affects every human being on this globe.

Not only is ours a government of limited powers. On the average of one out of every three years, those powers are divided between the opposing parties. That is the position in which we find ourselves at this moment. In the past it has tended to make for stalemate, and the present period is scarcely an exception.

This is not the fault of any particular party. It is almost inevitable in the very nature of our system. In 1931 the Democrats gained control of the House of Representatives. They elected John Nance Garner Speaker of the House. From that point on, their objective was to worry and harass the President in the White House. Poor Mr. Hoover has never recovered from that ordeal. I have always believed that if he had had the most perfect program in the world for checking the depression, it would have had no chance of adoption by Congress. The Democrats in control of one of the branches of Congress were looking to the election of 1932. They would not confirm the nomination of officers for the executive branch of the government.

In the same way the Republicans are looking to the election of 1948. It happens that this time the crisis is not a domestic one. It is a world crisis. But it is too much to expect that human nature will be altered overnight. It is too much to expect that the leaders of the party rising to power should suddenly behave like nonpolitical angels. They have been out of power for more than fourteen years. Their desire to return to power is natural and proper.

We have heard a great deal of brave talk about a bipartisan foreign policy. We have such a policy only in a limited sense. Mr. Truman obtained approval of the Greek-Turkish aid program;[4] but as former Governor Harold Stassen pointed out, it is largely a negative program. If the Soviet Union did not exist we should have to invent it in order to have a foreign policy at all. That is a measure of the negativism of our policy.

What we need above all is a positive and constructive foreign policy —a policy prepared to utilize America's great economic supremacy, to strengthen the forces of the democratic middle, and to bring order and stability to a world in perilous disequilibrium.

We shall not, it seems to me, have a government capable of making swift and effective decisions until we face up to the necessity of making some changes in the great charter of our government. It was Brooks Adams, the philosopher and historian, who foresaw years ago the tragic limitations of what he called our antiquated government.

The framers of our great charter believed that we should frequently want to amend it. If you read the writings of Thomas Jefferson, you realize that he did not regard their handiwork as an immutable document that was never to be altered.

First of all, it seems to me, we must change our laws or amend our Constitution in such a way that mid-term elections will be possible. They should be possible in order to correct the kind of double-jointed stalemate we now have in Washington. Further than this, we should begin to examine the basic structure of our government in relation to the parliamentary form which almost every other democracy in the world has today. Even when the two chief powers of the government are held by the same party it is difficult enough to execute important decisions. But when we have the kind of division that exists today, Congress scarcely speaks to the White House. You have an unending rivalry and jockeying for power that affects all the business of government, big and little.

Because they have no fixed constitution, the British can alter their government by an act of Parliament. Because British cabinet members are also elected members of Parliament, they can go to the floor of the House of Commons and answer the Opposition. It has been said that the presidential press conference is a substitute for the question hour in the House of Commons. This analogy seems to me very farfetched. The president at a press conference has all the advantage. The questioner cannot drive home a question.

I do not say that we should adopt the parliamentary system. But I do say that we must consider the structural weaknesses inherent in our form of government. I say that we must quickly begin to consider the direction in which we are moving.

We must decide whether we have the capacity to make our government responsive and responsible. It is neither responsive nor responsible today. We shall soon determine, I believe, whether we have something of the political courage and the political initiative of the men who framed our government; or we shall, in the words of Robinson Jeffers, "thicken to imperialism." And the time left to us to make a decision is very short.

It is difficult to be optimistic at this moment. We have just come out of a war that has meant a fearful toll in men and resources. We are tired. We are distracted. We are confused. But I come back to the particular obligation of those of us who are concerned with information and opinion. It seems to me that it is our special duty today to report on two attitudes of mind destructive to everything we value as Americans. Perhaps political labels could be applied to these attitudes, but it sometimes seems to me that our political labels have worn dangerously thin so that they are not so much used as constantly misused.

The first attitude of mind is that of the individual who believes that nothing good can happen in the present. He or she believes that change is inherently bad. He believes that everything good happened in the past, and apparently in the remote past. Of course we know that this attitude must mean death. For change is the very nature of a living organism. Perhaps the political counter to describe this attitude is fascism.

Our obligation in this respect is not merely to examine and expose this attitude. That is perhaps the smallest part of our responsibility. We have an obligation, constant and ever more pressing, to show that progressive change is in the great American tradition. It is a vital part of what is truest and strongest in our past from our own revolution down through the bold thinkers of the flowering of New England, through Whitman, through such voices of protest as Thorstein Veblen, through such fiery challengers as old Bob La Follette and the other dissenters who have come up in the West. These men were not parroting any European philosophy. They were speaking out of the challenge of America, a challenge that echoed across the world.

The second attitude is that of the individual who believes that all change must be made to conform to an intellectual pattern. He would superimpose an intellectual matrix on all of human life. He would crush this pattern down on all human beings, regardless of what cruelties it might work. We have seen the outcome of this effort in two great explosions. We saw in the French Revolution how those who would compress human life in an arbitrary pattern made the streets of Paris run with blood.

Again in the Russian Revolution we saw the fearful cost of an effort to superimpose an arbitrary political pattern, and that cost is still to be paid. We know, of course, that any effort to fit human life within the narrow frame of an intellectual concept must inevitably fail, because the stuff of human life is too diverse, too full of ferment. Perhaps the political counter for this attitude of mind is communism. But here again the political counter has worn very thin, and we find the word "communist" applied to almost anyone with whom the speaker happens at the moment to disagree.

And here again the negative side of our obligation—to examine and reveal—is the minor one. Our real obligation is to show that there is a pattern of progress and change within our democracy. It is one of the great sources of strength of our way of life and we must never be allowed to forget it.

I should doubtlessly have included a third attitude of mind. For perhaps apathy and indifference are the greatest enemies of political change in this country. We are not by nature political. We have not had to be. When I was in Sweden in 1943, I heard something that reminded me somewhat of our own political attitudes. Sweden was neutral. Swedish businessmen and Swedish diplomats moved freely between Stockholm and Berlin. That was in May of 1943, when ultimate defeat had become evident to informed Germans. I asked a Swedish diplomat what the attitude of informed Germans was. He told me that they were in a state bordering on despair. They said they had never thought anything of Hitler; they had regarded him as a kind of necessary evil. They had in any event looked down on all politicians and politics. But now they realized the terrible error of their ways. Now they saw that Hitler was not their creature, but that they were his captives sinking down to a common doom.

I could not help but think of similar expressions I had heard from Americans. Too often we have believed that politics could be left to the professionals. Too often we have regarded government either as a sinecure for the incompetent, or as a kind of decoration that we could take or leave as we chose.

The choice seems to me clear. I believe if we are able to present that choice in terms of America's great past, we need not fear what the answer will be. That puts on all of us a very heavy responsibility, a responsibility which we are only partially meeting. The technological means of communication in our time have been fabulously expanded. It is our supreme duty to see that these great new instruments of communication are used increasingly to bring a sense of the imminent urgency of the decision which lies before us.

THOMAS L. STOKES, JR.

Current Challenges

to Our Free Press

Those men, for whom these lectures are a memorial, gave their lives in a war which was fought, we are still sure, despite all the contradictions of today, to save the free human spirit.* That was the ideal for which they died, and for which so many like them died. We must cling to that. To preserve that ideal is the aim of every newspaperman in his daily work. It makes this calling of ours a continually inspiring one, even though we often disavow the fact with affected cynicism.

The newspaper never has had a larger field of potential service than today. The challenge is great. There has not been in our era a period when it was more difficult to pick your way about. It is, indeed, like being in one of those wrecked cities of Europe, its debris piled high where, in the comfortable days of peace, one could find his way in the dark. The path of the newspaperman is cluttered with obstacles, some of them vague and indefinable, like ominous shadows among the ruins, created out of the emotions and tensions of these days, mental and spiritual confusions out of which there seems no plainly marked path.

The war still hangs over us, like a shaky and rotting balcony. How it might help all of us if those in our profession who died might return and

---

* This lecture was delivered May 21, 1948.

take a look at the scene today and counsel us, point out what is wrong here and what is wrong there!

But the dead speak only to the dead. And the living must try to understand and live with each other. All we can offer one another is our own experience, what we have seen and felt. So, imposing that limitation upon myself, and with no special qualification other than that I have worked for newspapers for over a quarter of a century and in that time have acquired the brashness that is supposed—and usually correctly—to be the standard equipment of the reporter, I will talk for a few minutes about how things look from where I sit and about how they are related to newspapers and newspapermen. I will try to be tolerant, and I will try to be fair, although these qualities are hard to come by these days.

I find it necessary to make certain apologies in assuming the critical role which is natural to a newspaperman. That this is so is itself a sign of the trying times in which we live, and in which we seem to live especially in Washington. Out here there seems to be much more friendliness, much cleaner air, and so much more room, and that is hopeful. We live in Washington, figuratively, under the shadow of the FBI, the Un-American Activities Committee and loyalty orders and loyalty boards—a fetid atmosphere, although if some people there would stir themselves out of their committee room storm cellars they might see the Washington Monument and the fine, clear brow of Jefferson and the compassionate face of Lincoln. But what those men had to tell us is drowned out today by the noisy yappings of small men. These are very close. They hedge you in. And I can assure you they look no nicer closer up than they do far away. They create a condition in which it is not very pleasant to live and work, especially at this work in which so many here in this audience are engaged or are to become engaged. It does not seem truly an American atmosphere.

All of this prompts a reference to a personal experience. I have reported for many years on politics and the influences that shape it. That has been much easier in the past than it is today. You are aware of vague pressures against too frank exposition of economic matters and powerful interests that are at work in them. That is disturbing.

But what has disturbed me most recently was one day when I sat down to write about the Un-American Activities Committee Hollywood investigation,[1] after watching that frightening inquisition perhaps too long, and suddenly found myself wondering whether I should say certain things that I had it in my mind and heart to say.

That really scared me. What, I suddenly asked myself, are we coming to in this country? I went ahead and said them. I had to prove something to myself.

That is the experience. It is not much—and yet to me it is a great deal. Perhaps I am supersensitive. But it is a harrowing thing to realize that somebody is trying to invade the secret places of your mind, to ransack the temple of the intellect and the spirit. To me that has always been a sacred and private domain, and it has been considered so in our country. That is why that investigation into the private thinking of writers was to me such a terrifying spectacle. I was never able to understand why the newspapers of the country did not rise up en masse to denounce the whole episode to high heaven. For it came very close to the rights we cherish so in our newspapers. It may come closer yet unless we are watchful.

I did not come here to talk about the Un-American Activities Committee and got derailed longer than I intended. But it is the symbol of some things I do want to talk about. The fact that Washington now has provided such a favorable atmosphere for it tells a good deal about our capital city and, presumably, about our country. For the committee represents a concentration of the pressures that are at work today— pressures exercised also upon other committees of Congress, upon Congress itself, and through them, upon what the political scientists call the body politic. Newspapers also feel them. It is those pressures about which I want to talk tonight.

I think it only fair, so that we may understand each other, that I make some other explanations about personal experience. This will permit whatever discount seems necessary to environment and prejudice.

I got bit by a pressure bug early in my newspaper days. It was only a little pressure bug, nothing that would affect the fate of the nation or even the fate of that community, but the fact that I still remember it indicates, I suppose, that it impressed me very much. I was working on a small daily in the South. There were two of us who got out the paper. There was the managing editor who generally directed things, including the staff, which I was. I was a combination of city editor, sports editor, and chief reporter, and I also took want ads across the front counter and listened sympathetically to Mrs. Jones's complaint that the paper had not come.

One day the managing editor gave me a tip about one of our leading citizens who was also city solicitor and connected very prominently socially. His mother was quite a somebody in both the Daughters of the American Revolution and the United Daughters of the Confederacy. The story was that the city solicitor had run into a bridge about four miles from town the night before and wrecked his automobile. That would not have been much of a story. But he was drunk and the back of his car was loaded with whisky and prohibition then was the law of the land.

Some of you older people here can recall that and what we thought in those days of a prosecutor who was violating the law, himself. I went to see the local federal commissioner. I can still see the sly smile on his face when I told him what I wanted. He said he would give me the story, but it would never get printed in the paper. I told him I would like the facts and rather resented the suggestion that the story would be suppressed. He gave me all the facts and they bore out the tip in every particular.

I went back to the office and was about half-finished with the story when the telephone rang on the front counter. The business manager was wanted. He went over and listened a few minutes. Then he came over to me. He asked me what I was writing. I told him.

"Well," he drawled, "I don't think we'd better print that."

I protested, but we did not print it. And that day I learned something. I was very young.

A little later I learned more. Not so long afterward I went to Washington and a couple of years after that I was covering the Senate Teapot Dome and Justice Department investigations which exposed that shameful episode that came to be called "the scandals of the Harding administration." It was the so-called era of normalcy, but that was hardly normal. I saw all that as an impressionable young man. I saw also during those years how big special interests moved into Washington and literally took over the government. While the plunderers exposed by the two investigations stole outright and brazenly, the others got theirs in a more refined way through tariff and tax favors and by grace of officials who did not inquire too closely, as they were supposed to do under the law, into the trusts and combinations that were squeezing the public in one way and another.

That experience left a scar, too, at an early age, for whatever discount should be taken. The other night a friend and I were discussing a member of Congress from his native state, trying to ascertain why he was so conservative. He ventured an explanation that seemed to make a good deal of sense: that, as a young man, this member had lived through a very radical administration of affairs in his state, a very left-wing regime that also was corrupt and resorted to violence. He had reacted to that.

So perhaps with me who watched at close hand, day after day, the unfolding of a sordid era, one of the most sordid in our whole history, comparable perhaps only with the Grant administration. A conservative Republican administration was in power. The experience undoubtedly marked me. I do not apologize. I only give you the facts for your judgment.

And a final explanation which is hardly necessary, for it is plain with every word I utter. I was born a Southern Democrat, and there are nothing but Democrats all the way back in my family, not even a Whig, of which there were quite a number down South at one time. The fact that I was a natural-born Southern Democrat and have lived now so long away from my native habitat may account for something else, a sort of perversity that reacts in a resistance to some of the professional Southern Democrats we have in Congress of a certain flamboyancy and noisiness. They do not look so charming and guileless as they may have seemed when I was younger and lived among the reliques and followed the customs that they glorify often to excess to cover up certain delinquencies in that land below the Mason and Dixon Line, which is in so many ways so fair.

But enough of explanations. We all have our limitations and our preconceived notions and our prejudices against which we must constantly fight. Today they seem exaggerated in all of us everywhere, all over the world. That makes the job of all of us harder today, and particularly the job of the newspaperman.

History's greatest war has been over nearly three years now. Yet we still live under an armed truce in a disordered world. The world's two greatest powers, once allies, seem able to find new enemies in each other. There is no peace and therefore no stability, for peace is necessary to stability. There is another sort of war in the world. It is a war raging in our minds and spirits, all over the world, and it confounds us, makes us fearful, restless, inclined to believe the worst of each other and suspicious not only of people in other lands but suspicious even of our neighbors here at home. We even have to be careful with whom we associate, or we may be called to account.

How this sort of spirit manifests itself is evident today in what has been done by the Un-American Activities Committee to a distinguished scientist, Dr. Edward U. Condon, director of the Bureau of Standards. [2] It is manifest likewise in what was done a year ago to David Lilienthal, who was persecuted shamelessly for no reason whatever except that he had offended an aged Senator because he had refused to play politics with TVA. [3] He was opposed by some other Senators because he had been identified with the Roosevelt administration and was therefore a New Dealer, and he was anathema to great private interests, including utilities, because of his success in administering a great public power project. Some among them did not want to see him in charge of development of the amazing new form of energy that we found when we made the atom bomb because he had demonstrated that he believed in utilization of our resources in the interest of the public rather than selfish private interests. Again Lilienthal is a target, as you can see from your newspapers, and the Republican leadership in Congress has worked out a compromise for a two-year term for all members of the Atomic Energy Commission to prevent him from taking the five-year tour of duty that President Truman designated for him. This is symptomatic of the spirit abroad in Washington. There is no question of David Lilienthal's fitness and ability. That is proved. His management of the Atomic Energy Commission won wide commendation.

Dr. Condon and David Lilienthal are prominent men and you hear about them. But there are many lesser figures in government about whom you do not hear who have been hounded and persecuted. Their cases are never brought into the light. It is only possible to hear about them when you live and work in Washington. They are minor figures, but they are human beings.

The war that goes on today is a war of ideas, of philosophies. It is, broadly, a war between Capitalistic Democracy and variations of that to Democratic Socialism, on the one hand, and on the other, Communism of the Russian totalitarian variety. Since it is a conflict of ideas, it has to do with men's minds, and no man can ever know what is in another's mind. Therefore he can believe all sorts of things are there. Anxious times such as those in which we now live breed tension. So people begin to worry about what other men believe. There are all sorts of shadings and degrees in the rules which one man or another would have society impose on itself, a fact which leaves room for all kinds of doubts of the intentions of those who have to do with the regulation of society or seek to have something to do with it. The temptation in the stress of the confusion of today is to see ideas in terms of black and white. This, of course, is never possible. But it is an easy refuge to which so many try to escape. There is, indeed, no kindly climate today for fluidity of ideas, for readjustments, and for men who think of society as being in a state of continual change to adapt itself.

This makes it hard for newspapers also, for newspapers are human institutions, run by human beings and read by human beings. They have a sense of social responsibility. Therefore they must be careful of that responsibility. In times like these some incline to become cautious, nervous, and timid in the face of passions and prejudices that are stirred up by a war of ideas, and some tend to become blunt and cocksure often on the basis of prejudice or too little evidence, when there is nothing certain or positive, except the one fact that the world is in the process of change (or revolution, if you would like to call it boldly by its real name).

It is made even more complex for newspapers, as for other institutions, because we have just come freshly from a war fought over an idea. The idea against which we fought demanded complete allegiance of mind, body, and soul to the state and such a system proceeds from one cruelty to another to impose its authority, for men will not long submit supinely to such a system, as history has demonstrated. From that war we got certain tags and a certain procedure. Because we are in another war of ideas, these tags have been taken over conveniently into this war, and we assume the same chain of procedures, often, I think, without stopping to analyze whether they are always applicable. Communism is said to be the same as Fascism. I will not pretend to debate that, and there are similarities in methods and end results, but there also are differences. Perhaps the most unfortunate carry-over of a tag is "appeasement" or, as it is more dramatically put "Munich," since that raises up a certain picture of certain men in a certain set of circumstances that we have come to deplore.

So today when it is suggested that it might be possible, if another effort were made, to work out an adjustment with Russia, there arises the cry of "appeasement" or "another Munich." So, recently, we found our government becoming very cautious and resorting to diplomatic protocol and doubling back into its shell, like a frightened turtle, when Russia offered the first real opening since what we call the "cold war" began. I cite that merely as an illustration.

Another difficulty in a war of ideas is that nobody agrees exactly what democracy is. We all have our opinions and there is a broad general agreement, else we could not have preserved ours for so long. But there are variations so that what one man defines as democracy is different from the definition of another. That is our greatest strength ordinarily, but in times such as these it is likely to be our greatest weakness.

In such times anyone who does not conform to the norm may become, figuratively, an outlaw. The term is not used in its literal sense. The norm is fixed by the idea prevalent in society at the time. Just now in our country the norm seems to be a cautious sort of conservatism that bridles at change and would like to reverse some of the changes we have established already by law. In government it is fixed for us in Congress which has become the most powerful branch in one of those periodic shifts through which our government process goes. So we have our vigilantes of the existing order.

The bellwether is the House Un-American Activities Committee. It is, in many respects, a vigilante operation and, like all vigilantism, rationalizes itself from one step to another until it assumes the arrogance of an inquisition, confident of its rightness, its righteousness, and its power. It was created to investigate and expose subversion of both left and right. But it has gone far beyond that. It has now become the avenging posse of reaction. This is exemplified in its latest adventure in the Mundt bill [4] which, luckily, has become the subject of a great national debate. It is apparent that under its terms persons who are not Communists at all could be hounded down and stood up for public display in the pillory because of personal beliefs.

There are other manifestations which are signs of the times, and created by pressures.

There was President Truman's loyalty order.[5] It was his concession to the vigilante movement which, as demonstrated by the 1946 elections, was becoming effective politically. He sought to keep it within bounds, tried to substitute a legalized police force for vigilantism. This moderation, of itself, has been criticized as weakness and appeasement. But the rules under which the Loyalty Review Board operates leave much to be desired in the way of protection for the individual, at least according to our conception of original Anglo-Saxon justice, as has been pointed out by eminent legal authorities who are not radical at all but very jealous of the inherent rights of citizens under our Constitution. There was the Hoffman bill [6] passed by the House the other day requiring the President to give up confidential executive papers, which is aimed at getting the FBI to turn over its reports on Dr. Condon—reports which, as anyone knows who knows anything about FBI and other investigative agency methods, would contain all sorts of hearsay, gossip, and everything else that is collected by investigators in their routine work and is assessed and checked afterward before any judgments are made.

All of this has embodied pressures upon newspapers, incipient threats to freedom of the press. There was in President Truman's loyalty order some phraseology restricting certain types of information (pointed out first in articles by Ed Lahey, for many years a star reporter for the Chicago *Daily News* and now with the Knight newspapers) which might be interpreted to keep from the press all sorts of information, including information about war contracts. How correct he was in his very keen diagnosis was exemplified later in the interpretations and directives worked out by an interdepartmental committee for government press officers which restricted all sorts of information, even going to the ludicrous extreme of anything that would "embarrass" officials. For exposing this second phase, Nat Finney of the Minneapolis *Star* and *Tribune* was awarded both the Raymond Clapper Memorial Award in 1947 and the Pulitzer Prize in 1948. The Pulitzer award in 1948 was given also to another Washington correspondent, Bert Andrews, chief of the New York *Herald Tribune* Washington bureau, for a very revealing series of stories detailing just how one minor employe of the State Department was trailed and harassed and never allowed to know what the charges were against him. He was one of the ten who had been dropped by the State Department on vague allegations of disloyalty. Seven of the ten later were permitted to resign without prejudice since no basis for disloyalty could be established.

The Hoffman bill also had its hidden threat to freedom of the press which was exposed and removed on the floor. It was discovered that newspaper reporters who divulged in Congressional Committees information that was supposed to be confidential could be jailed and fined under its terms. A newspaper publisher member of the House, Representative Clarence Brown of Ohio, one of the Republican leaders, had this deleted by amendment in the House. But the extraordinary penalties of jail sentence and fine imposed on members of Congress who reveal confidential information, as well as officials in the executive branch who do so, is not only a dangerous threat to our fundamental freedoms, for congressmen and officials are citizens also; but in its operation it might also constitute an indirect threat at least to freedom of the press since it could close up avenues of information usually open to reporters of initiative by providing an excuse to officials through a very broad interpretation of "confidential information." Beyond that, of course, the bill is clearly an unconstitutional invasion of the rights of the Executive, as established in numerous Supreme Court decisions, as well as an unconstitutional invasion of the rights of citizens.

It is interesting, if not significant, that the author and sponsor of this bill, Representative Clare Hoffman of Michigan, not long ago haled two newspapermen before the House Expenditures Committee of which he is chairman, a reporter of one Washington newspaper, and an editorial writer from another. He tried to worm from the reporter the source within the committee from which he got information for a story he had written, and of course failed. He objected to an editorial written by the editorial writer about his committee, and gave him a grilling. He was threatening proceedings against newspapermen for such activities, but a barrage of protest was laid down against him and he dropped the matter. He turned up later with the bill aimed at Dr. Condon and the President.

The tension over our relations with Russia, with all the emotions that have been whipped up and released, is easy to capitalize for those who are so inclined, and it is being capitalized and exploited. We are still in a war and emergency atmosphere around Washington, as it must be easy to sense from here. Our National Defense Administration is very sensitive about its plans and secrets, and this has been intensified by the voting of additional billions for the expanded military and naval program. Some weeks ago top defense officials put out feelers for a voluntary censorship system such as was in effect during the war. One proposal advanced was to put a censor in newspaper and radio offices in Washington. This shows how far officials will try to go when circumstances permit. Such proposals were resisted, of course, by a committee of newspapermen who were called into consultation. Defense officials had no real justification. Newspapers have been most careful. Only two incidents were cited by defense officials over a long period where supposed secret information had been published. One was the fault of the government itself, the other was an innocent error in a magazine.

All of these things indicate the necessity these days of constant alertness by the press to protect itself. These are threats from the field of government. There is another large area of pressures to which newspapers are subjected which are much more vague and go into the field of ideas about what part government should play in the lives of its citizens—in brief, how far it should go in what we generally know as social and economic welfare measures.

We went through a peaceful revolution in this country beginning in 1933, something that its sponsor called the New Deal but which was only a continuation, after recurrent lapses, of the Square Deal of Teddy Roosevelt in the early part of the century and the New Freedom of Woodrow Wilson a few years later. Every so often we as a people are compelled to stop, take account of our democracy, and readjust it to the swiftly moving demands of a mechanical civilization. We were forced to stop and to make this readjustment the last time because our system had become paralyzed, failing for the moment to meet the simplest needs of our people for food and clothing. Something had to be done in a hurry. After the necessary emergency measures to provide jobs and shelter and food, the basic necessities, the Administration and Congress moved ahead on a broad front of reform to patch up our economic machinery to meet the needs of the people. The object was to give the individual more economic freedom, greater opportunity, and more security. To do this, it was necessary to require those who could provide these things, the managers of our free enterprise system, to operate in a way to do it. This necessitated certain restraints and curbs on the power they had acquired, for it is very natural for the possessors of power to use it for their own benefit. All of this stirred up a ferment and conflict, with excesses on both sides. It was a great and dramatic story, this peaceful revolution, and it was covered day by day in our newspapers as a great story. There was imagination in it and the stuff of dreams—the great American dream.

We are now in the counterrevolution, the reaction against that other era. It is the historic swing of the pendulum with which we are familiar. It, too, is a great story and a dramatic story.

We now have back in Washington, back at the battle again, the big economic interests that were restrained somewhat, though never to a degree, as their current balance sheets show, that in any way restricted their own freedom or in any way endangered fair profits. This counterrevolution is on in earnest. It is well financed. It is directed in Washington by skillful men who know their way around.

So we see the utilities pecking away on various fronts to check the further expansion of public power. They are trying to prevent necessary further extension of TVA, the great model, to meet power needs for industry, including national defense industry, in the Tennessee Valley. They are exerting their influence against proposed duplication of TVA in an MVA for the Missouri River and a CVA for the Columbia River, and other such regional developments, although it is a stark fact that the nation is faced by a power shortage. They again defeated the St. Lawrence Waterway, and Governor Thomas E. Dewey of New York now is trying to take that over as a state project, since he knows full well the value of that development, both for the nation and for his own state. They have been successful in delaying the needed expansion of great power and reclamation projects in our Pacific Northwest by their success in getting appropriations reduced. They are pushing measures to prohibit the government from building transmission lines from its public power projects so the private utilities may have control of power distribution. They are seeking to weaken federal regulatory agencies, such as the Federal Power Commission, by depriving them of authority to go fully into the books and accounts of private utility companies which has enabled these agencies to reduce rates for the consumer —household, farmer, and industry. It is a big fight along a broad front.

But there is similar activity along other fronts. There is, for example, the Bulwinkle-Reed bill to exempt railroads from the antitrust laws which has passed both branches of Congress and is now awaiting action by President Truman.[7] There is the bill to remove lands in our coastal areas from the control of all the people through their federal government and return jurisdiction to the states, where the big oil companies behind this measure hope to have more success in getting their hands on oil deposits in coastal areas.

Social security is being attacked from several directions—by an attempt to remove from coverage by specific act of Congress hundreds of thousands whom the Supreme Court has ruled should be included, and by reducing appropriations for the administrative agency—all this despite Republican platform commitments to enlarge coverage to many not now covered. Some months ago we saw the bill designed to regulate portal-to-portal pay and to check a flood of labor suits used also to restrict the benefits of the wage-hour act, and now Senator Joseph H. Ball, under the guise of a measure to increase the minimum wage, is seeking to restrict the wage-hour law still further so that one to three million persons now protected by it would be removed from its protection.[8]

The real estate interests have been busy also, working through one of the most effective and highly financed lobbies now operating in Washington. They wrecked the veterans' housing program, with some help from President Truman, and now they are trying to kill off the Taft-Ellender-Wagner housing bill [9] because of its incidental assistance, and on a minor scale, to public housing in local communities. And the high tariff interests are having initial success in trying to weaken our reciprocal tariff program, one of the keystones of our policy of international cooperation and a necessary complement to the European Recovery Program.

The battle rages along the whole front.

It is, truly, a great story, whatever may be the views of any newspaper about the merits of one side or the other. It deserves much better coverage than it is getting in our newspapers today. For at stake are the future course and progress of our democracy.

The successes thus far achieved by the counterrevolution would indicate that there is a favorable reception in Washington. There is. It is getting encouragement from one end of Pennsylvania Avenue, the Democratic administration, to the other end, the Capitol where Congress sits and deliberates.

To meet this counterrevolution and cope with it there are needed somewhat the same vigor and skill among what I may call the progressive forces that created the original revolution, for the same powerful forces must be combated. It is no news to you to say that such vigor and skill are lacking. That is quite apparent. While President Truman is in the progressive tradition—his Senate record was such—and while he talks the doctrine almost endlessly in speeches and messages that are wholly disregarded in Congress, he seems unaware of the nature of the forces aligned against him and does not have the knack of organizing a fight against them. He has surrounded himself, too, with amiable and comfortable men of no considerable ability who have no heart for a fight and are content to let well enough alone.

This is true not only of the top command, the general and staff officers, but also—and this is even more important if you are in a fight— it is true of what I might call the map room contingent, the men who plot the strategy. Long gone from the map room are the bright and zealous and clever young men who served Franklin D. Roosevelt so well, who arranged for the ammunition, prepared the propaganda, devised means of lining up this and that vote, and otherwise did what might be called, politely and with no particular offense, "the dirty work." They were energetic and they were tireless and they burned for a time with a sort of religion. Some have gone back home and retired into quiet lives. Others still stick around, making good livings for themselves practicing law, or practicing what we call "influence," or acting as economic advisers and consultants for those who can pay for such luxuries. In their spare time they sit and talk of the good old days, mourn their lost leader, call Harry Truman all sorts of names, and plot his downfall, and reveal what was often suspected—that without their lost leader they, too, are lost, so much that some of them are chasing off after General Eisenhower or anybody else but Harry Truman.

If President Truman had all the will in the world for a fight, and all the skill, and had at his command a staff that could organize and carry on a real fight, he still very likely could get nowhere, although it all might look better and help to keep the progressive forces in his party together. For he has a Congress packed against him, and it is doubtful if even a Roosevelt, Teddy or Franklin D., could do anything with it. It is a common saying around Washington that this is the worst Congress in the experience of whoever is saying it. That takes in a lot of experi-ence and a lot of time in some cases. It is, surely, bad enough. But it is perhaps a natural product of the times and of our own apathy and casualness, and, in the last analysis, we the people must take the blame. It is a Congress that was swept into office in the reaction after a long and hard war and expresses the irritations and nervous anxiety of the nation, its bitternesses and its prejudices. As we can recall, there was

37995 LIBRARY
College of St. Francis
JOLIET, ILL.

little discussion of the real issues in the last election. We were clamoring for meat and an end of war restrictions and regimentation and were chasing illusive Communists who might, somehow or other, rise up and take some of the money that burned in our pockets.

Well, we got our meat—and we pay for it—and we got rid of that old devil OPA and all such, and we are still chasing Communists and yet our souls are not at ease.

In the field of international affairs we have shuffled off our one-time isolationism and adopted an internationalism that is a peculiar sort of mixture, compounded as it seems to be of some parts of sound common sense, honest idealism and our native humanitarianism, and some parts of fear intermingled with selfishness. It is no secret, but very apparent when you watch daily events in Washington, that some former isolationists of both parties in influential places both in Congress and in civilian life have espoused internationalism and all the things that go with it in an administrative and legislative way because of a burning hatred and fear of Communism and what it might do to them. It is a negative matter. It is with such people a holy war and some of them are ready almost to go into a fighting war about it, atom bomb, bacteriological warfare and all. It was this spirit that helped to clinch the victory for the original Truman Doctrine for Greece and Turkey in Congress.[10] It also played its part in the success in Congress of the Marshall Plan, or European Recovery Program as we now call it.

From this group of what might be called dollar internationalists—for they seem to believe that money can buy them security, since they believe money can buy anything—you get some very incongruous and illogical attitudes. They would check the Social Democrats in Europe who seem to be our natural allies against Communism, and some would even take to their bosoms former Nazi industrialists in Germany who created Hitler's war machine and build them up again as a bulwark against Russia, which was the way it all happened after World War I. It is not democracy as most of us think of it that they want, but an antiquated sort of free enterprise close to freebootery that went out in this country a long time ago, and went out in England and some parts of Europe even before that.

What makes this situation dangerous for the peace of mankind is the influence of military men in the shaping of our foreign policy. They think of foreign policy in terms of military strategy. They cannot help that. That is their training. You only have to sit and listen to them talk about foreign affairs to understand that. It is not a pleasant experience. Military men have to think always of a potential enemy and how to fight that enemy. For that they want plenty of guns and airplanes. They will take all they can get. When there is a disposition to vote some money for national defense, they come in to demand as big a chunk as possible. That is natural. Money buys guns and airplanes for them, just as the dollar internationalists would use it to buy security for themselves. They have a community of interest. The combination is not a healthy one. To keep these influences in bounds is one of the chief problems in Washington today.

All in all, our situation today is something of a paradox. We are the most fortunate of people. We have prosperity such as we never had before. A visitor from another planet would consider us the happiest of people and would be puzzled by the mental and spiritual torment he would find among us. The trouble is not with us, but with us as situated in the world. Formerly the troubles of the world beyond our shores did not concern us too much. But now, really for the first time, we have assumed our place, our rightful place, in the family of nations. But not only that. We have become the leader in the family of nations. That is a grave responsibility. It is hard at first for a once insulated people. From that arises so much of our confusion today. We are not only managing a nation. We are, literally, running a planet. That planet just now is in a sad state, and we are a harried Atlas.

But we are learning, and we will continue to learn. It is a trite thing to say, but I, for one, have an unbounded faith in the good sense of the American people and I am just as confident as that I stand here that it will assert itself, and not be too late. We have, thank God, a way of talking things out among ourselves, talking very freely, and we usually come in the end to a sound solution.

It has seemed to me a very healthy thing in this connection, for instance, that our presidential campaign already is producing a great debate on the subject that seems to plague us most just now. I refer to the debate started by two Republican candidates, Harold Stassen of Minnesota and Governor Dewey, on how far we should go in handling Communism. Their discussion was confined to the question of whether we should outlaw the Communist party. But it has started discussion on the whole subject of Communism and our democracy and how we can best protect democracy. It is going on, too, in Congress, and in public forums, and in schools and colleges and in the living room. It is a good sign.

I think something else that has happened lately which is somewhat related is also fortunate. I refer to the break, even if a tiny one so far, in the clouds that have hung over our relations with Russia. Even though the peace offer was initiated in a strange way from Russia, and we fumbled around on our end, the way has been opened for getting together on negotiations out of which some adjustment may come. That also seems a good sign.

As a matter of fact there appears a faint glimmer of the dawn after the dark that descended upon us so soon after the war. Optimism seems to be in order. The dawn is sure to come slowly, and there still will be clouds here and there from time to time. We must be patient and tolerant and sensible.

It is hard for us to realize our place in the world and our responsibility. It is equally hard for us to realize the individual responsibility upon each of us that this larger responsibility imposes. It requires that each of us become world-minded. That is something about which to think and think hard.

That imposes a responsibility upon the press, and that is something for many of us to think about. For the press is one of the chief instruments of our democracy. That responsibility goes to keeping our democracy here at home a living and growing institution, so that it may influence the spread of democracy elsewhere. And that means alertness by the press to bring to light some of the influences to which I have referred tonight that seem to me to threaten our progress, both here at home in our domestic affairs and abroad in our international affairs. They are all of a piece now.

This brings me back to the three newspapermen for whom this memorial was ordained, and to us who are living. It brings me back to reporting, which is the life blood of the newspaper. There was never more need for good reporting than today. If we reporters tell the American people the story, the full story, we need not worry about their decision.

The Press and

World Affairs

The foreign policy of the United States has received unusual support from the American people since 1945.* Never in history has a nation which depended upon common consent for its action accepted so quickly such unprecedented world responsibilities. The people of Spain and France and Britain had generations and even centuries to assume comparable burdens. The people of the United States have assumed their decisive role within a single decade.

This accomplishment was not due primarily to any superior wisdom on our part. The compulsions have been terrible. Our hesitations have been many. We have been swept along by events which we sometimes did not understand and could not always control. But in the last analysis, we did meet our responsibilities. I do not think we reacted wisely when Fascism threatened liberty from 1933 to 1941, but the Communist threat to liberty has been challenged by the policy and power of the United States.

A new balance of power has been achieved in Europe. Power has, I believe, been wielded by this country in defense of justice. A start has been made toward the economic and political coordination of the whole

---

* This lecture was delivered May 13, 1949.

Atlantic Community, and these things are in large measure the result of the revolution in the foreign policy of the United States.

The values of a newspaper and of a reporter can often be measured by their capacity to remain dissatisfied with things as they are. Therefore, although my premise is that the nation has made unprecedented progress in world responsibility in the past decade, I want to raise certain questions about the present and future.

It is easier to change a policy than a people. McKinley changed our policy at the beginning of this century when he moved the responsibilities of the United States 7,000 miles across the Pacific to the Philippines. Woodrow Wilson, for a time, changed the foreign policy of the executive branch of the government. In both cases, however, a gap remained between the thinking of the government and the thinking of the people. McKinley and his successors did not keep our power equal with our commitments in the Pacific. Wilson could not command the support of the Senate. And throughout this period, many of our institutions have lagged behind our policy.

In some respects, these things are still true today. The question now is not whether we have made progress but whether we have made enough progress. The issue is not whether we have run a good race but whether we can stay the course—which will be very long indeed. The point is not whether we have had a revolution in our policy but whether that revolution—which has in many ways been merely an intellectual revolution—has seeped down into the conviction of the mass of the people and influenced sufficiently the habits and methods of our government, our newspapers, and our other institutions.

These are questions which can be applied to the thinking of every adult American: to our schools and universities; to our methods of selecting careers; to our churches; to the whole fabric of American society, which is sounder in some areas than others. I want to apply them narrowly to the newspapers of the country. I want to discuss how our foreign policy is explained, first by the government to the newspapers, and second, by the newspapers to the people.

In doing so, let me start by stating some personal opinions:

First, I believe that our foreign policy is based on the realities of the world as it is; that since sovereign states still control the physical forces in the world, this policy corresponds on the whole to the material interests and moral beliefs of the vast majority of the American people; and that if it is carefully and patiently explained, the people will understand and support that policy over a long period of time.

Second, I believe that, while our foreign policy is now widely supported throughout the country, this support has been due, in part at least, to a popular emotional reaction against the foreign policy of the Soviet Union.

Third, I believe that a foreign policy which relies on emotion and on reaction to another nation's policy is not the most reliable instrument; and that if our leadership in the world is to remain effective, it must rely more on reason than it has in the past.

Finally, I believe that while both the government and the newspapers have made enormous progress in explaining policy to the people, they are both the prisoners of old techniques and prejudices which minimize their influence and may in the long run threaten the progress that has been made.

In the days of our isolation, statements by the President on foreign affairs were less frequent and less important than they are today. President Taft and even Franklin Roosevelt could talk off the cuff without much danger of upsetting events and policies all over the world.

This is no longer true. In the last decade, the foreign policy statements out of the White House have been studied down to the last comma by every foreign office in the world. Not only is the United States more important, but the power of the President is greater. Executive initiative has increased. It is necessary merely to remember, first, that it was the executive branch of the government that dispatched the *Missouri* to the Aegean during the Greek-Turkish crisis of two years ago,[1] and, second, that it was the executive branch that had to decide whether to push an armed convoy through to Berlin when the Soviet blockade was imposed,[2] to recognize that the issue of war and peace is more in the President's hands today than ever before.

Nevertheless, the President continues to shoot from the hip in his extemporaneous answers to intricate foreign policy questions in his press conferences. You will remember his offhand comments about the foreign policy views of Henry Wallace a few years ago, which disrupted the Council of Foreign Ministers in Paris and eventually led to the resignation of Wallace. You will remember, too, the President's remarks on foreign policy during the campaign, particularly on Palestine. If you will look in your newspaper files at the beginning of June, 1947, you will see that General George C. Marshall's announcement of the Marshall Plan at Harvard[3] was overwhelmed by a couple of press conference announcements on the same day by the President on Senator Robert Taft and on the new regime in Hungary.[4]

The Truman Doctrine[5] was not a press conference announcement, but it was evidence of the same kind of sweeping policy announcement, obligating us to oppose Communism all over the world without qualification. For lack of prudent qualification, there is today considerable confusion about why we are not opposing the Communist drive in China, and why we are not explaining our failure to oppose it actively.

The remedy for this is not to abandon the White House press conference or limit it to domestic issues. The need is not for less explanation, but for more careful explanation. The tendency too often is for the President to answer too quickly or to dismiss legitimate questions with "no comment."

Unfortunately, the "Fireside Chat" and the "Notice Question" disappeared at the White House just when they were most needed. In the former, which Roosevelt used to such effect, an opportunity was provided for the President to explain intricate questions in simple terms, but President Truman has seldom used this effective Sunday-night device. Similarly, there was a day at the White House when the President would respond to a difficult question by saying that the question was legitimate, that he would provide an answer to it when it was carefully prepared, but that he was not prepared to give the answer casually at once.

It is not surprising that the habits and institutions of a large democratic country lag behind a revolutionary change in its foreign policy. I am suggesting, however, that it is dangerous for them to continue to do so, and that we should be asking what our institutions can do to prepare the country adequately for its decisive role in the world affairs.

The habit of debate in Congress, for example, like the White House press conference, has not kept pace with a foreign policy which now affects the lives of people all over the world. Our overworked Congressmen are remarkably casual in their debates on foreign policy. Like many newspapers they play heroes and villains with the facts. The quality of fair, open-minded study of intricate foreign policy problems is mighty scarce on Capitol Hill. We have not really had an objective exhaustive debate in the Foreign Relations Committee on the North Atlantic Treaty. Members have not really chosen to explain all the important aspects of this legislation. They have chosen up sides—for and against it. They are concerned, many of them, not to explain the treaty with all its serious and important implications, but to get it through or to keep it from getting through the Senate. What many of them are doing now is not studying the question, but scoring debating points against the opposition.

This gap between policy and the methods of explaining policy exists in the State Department as well as in the White House and Congress.

No official in the world has better reason than the State Department official for knowing that a foreign policy is no better than the public understanding and support behind it. Yet the State Department is still trying to implement a modern foreign policy without an adequate system for explaining it to the people.

It is true that the jobs of responsible officials at the State Department and responsible reporters there are in direct conflict, maybe 10 per cent of the time. Our job is to report, to explain, and to disclose. Their job, part of the time, is precisely the opposite: in the general interest, they cannot always disclose or explain. But 90 per cent of the time, the job of the responsible foreign policy official and the job of the responsible foreign policy reporter are complementary, not antithetical.

Most of the time we are the means to the public understanding and support on which their policy in the last analysis rests. Perhaps 90 per cent of the time, therefore, the reporter is an *opportunity* for the State Department, not a *problem,* though the tendency is to treat the reporter as a problem most of the time.

It is a fact of some importance, I think, that a reporter for a responsible newspaper like the New York *Times* gets more reliable factual guidance on international issues from the representatives of every other major Western country than his own.

There cannot be an adequate system of explaining foreign policy if there is a lack of confidence between officials and reporters at the Department of State, and this confidence does not exist. The negotiations which led to the ending of the Berlin blockade came directly as a result of the enterprise of a reporter's questions to Premier Stalin. Yet when that reporter (Kingsbury Smith of the INS) sent his questions to the Kremlin, the reaction at the State Department was that his questions were an annoyance, an invasion of the province of diplomacy, and an instrument of Soviet propaganda. In the long run, Smith's questions led to the Jessup-Malik conversations, and when reporters sought to check reports that these conversations were proceeding, they were not only evaded (which was all right in the circumstances), but they were misled by a series of half-truths and worse.

Let me emphasize a point here: Reporters have a tendency to wail too much about the barriers placed before them by officials. Our job is to get all the facts the people need to reach correct judgments, and we would be deceiving ourselves if we thought that anybody cares very much about the problems of newspapermen except other newspapermen.

The question of whether these major questions of foreign policy are fairly and adequately explained to the American people, however, goes far beyond the problems of reporters. It is a question which affects the understanding and support of American policy, and I take it this is a fairly wide and important subject.

The problem at the State Department is not that there is a conscious conspiracy to conceal or mislead, although that happens more often than is necessary. There is, however, nobody working directly and intimately with the Secretary of State who knows the needs of newspapers, the strengths and weaknesses of newspapers, or what to expect from newspapers when information is concealed or disclosed. There is nobody in that position who can look over the vast flow of information coming into the department and define accurately and fairly what part of the information properly falls within the 10 per cent that has to be concealed and the 90 per cent that can be disclosed, to the benefit of the department and the public.

On routine questions of getting out texts of speeches and communiqués, the system at State works all right. The difficulty is that the system of *explanation*—which is what we are talking about—always breaks down at the most critical time. When things are going along in a routine way, which is not often these days, officials who know what is happening are available to reporters. But when the big story breaks, the officials you want are almost always tied up on policy matters and very properly cannot take time out in the crisis to explain sensitive questions to reporters. This does not solve the problem, however, for at such times, the officials who are available to the reporters do not know what is going on, and those who do know what is going on are not available. Therefore, for lack of a well-informed officer dealing with reporters at such times, the reporters either write inadequate or misleading stories, or if they are wise, get their information from reliable officials of other governments.

The State Department has spent a great deal of time studying the technical problems involved in transmitting information abroad. This is important, but it is secondary. The primary problem is not *how* you transmit information *abroad,* but *what* information you transmit at *home and abroad.* It is the old question of form and substance. The substance is the important thing, for unless you get the substance right, a good transmission system will probably do the nation more harm than a bad transmission system. After all, the Voice of America is the President of the United States and all the myriad voices beneath him; it is not merely a radio station.

If we in the newspaper business are to raise questions about whether the government and other institutions are meeting the challenge of the time, we should certainly raise the same question about ourselves.

The question we have raised here is whether those who have a responsibility for explaining the foreign policy of the United States are keeping pace with the requirements of what is an unprecedented and even revolutionary foreign policy for America. I have suggested that responsible officials and representatives in the executive and legislative branches of the government have not kept pace. I suggest that the newspapers have not kept pace either.

Again the question is not whether we have made progress but whether we have made adequate progress. Of course we have made progress in the past decade. The coverage of foreign policy news in the American papers is more detailed, better informed, and in truer perspective than it was in 1939. Like the White House, the Congress, and the State Department, however, we are often the prisoners of old techniques and prejudices, which color our judgment of what is news, and how it should be written and displayed.

The news we have to report and explain these days is not only more important because of America's decisive role in the world, but it is more intricate and many-sided. It does not fit easily into the short news story with the punch lead. It often defies accurate definition in very short space. Very often it rebels against our passion for what is bright and brief.

Nevertheless, we still have a tendency to make this complex modern news conform to our old techniques. It is a natural reaction—space is limited and type will not stretch—but you cannot often make an intricate debate on the European Recovery Program sparkle without distorting the whole picture.

In the past, we in the newspaper business have been satisfied too often with reporting the literal truth instead of the essential truth. It may be literally true to report that "Ten Soviet Yak fighter planes roared into the American airlift corridor today outside of Berlin," but if you do not also report that the corridor is twenty miles wide, that the fighters did not come near our cargo planes, and that the incident was only the eighteenth reported in some ten months and 200,000 cargo flights into the former German capital, you do not report the *essential* truth.

The bright, the startling, the bold, the sharp, and the clear simple fact may make the most interesting reading; they may be "literally true"; but unfortunately, the material we have to report in this field is not always simple or bright or startling, although it may be vital to men's lives and therefore important and newsworthy.

We have no right, therefore, to twist the mass of facts into forms which are exciting but misleading; to take out of it that portion that conforms to our prejudices, to preserve the shocking or amusing, and to leave out the dreary but important qualifications which are necessary to essential truth.

Our preoccupation with what happens today, like our passion for the bold and simple, also often minimizes our value as reporters and recorders of great events. If a detailed study of the economy of Europe or the state of the federal government is released on a Tuesday afternoon, our tendency is to skim it, summarize it briefly, and forget it Tuesday night. Wednesday's news may be a compilation of trivia; it may be far less important than the ill-digested document of Tuesday, but because it happened on Wednesday, we tend to devote all our space to it and abandon the more important question of the day before.

There is another aspect of this today-angle story. It often happens these days that government decisions are taken in private and never reported until some official decides that everything is buttoned up and ready for publication. By that time, however, government commitments may be taken and disclosure cannot lead to objective appraisal by the nation.

Sometimes this is essential, but sometimes it is not. The veto in the United Nations charter was negotiated in private. A commitment was taken by our government to support that veto at the San Francisco conference. By the time an announcement was made about the veto, it was difficult to have an objective debate about it without repudiating the government and embarrassing the President in his conduct of foreign policy.

The time for enterprising reporting in that case was not after the announcement was made but before the commitment was taken. The same thing was true during the negotiations on the text of the North Atlantic Treaty. In that case, Senators Tom Connally and Arthur Vandenberg objected in a private meeting with Secretary of State Dean Acheson about making any reference in the treaty to the possibility of using military force against an aggressor. On their objection, the reference was struck out. This fact, however, was ferreted out; a public debate ensued, which indicated that there was considerable opposition to the timid position of the senators, and in the end, the reference was restored, with their consent.

I am not arguing for less aggressive reporting. Nor am I arguing, believe me, that only the irresponsible can be bright and that to be accurate you must be dull. I am arguing for a more modern test of what is news; for keeping on top of these momentous foreign policy developments *while they are developing* and not merely after they are announced; for the *explanation* of intricate and fundamental issues, even if they have no "gee whiz" angle.

Good enterprising reporting of ideas on basic issues can in many cases be as important as the reporting of action. The decisive point in many great events comes long before the event happens. It comes in what the diplomats call the "exploratory stage," when influential officials and legislators are making up their minds what they are going to do. The Marshall Plan was a great story in Washington before General Marshall ever heard about it. Few papers, however, paid any attention to it because "it was just an idea." In fact, the *idea* behind it was all laid out in a speech made by Dean Acheson weeks before General Marshall ever announced the plan at Harvard, and the only paper in the world, to my knowledge, that carried the text of that speech was the *Times* of London.

It will take a conscious effort on the part of those who run newspapers to meet the new responsibilities imposed on us by the new responsibilities of our country. The problem, I suggest, is not that anybody in the business is willfully trying to mislead the public or distort the truth. The problem is that we are busily engaged, like congressmen, and State Department officials, and even Presidents, in acting the way we have always acted, in using techniques we have always used, without asking whether they are the best techniques for America *today*.

In many ways, the criticisms we make of our officials and our representatives in Congress can fairly be applied to ourselves. They are so busy, we say, that they never have time to inquire or look where they are going. Is this not also true of ourselves?

They are flighty in their criticism; they get all excited about a subject and whoop and holler about it, and then they drop it dead, although the problem remains very much the same. Do we in the newspaper business not commit the identical mistake?

The President, we say, pops off without weighing his words; the congressmen spend their time scoring debating points against the opposition; the State Department pronounces without explaining—are we not honestly guilty of the very same conduct?

I think we are. I tried to emphasize at the beginning that it is natural that we act as we do—Americans having been required to change their policy so much so fast. But now that we are appraising everybody else, and everybody else seems to be appraising us in the newspaper business, maybe the time has come for a little serious self-appraisal.

We have always been good at reporting wars. We have always been pretty good at winning wars. But the problem is to prevent wars, and the question before all responsible men and institutions is whether they are doing that as well as they could.

The Role of the Newspapers

in America's Function as

the Greatest World Power

The press represents the eyes and ears of a nation. The American press has the rather terrible responsibility of acting as eyes and ears of a remarkable giant, living in quite startling historical circumstances.* Consider our situation:

As a nation we are not two centuries old. Our infancy lasted until the turn of the past century—indeed, it lasted until the First World War. We became involved in that world conflict, as we thought, rather fortuitously; or, as some affected to believe, by the mistakes of the pilots who steered our ship. In the period between the two world wars we revealed characteristic adolescent illusions. We thought that we might be able to preserve a continental security in a period of historic upheavals of world-wide scope by rigorous covenants of irresponsibility, entitled neutrality laws. They proved unavailing and may in fact have contributed to the fury of the second conflict, since they gave the foes of civilization the false hope of our abstention. We were nevertheless drawn into the second world conflict inevitably, and we emerged from it the strongest power on earth. We sustained armies of millions, operating in every part of the world; we built a navy twice as strong as the other great naval power,

---

* This lecture was delivered May 26, 1950.

which only yesterday had somewhat reluctantly granted us the right to match its strength. We spent some forty billion dollars beyond our military endeavors in aiding the cause of our allies. We emerged from the conflict as the only nation whose economic resources had been enhanced rather than diminished by the terrible conflict.

Thus we have, in the period of one brief decade, achieved a precarious hegemony in the Western world. Our leadership is precarious not only because we are called upon to exercise great power and meet tremendous responsibilities with only the briefest period of apprenticeship to prepare us for our task, but also because we have come upon this scene at the precise moment in world history when a latent civil war in the heart of Western civilization has become nationally localized. We have become the senior partners in a vast alliance of free nations, seeking to preserve their freedom against the machinations of a tyrannical power. It is a power, moreover, which counts its greatest resource not in terms of military strength, but in terms of utopian dreams by which it beguiles the impoverished peoples of the world and in terms of political chicane by which it seeks to undermine the order and government of the world. This power can obviously not be defeated merely by the show or the use of military might. We can hold our own only if our intellectual and moral resources are adequate to give unity, a sense of purpose and justice to the free world.

It is in this situation of gravest perils and possibilities that the American people must find themselves and learn to understand both their friends and their foes. There is not a single organ of the cultural life of a nation which may be held solely responsible for helping the nation to acquire both the knowledge and the wisdom which our task requires. There are many organs—schools, colleges, churches and every other instrument of communication and guidance. But no organ is more important in this task than the press of the nation.

We have spoken of the press as the eyes and ears of the nation. We must count on it for the knowledge of what kind of world we are living in and what our duties in it are. But we need not only knowledge but wisdom; not only the raw materials from which opinions are made, but the capacity to digest what we have observed until it issues in effective action. For this latter task of interpretation and digestion the press is not alone responsible. It shares that responsibility with many other organs of the community. It is nevertheless a responsibility which it cannot disavow or trade off to others. Let us therefore consider both of these responsibilities in turn.

The first responsibility is to help the largest possible number of our people to see the world-wide realities in which American policy operates. Even if there were not peculiar difficulties for a nation living on a continent far removed in space from the scenes where its actions must take effect, the knowledge of foreign affairs would be important. Foreign affairs is the Achilles heel of democracies. Democracy rightly places the arbitrament of the principles, though not the detailed strategy, of all national affairs in the hands of the people. In domestic policy this means that the people judge the effect of governmental policy by gauging its consequences in their own lives and those of their neighbors. One reason why democracy has proved more just than government by elite is that not even the most intelligent group of rulers is able to judge the effect of a policy upon the people as well as those whom the policy actually affects. Even the most ignorant man knows better than a cobbler whether or not the shoe which the cobbler has made pinches the foot.

But these great advantages of democracy in domestic policy are partly lost in foreign policy. There the people are able to judge the effect of a policy in their own lives only in the most indirect and ambiguous manner. Democracy in foreign policy has only one primary advantage: the reluctance of the common man to engage in war. But the obverse side of this advantage in a world in which democratic societies are locked in combat with dictatorships is that the reluctance of the common man to engage in war may also mean a reluctance to take the risks and precautions without which it is not possible to defend a nation against threats and bluffs in which tyrannies indulge without any check from the reluctance of their subjects.

A favorite illusion in democracies about war, which persisted in this country until very recently and was perfectly expressed in the proceedings of the Nye senatorial committee,[1] was that wars are merely the consequences of the machinations of kings, diplomats, and munitions makers and that they could be eliminated if only all centers of both economic and political power could be brought completely under social control. We need not deny that wars have been caused by the pride of kings and the dishonesty of diplomats. But in the present century they have been more frequently caused by the failure of the common man to countenance risks, to make sacrifices, and to support policies which were intended by those who understood the situation to prevent the aggression of the foe. The Kaiser went to war partly because he hoped that Britain would remain neutral. He hoped this partly because the British public itself indulged in the illusion that neutrality in a continental struggle was a live option. It was in fact not a possibility. Who can say whether

Hitler would have dared to move had he known that the whole weight of America would be thrown against him? He did not know this because our own American people hoped rather desperately that we might preserve our neutrality.

It is fair to say that our responsible leaders had fewer illusions about this possibility than the people. In a sense the war was the more sanguinary, and the issue for a time in grave doubt, because the attack at Pearl Harbor was required to convince the American people that we could not preserve our freedom if the rest of the world became enslaved.

One of the reasons why the political wisdom of the American people has matured rather rapidly is that we have not forgotten that lesson. Our people have been ready to bear exacting responsibilities in peace time because they are convinced that our fate is interwoven with the destiny of the whole free world. But there are increasingly clamant voices among us trying to persuade our nation that the sacrifices required of us are excessive, that other nations are taking advantage of us, that such help as we are prompted by prudence to give to our allies represents in fact a simple-minded and imprudent generosity. How can such theories be disproved? We must first of all make the facts available.

The evidence is abundant that a wealthy nation in an impoverished world can neither preserve its own health nor contribute to the economic and spiritual health of the vast alliance of which it is a part if its policies do not defy the market-place prudence of yesterday. These facts must be given to our people in the most vivid possible terms. Nothing is more important for any nation to learn, particularly one so fortunate as our own, as the simple fact that the morality of a nation never rises above the level of finding the concurrence between its own interest and the general welfare. What seems to be generous from our standpoint will be recognized by even our most friendly allies as prompted by a wise self-interest. This is one reason why we had better not count too much on the gratitude of the nations whom we are seeking to help. Gratitude is not only a grace which is beyond the competence of collective man; it is also never quite as deserved as it seems to the donor.

If we are to be preserved from illusions and frustrations in this matter, our people need the facts about the vast interwovenness of the world economy and about the mutual advantages which accrue from a seemingly generous policy.

We need facts too to give our people a proper respect for the moral and spiritual quality of the great nations allied with us. Our nation has the freest economy in the world. Whether we are so productive because it is so free, or whether it is so free because we are so rich, is a question which cannot be settled in a simple argument or debate. It is true, however, that the poorer nations of Europe and of Asia regard our particular combination of democratic institutions and a free economy as beyond their reach. They are as fiercely devoted to liberty as we are. They have suffered, in many instances, from totalitarianism and bear the scars of tyranny upon their bodies and souls. Any American prejudice which obscures the moral quality of their collective life or even creates the suspicion that they are slipping down the slope which leads to totalitarianism is a threat to the vast alliance of which we have become the leaders. It is worth remembering, moreover, that we are the leaders in this alliance not because we have proved ourselves wiser than they but because we are economically the stronger. And the strength of our economy, which has many causes, is certainly not merely the fruit of our superior virtue.

We need facts not only that our people may be oriented to the total world situation in which our decisions have such fateful consequences; but also because we must know more about specific issues in particular situations. American power impinges upon almost every critical point in the world. What shall we do about Germany? How much residual health is there in this nation, so recently corrupted by Nazism and now distracted in its convalescence by a vast power conflict over its prostrate form? Can Germany be restored to health without being integrated into the Western economy? Can this integration take place within western Europe itself or must it be a part of a wider integration of the so-called Atlantic Community of which we are necessarily a part? These questions are not answered in detail by the man in the street. But if there is not some knowledge of what is involved in these questions among the general public, demagogues and visionaries may be able to upset the handiwork of the most resourceful statesmanship.

We need facts about Asia, more and more facts. Vast revolutions are taking place in Asia. Recent events in China have been neither to our advantage nor for the world's good. But is it true that this or that mistake on the part of our leaders was what caused the disaster? Is not a powerful nation periodically tempted to imagine itself in the role of the Lord God Almighty? China has found it difficult for centuries to achieve cohesion and order on a wide scale. The last attempt failed for many reasons; but there is a good deal of evidence that the Chinese government was morally and politically impotent beyond our capacity to restore it to health. Foreign help to a government becomes progressively less helpful when the government lacks sufficient authority of its own to refute the charge that it is a stooge of a foreign power.

Meanwhile the Communists have been able to take over the vast democratic movement which was seething in all Chinese villages. We have enough facts to know that these leaders are real Communists and that they would, if they could, harness the discontent of the Chinese peasants to the engines of totalitarianism. But we do not know what their prospects of success are. Nor do we know what hazards attend a policy which deflects their resentments against Russian encroachments upon their sovereignty to us.

These questions are debated in Washington; but they are finally debated in our towns and cities when the proponents of this or that policy bid for our suffrage. We must know more than we know now if we would reach intelligent decisions upon such issues.

One could multiply the instances of specific policies which will either be reviewed by the American people or will by default be decided by a few bureaucrats. Is the secrecy surrounding the manufacture of atomic weapons necessary in the extent to which it is practiced? Has our military strategy placed such great reliance upon atomic weapons that we are in danger of inability of winning a war except by their use? Is there any danger that we might seek occasion to begin a war while we still hold an essential advantage in atomic weapons?

On all such issues the details of tactics and even strategy cannot be brought down to the level of the polls. But in every case there are questions of principle which will finally be determined by the people.

This plea for "facts" may have seemed to some a little dishonest. For it has not been possible to plead for more facts without betraying a particular bias and revealing how the writer expects facts to validate particular theories about our national responsibilities. Let it be admitted: There are very few naked "facts" in history. Facts consist of hardly more than names and dates. There are events in history, and these events cannot be understood except in relation to a whole stream of previous causes. Every record of events is therefore also an interpretation of this stream of causes. In the strict sense there is therefore no unbiased account of either past or contemporary history.

We do have a healthy scorn for obviously biased and partisan accounts of events in newspapers. We can detect flagrant distortion. This means that there is a genuine difference between honest and dishonest reporting, even as there is a difference between honest and dishonest debate in Congress. Some of the most flagrant distortions, prompted by obviously ulterior motives, have occurred in the debates of government rather than in the press. It must be admitted that a portion of the press has given itself to the ready dissemination of obviously corrupted views of our national situation. But after we eliminate these patent dishonesties we still have a very large problem upon our hands.

The problem is that our nation, like every nation, needs not so much isolated facts to inform its mind as the understanding of facts in their setting. This means the interpretation of facts. Facts without interpretation may more easily lead to erroneous conclusions than interpreted facts. This is particularly true in the reporting of foreign affairs, of which the reader does not possess the background of general knowledge to put isolated facts into a proper setting. If a lynching occurs in this country the average reader has some knowledge of the problem of race relations and of the not inconsiderable progress which has been made in bettering them, so as to assess the symbolic significance of a single incident. But that is not true when we judge events in other nations or when they judge happenings among us. Some time ago I saw a film prepared by Dr. Joseph Goebbels' propaganda ministry during the war, intended to discredit us as a nation of morons. The film consisted of "shots" of ridiculous and lurid events in our national life—pie-eating contests, mud fights, bathing beauty contests, and so on. Every shot was taken from an authentic newsreel; but the total effect was a complete libel on our life in the mind of anyone who could not put these facts in their setting.

Obviously we cannot solve the problem of bias in foreign news reporting by sticking to the "facts." Nothing is more disconcerting to an American visitor in Britain than to find that the afternoon press in that country has no other news from this country than little snippets of sensational items which cannot possibly give the reader a balanced view of our nation. I would not claim that our papers of similar stripe do any better for Britain or any other continental nation.

Let us postpone for the moment the problem of the special bias from which every observer must observe, the inevitable framework of meaning which he uses to string his facts together, to plead for more interpretation. Genuine interpretation includes not merely the present fact but something of the history which explains the fact. I rather hope that the quasi-editorial interpretative article on the editorial page, more common in the best European journals than in our own but increasingly popular in our more thoughtful journals, will become a standard form of journalism. While I do not want to decry the contributions of the conventional columnists, mostly writing from Washington, I should think we could dispense with a few if space were needed for these interpretations, not usually to be written in the editorial office but from foreign lands.

This is of course only a minor suggestion. Such a single feature cannot obviate the necessity of the greatest possible flow of news on foreign affairs in our newspapers. Let us admit that if these news reports have any significance they will be written from some viewpoint. Let us therefore consider the matter of bias more fully.

The first guard against bias in a free society is the possibility of stating alternative viewpoints. In the ultimate sense this is the only guard, for we have long since made up our mind that the political control of journalism is a cure worse than the disease. A democratic society must assume that even the best possible government must stand under scrutiny and criticism. With John Stuart Mill we trust the free market place of ideas to provide a sifting ground between truth and error. It must be noted, however, that in foreign affairs the reader has less chance to separate truth from error than in domestic policy. He lacks information of his own to arrive at reliable judgments. Furthermore, there is not enough competition in local communities between papers with adequate foreign news coverage to create a possibility of selection between rival interpretations.

Our guard against bias cannot consist therefore merely in the competitive situation. Perhaps it would be better to consider the quality of the bias, rather than its presence or absence or its elimination through competitive screening.

Essentially the problem of bias in journalism is no different from the ideological problem in the whole of the humanities. Every historian and social scientist, every philosopher and scholar, with the exception of the natural scientist who needs only the framework of the formal principles of science and reason, confronts an identical problem. Historical events cannot be interpreted except in a framework of meaning. The observer supplies the framework. The framework inevitably determines the manner in which the facts are assorted, emphasized, and interpreted. But this does not mean that all news of contemporary history and all records of past history are hopelessly distorted in their interpretation. The honesty of a journalist or historian depends upon two qualities in regard to the framework. The one is its breadth and width. The other is the ability to alter some elements in the presuppositions of interpretation, if the facts make them untenable.

In regard to the breadth and the width of the framework, one naturally must consider first the necessity of eliminating party prejudices in the consideration of foreign affairs. The viewpoint must be in the best sense patriotic, rather than partisan. It may be a counsel of perfection to ask journalists not to consider the impact of foreign affairs upon the fate of political parties. But the more a genuinely bipartisan foreign policy is achieved in both Congress and in the press, the less can changes in foreign policy be of particular advantage to either party.

Yet the framework must be wider than simple concern for the national interest. Every nation is tempted, in encounter not only with its enemies but with its friends, to be too uncritical of its own motives and achievements and too critical of the others. Good journalism has some responsibility to function as a conscience of the nation and to supply the material through which a healthy national self-criticism is possible. Many of our journals in recent years have engaged in a kind of ritualistic anti-Communism, with lesser or greater hysterical overtones, which does not even have the merit of awakening the nation to the great danger with which Communism confronts it. For this type of uncritical journalism would make it appear that our primary peril arises from traitors in our own ranks. We have less cause to fear such treason than such nations as France and Italy, for instance. Yet we are more hysterical about it. The real peril is that Communism as a great utopian illusion should still be able to win the hearts of many impoverished peoples in the world. That danger can be averted only if we play our part in achieving economic, moral, and spiritual health in the whole free world. A very considerable portion of national self-criticism is necessary for the achievement of such an end.

Our patriotic bias need not be corrupting if we are wise enough to know, as surely we must, that the welfare of our nation is intimately related to that of a whole free world. We are in the rather unenviable and yet enviable position that we cannot save ourselves without saving cherished values which transcend our national existence. A patriotic bias which is broad enough to include these considerations ceases to be a nationalistic bias. It becomes the framework in which loyalty to a total civilization is expressed. That is after all the final framework of meaning for us as citizens of a free world. As devotees of various religions and faiths we have other and various frameworks for expressing the total meaning of our existence. But the meaning of our common existence is expressed in our desire that we achieve a society in which both freedom and justice prevail. If all our journalism and historical science is informed by such a bias as the most determinative force, we can afford the expression of many subordinate biases, provided they do not hinder us from always seeking for the truth.

The other check upon our bias must be a sufficient freedom from our own presuppositions to permit facts to speak and to entertain interpretations, even if they run counter to our presuppositions and may prompt their revision. In journalism it is particularly important that the journalist who is in the field have the opportunity of examining the facts without too many directives from the home office. In the newspaper which I read several first class reporters have given quite contradictory accounts at different times of events in Germany. As I happen to know affairs in Germany rather better than in some other parts of the world, I have my own opinion which of these reports is the most trustworthy. I suspect one, in fact, because he has expressed his presuppositions in a full length book. But I am grateful for a newspaper which gives its reporters that much freedom. They must of course stand under some final judgment as certainly as a statesman. Does their interpretation of the facts fit tolerably well into the total picture as we know it from other sources? Reporters require this freedom not because they are more intelligent than the home office but because they are closer to the facts.

This discussion of the place of interpretation in the transmission of news and of the inevitability of bias and of the necessity of broadening the bias as far as possible until it is identical with loyalty to our whole civilization, assumes at every turn that there is a genuine desire on the part of the great organs of journalism to serve our nation and our civilization. Newspaper people, being human, undoubtedly have other motives beside these very exalted ones—motives of gain, of loyalty to party, and so on. Usually we assume that a mere moral appeal is not sufficient to achieve the kind of disinterestedness or, more exactly, the breadth of bias —which our nation requires of its journals. The political order is built upon efforts to deflect, harness, transfigure, and repress narrow interest for the sake of the wider good.

But there is little possibility of solving the problem of an adequate journalism politically. The eyes of our body politic cannot be forced to perform their proper function, as other organs may. The eye must be free. We might pass laws to suppress very irresponsible forms of journalism, or to bring very extravagant forms of lying to book. But there is no way of correcting these abuses without some danger of destroying essential freedoms. In any case, the main problem is not solved. No correction of abuses can solve the problem of giving the American people a sufficient amount of news and interpretation of our world to permit them to exercise their vast responsibilities intelligently. We do therefore return to a simple moral situation.

American journalism faces a vast responsibility to a powerful nation, holding a precarious eminence in the world community. No political coercion can force it to fulfill that responsibility.

The press, together with other organs of opinion, is therefore in a very special situation. Other organs and instruments of the community may, within limits, be coerced, if necessary, to serve and abide by the common good. It is of course an advantage in every society to have a high sense of responsibility to the common good in all organs of the community so that coercive measures may be reduced to a minimum. But only an anachronistic libertarianism would insist that a community ought not take such measures as are necessary to achieve minimal standards of justice in all our economic relationships. Any healthy society will do this, no matter how much those affected by such coercions may cry that these restraints are a halfway house to totalitarianism. The good sense of a free society usually supports the thesis that it is as important to achieve justice as to preserve liberty and that the preservation of liberty is no certain guarantee of the achievement of justice. In our economic problems every healthy society will insist on both liberty and justice, will know that the one cannot be unduly sacrificed to the other, nor will one flow inevitably from the other. In short, we need not depend solely upon a voluntary sense of responsibility in the economic life of the nation.

The cause of our organs of opinion is strikingly different. In this realm we are forced to be purer libertarians than in economic life, although it is silly for the press to claim (as it sometimes does) special economic immunities in the name of the principle of the freedom of the press. We cannot use very much coercion on the press any more than we can upon a college. We may be tempted at times to strengthen our libel and slander laws in order to discourage flagrant violations of the commandment: "Thou shalt not bear false witness against thy neighbor." But nations which have more rigorous libel laws than our own have experienced some great disadvantages from their rigor. In several instances the rigor of British libel laws has discouraged a journalistic airing of public scandal.

In any case something much more than a suppression of flagrant falsehood is what is needed. We require a fuller and fuller account of the world we live in. That achievement by the press belongs in the realm of grace rather than law. Political coercion has little positive effect, although in the realm of economics its negative effect may be beneficial. But in the realm of opinion any kind of political coercion bears within the danger of political corruption. That is why we are determined in our nation to preserve the freedom of the press as one of the cornerstones of an open society.

The moral consequences of this position are enormous. We are driven to the conclusion that the press of America must perform a function for our nation, which the nation desperately requires but which it cannot secure by coercion. It is a function upon the proper performance of which our whole future may depend. A partly blind and deaf America is doomed in this complex modern world. It would be doomed if it had less power. It will be the more surely doomed because it has so much power that the significant decision must be made or underwritten by us. We might be doomed by false policies. We could be as certainly doomed by sins of omission. If our free world is to be saved, this nation must bear great burdens for many decades to come. The patience required for bearing them and the courage necessary for facing the uncertainties and hazards of a tragic world must come from many sources. But one of the sources is undoubtedly the fullest possible knowledge of all the facts and factors in the world situation which are the presuppositions and consequences of our action.

This resource must be furnished the nation by the press without any whip of compulsion to hasten the laggards or awaken the sluggards. It must be furnished purely by the prompting of conscience, by a sense of responsibility to both our own nation and to the free world in which we have achieved such a fateful eminence. There is good evidence that this service can be rendered without financial sacrifice. The evidence consists simply of the fact that the newspapers which conscientiously act as the eyes of our nation are on the whole the more, rather than less, successful journals. A good account of the most exciting drama in which any nation of history has ever been involved need not cost the loss of a single subscriber. Even the indifferent may be taught by good journalistic teachers to take the tasks and responsibilities of our nation in the world seriously. It is not financial sacrifice which is demanded. The "godliness" required in this instance may "be profitable in this life." What is required is not financial sacrifice, but moral and political imagination.

ELMER DAVIS

Must We Mislead

the Public?

A couple of years ago Christmas, having to take an early plane the next morning, I found myself sitting up all night in the Berlin Press Club, listening to an impassioned debate on the question whether journalism is an honorable profession.* The negative was upheld by one of the most distinguished of American foreign correspondents, who has since admitted to me that the vehemence with which he maintained his argument—if not the argument itself—might have been due to Mr. I. W. Harper.

Nevertheless he maintained it most stoutly, reasoning as follows: It is never possible to know everything about a situation, whether individual or public; as your deadline approaches you have to sit down and write a story, write as if you knew everything about it, thereby deceiving your readers; hence journalism is not and cannot be an honorable profession.

This has a certain plausibility; and I confess that I was too tired that night to break in on the dispute and offer considerations against it. But the fact is that the problems underlying this debate had been thought out, and talked out, nearly twenty-four hundred years ago by a cantankerous character named Socrates, who was in the habit of needling his young

---

* This lecture was delivered November 3, 1951.

friends into asking him questions, so that he would have an excuse for spending all afternoon answering them instead of doing his work.

After tossing this particular question into the air and hitting fungoes with it all over the lot he finally came around to the conclusion that it is forever impossible for the human mind to have knowledge of anything—for instance, of the road from Athens to Thebes; but that you will get completely satisfactory practical results if you have a correct *opinion* of the road from Athens to Thebes; and that the way to find out whether your opinion is correct is to start from Athens, and see whether Thebes is where you get to, or some place else.

On that distinction the honest reporter can take his stand. He may never have genuine knowledge of a situation in the sense of knowing all about it; but if he knows enough about it and has conscientiously endeavored to verify what he knows, he has a sufficiently correct opinion to write a news story. Unfortunately it is not always possible for him to verify the correctness of his conclusion—at least very soon—by experiment, by starting out from Athens and seeing if he gets to Thebes. He will have some other assignment tomorrow; indeed there may never be opportunity for verification at all, unless the paper is sued for libel, and the publisher's lawyer is not smart enough to stall off the suit and keep it from coming to trial until the plaintiff has died of old age.

Nevertheless, for a man who has to turn in a story every day, and who seldom has time to go back to what he has written in the past and find out how far it is right and how far wrong, there is no better prescription than to do his utmost and conscientious best to form a correct opinion and then to go ahead and write his story.

That is what honest reporters do; that is what honest editors encourage. Yet in spite of that it seems to be more and more difficult to give the reading public a correct impression of what is going on; more and more, it seems to me, the front pages are being filled up with material which is only partially true if true at all. And this not with any evil intention.

I am not talking about the minority of newspapers, and the smaller minority of newspapermen, that do not want to tell the truth, that indeed make a career of publishing and disseminating incorrect opinions; I am talking about the honest papers, the honest reporters, who want to tell the truth but too often fall far short of doing so.

And why? Partly because of some of the conventions of American reporting, editing, and make-up; partly too because of the vast and continually increasing complexity of modern life with which the news must deal. Every day it becomes harder and harder, not merely to know enough about any given situation, but to remember what has been done and said about it in the past and to check what is done and said now against that. This is something of which I suppose we are all conscious in every field of human activity, and in the gathering of news about it. But it happens to have become particularly acute in Washington in the past year or two, thanks to the new doctrine of Congressional jurisprudence which might be called perpetual jeopardy.

The Founding Fathers wrote in the Bill of Rights that no person shall be subject, for the same offense, to be twice put in jeopardy of life or limb —and thought they had taken care of that. If a man was acquitted in court, that ended it. They did not foresee that Congressional committees would take over a considerable part of the judicial process and would hold that they are not bound by the limitation which the Constitution imposes on judicial agencies. Technically this contention is no doubt correct, since a hearing before a Congressional committee does not put a man in jeopardy of life or limb. The only penalty he can suffer, ordinarily, from Congressional condemnation, unless he is foolish enough to perjure himself, is the loss of his reputation and standing in the community—a deprivation which the average senator or representative seems to regard as trivial, at least when it happens to somebody else. The victim may also of course suffer the loss of an opportunity to make a living, at any occupation that he knows; but the Constitution says nothing about that.

In any case, Congress seems to have established the principle that no man is ever acquitted, so long as a single influential member of either House is out to get him. If a committee—or three or four committees— have investigated him and found him innocent, that only means that they keep on setting up hearings before other committees, until they find one that will pronounce him guilty. Double jeopardy has been ruled out in the courts; but before Congress any man may be in multiple and perpetual jeopardy for the same offense, actual or only unconvincingly alleged.

The juridical and ethical implications of this new doctrine are beyond the scope of this argument. What I am concerned with is its effect on news reporting, on the endeavor to give the public a reasonably accurate picture of what is going on. This is getting harder and harder to do, and one thing that makes it harder is the fact that this doctrine of perpetual jeopardy has been implemented by a couple of fantastic new weapons— what is called the pertinent excerpt and what might be called the seven-shot automatic repeating witness.

The pertinent excerpt is an improved version of our old friend, the sentence taken out of context. As it has appeared in the operations of

Senator Joseph R. McCarthy, and of Senator Patrick McCarran's Internal Security Committee, the pertinent excerpt is two or three sentences taken out of context—perhaps from two or three different pages of a letter, or a report, or a book—and put together with no indication that it is not a continuous statement, that a great deal of qualifying or even contradictory material may have been interposed between its parts.

We had one case this fall of a pertinent excerpt that turned out to be two sentences eleven pages apart, but put together.

Counsel for the committee reads this off to the witness: "On April 14, 1938, you wrote so and so; why? What did you mean?" If it comes from a book or a published article the witness may be able to refer back to it and read the context too, but if it comes from a letter that he has not got he is in trouble. For who of us can remember all the letters we wrote a dozen years ago—or why—without the text?

Officials of the Institute of Pacific Relations were asked questions like that again and again about documents from their files, which had been taken over by the committee; the men who had written the letters were not allowed to look at them and see all that they had said, and in what circumstances, when they wrote these snippets that counsel had read to them. Sometimes they remembered, but not always.

But the most effective use of the pertinent excerpt was reading it off to somebody who had never seen it before and asking him what it meant. So pertinent excerpts were read to General Albert C. Wedemeyer from reports on China by State Department officials made several months before he went to China—reports which apparently he had never seen before—and he was asked for comment. He had seen enough of the committee's operations to know what kind of comment was wanted: Is this party-line stuff or is it not? He did not know that these were disconnected snippets from a long report, whose general tenor was quite different from what the phrases quoted would suggest, and neither did the reporters who were covering the hearing.

Naturally, then, he came up with the right answer, and neither he nor the reporters knew it was the wrong answer. But because General Wedemeyer had said it, it was news.

As for the seven-shot automatic repeating witness. He shoots and misses his man; but then he remembers something else, or thinks of a different line of attack; and there is a fresh cartridge in the firing chamber, and better luck next time. We first saw this weapon demonstrated by a rather primitive type, Louis Budenz—slow-firing; when his first story did not hit the target it took him months to get a new one.

Later we saw a much improved model with smoother magazine action and a more rapid rate of fire—Harold Stassen, who could turn up next morning with a fresh story after yesterday's story had blown up in his face. And a great field for both these weapons was offered by the Mc-Carran committee, which seems to have undertaken to correct any errors of moderation that have been committed by any other committee in the past.

This fall it was engaged in what must be the fourth or fifth Congressional hearing dealing, in whole or in part, with the Institute of Pacific Relations. Pretty much the same witnesses come up every time—Stassen was an added starter—but they do not always tell the same old story. A witness before the McCarran committee knows what is expected of him. Even if he has not been rehearsed in secret session—as many of them have been—the answer is usually handed to him wrapped up in the question, and only an imbecile could miss it.

No wonder that this stimulating atmosphere sometimes refreshes a witness' recollection and enables him to recall picturesque and damning details that he had forgotten when he testified on the same subject before some other committee a year ago—or even before the McCarran committee a week ago.

But I venture to believe—though Senator McCarran has made it clear that he does not—that an accurate news report would include not only what the witness says now, but the fact that he told a different story last year. And for a reporter who has had to do many different things in the course of the last year it is pretty hard to recall whether the witness is telling the same story or not—especially if the reporter did not cover the earlier hearing. Once in a while it happens.

Joe Alsop happened to remember that what Louis Budenz said before the McCarran committee, about John Carter Vincent, was much more precise and damning than what he had said about him before the Tydings committee; Bill White of the New York *Times*—one of the many Bill Whites, William S.—happened to remember that there were material discrepancies, in emphasis if not in content, between General Wedemeyer's testimony before the McCarran committee and his testimony in the MacArthur hearings three months earlier.

But these were pieces of luck. White remembered because he had covered the MacArthur hearings too. Alsop remembered because this incident dealt with matters of which he had first-hand knowledge and with which he had concerned himself before.

There must be a good many similar instances in these reiterated hearings on the same subject which escape notice; yet these discrepancies seem to me to be part of the news story, to have some bearing on how much weight should or should not be attached to the value of the witness' recollection.

The McCarran committee is likely to be prolific in cases of this sort because it is going over familiar ground, but there have been other similar episodes. Before I leave the McCarran committee, however—a fascinating topic, really it must be seen to be believed—I should make it clear in all fairness that its witnesses do not always come up with the right answer. Senator James O. Eastland asked William L. Holland if he had known the traitor Harry White; Holland said he had known Harry White but had no reason whatever to suppose he was a traitor. Raymond Bennett volunteered some favorable observations about Philip Jessup only to be sharply reminded by counsel for the committee that they had not asked him about that.

General Wedemeyer was on the whole a very satisfactory witness; he even closed his testimony by volunteering some high praise of the committee's objectivity and the observation that any criticisms of its procedure were a smear campaign instigated by the people they were investigating. They had not asked him about that, but he was not rebuked. Yet he declined clear invitations from Senator Homer Ferguson to read meanings and motives into other men's words and to assume that opinions which he regarded as mistaken were proof of disloyalty. And within a few days two witnesses had turned up who said that Wedemeyer himself had at one time been suspected of being pro-Communist. This, however, seems to have been sheer coincidence. For Harold Stassen was an even more cooperative witness than Wedemeyer, but even he fell short of perfection. The first time he mentioned Owen Lattimore, counsel for the committee interjected, "He has been identified here as a Communist." Stassen said, "That's your statement; it is not mine." No witness, however, accused Stassen of having been regarded as pro-Communist.

But that is beside the point. The question is, what is a reporter to do who has sat through a hearing till five o'clock and then has to go back and write a long story? What am I to do, being responsible for taking note of the most important news of the day all over the world which keeps coming in right up to my deadline? What are we to do if one of the old familiar faces—Budenz, or what have you—turns up and gives testimony which stirs a vague recollection that he said something quite different in times past?

What we ought to do, obviously, is check everything this witness ever said in the past and see how it squares with what was said today; that is to say, go through thousands of pages of hearings of various committees, looking for a needle in a dozen haystacks. Ordinarily, it just cannot be done.

What can we do when McCarthy gives his kaleidoscope another turn and comes up with his ingredients rearranged into a very different story? I have on my office shelf a stack of McCarthy's speeches two feet thick; but it is seldom that I have time to run through them all between five and seven o'clock with half a dozen night leads coming in. It would take a full-time research historian to keep up with all the different stories McCarthy has told in the last year and a half.

Maybe it would not be worth it, since people who want to believe him go on believing him, no matter how often he is shown up. But the discrepancies and contradictions are news; news to which the public is entitled, and in so far as we reporters do not call attention to them, we are falling down on our job.

Aside from these twice-told tales, the immense complexity of the news is often too much for adequate presentation, and once in a while leads to downright, although quite unintentional, misrepresentation. An example: I read three morning papers, the Washington *Post,* the New York *Times* and the *Herald Tribune*—three of the best papers, and three of the most honest papers, in the country. Yet one morning last May they all made the identical mistake—and a mistake which happened to give support to their editorial policies. General George C. Marshall had been testifying in the MacArthur hearings, talking about MacArthur's personal and unilateral peace proposals of last March. And the next morning the top line of the *Times*'s eight-column head told us, "Marshall Says MacArthur Upset Peace Move." The *Post* and *Herald Tribune* also had eight-column heads and the top lines were substantially the same as that in the *Times.*

Now in the first place, General Marshall never said that. What he said was that MacArthur had lost whatever chance there may have been of making peace at the time, which is rather different. That verbatim quote appeared, of course, in the lead of every story; but you could not fit it into a headline, and the too numerous readers who look at nothing but the headline were accordingly deceived.

Furthermore, the chances of making peace at the time MacArthur offered his proposal were infinitesimal—almost nonexistent. There had been as yet no agreement among the sixteen nations with troops in Korea as to what the terms of peace should be, and there was no reason to suppose that the Chinese would have made peace at that time; they never even began to talk about it until they had taken a couple more first-class lickings.

Now this fact was known to the diplomatic correspondents of the *Times,* the *Post,* the *Herald Tribune*—to Scotty Reston, Ferdie Kuhn, Ned Russell—but they were not covering the MacArthur hearings; they were busy on their regular beats. The men who were covering the hearings, and the copy readers who edited their stories, did not know it; and it was nobody's business to tell them.

Here is a case where three of the best papers in the country gave their readers, particularly the headline readers, a seriously mistaken impression —partly because the American headline, with its rigid limitations of space and balance, very often invites misunderstanding; partly because the news has become so complex that it is just good luck if a man knows all the things he ought to know to cover some stories satisfactorily.

There were of course far graver distortions of testimony in the MacArthur hearings in other papers—distortion both in headlines and, sometimes, in the new stories. I have picked out this case only because the papers involved are technically among our best and ethically above suspicion of slanting the news to support their editorial policies. Yet, inadvertently, that is what they did.

Another example from the MacArthur hearings, which illustrates a habitual nonfeasance that has become a part of newspaper practice:

On June 21, 1951, General Pat Hurley was testifying; he had been testifying about some matters in connection with his official service; he had offered his opinion on some matters he knew about only from hearsay, and then all at once he went off into something that had nothing to do with the case and said this: "We have had a lot of secret hearings by committees; proceedings in all of them have been kept secret from the public. For instance, the hearings on the atomic energy organization; I read the report of the committee that heard that case and it was a clean bill of health, a certificate of purity and patriotism for everyone in the organization; yet less than six months, just a little while after, Dr. Klaus Fuchs confessed in London, and the result is that they were not pure, they were not patriotic in that organization, and two of them are under sentence of death at the moment."

Now this of course was completely false—though it may charitably be assumed that General Hurley, a highly emotional gentleman with a very erratic memory, did not know it was false. The two people under sentence of death never had any connection with either the Atomic Energy Commission—which was the subject of the committee report that General Hurley was talking about—or with its predecessor, the Manhattan Engineering District under General Leslie R. Groves. Furthermore, the espionage for which they were convicted, and for which Fuchs was convicted, all took place in General Groves's day, two years or more before the Atomic Energy Commission was created and took over from the Manhattan District.

You would think any senator would remember that much, but if anybody did, nobody mentioned it. The two members of the combined committees who would certainly have remembered it, Senators Brien McMahon and B. B. Hickenlooper, both happened to be absent when Hurley said that. Senator McMahon was told about it, and he came back into the hearings that afternoon while Hurley was still on the stand and got the facts on this point into the record. From this they were correctly reported in the morning papers—and maybe even in the last edition of the evening papers, that same day. A senator had brought it out; so it was news.

But in the meantime Hurley's story had run through one or maybe two editions of the evening papers without official challenge. Any competent news editor must have known that it was false, and so should most of the reporters who collected the transcripts of testimony. But unless a senator says so, it is not news. I do not see all the evening papers published in the United States; but I should be very much surprised if there was a single one, from coast to coast, which in its story of that morning's hearings followed up the report of Hurley's testimony with a bracketed paragraph saying, "This simply is not so." To do that would have been interpreting the news, editorializing—falling short of that lofty ideal, objectivity.

Objectivity is indeed a noble ideal; but try and get it. I have heard Fulton Lewis tell a Senate committee that complete objectivity in the presentation of news is impossible—a matter on which he should certainly be the world's greatest authority. I must say that I agreed with at least part of his statement on that occasion (for perhaps the only time in my life); for he pointed out that personal predilections can have their influence even on the selection of what news is most important—what deserves the front page, what is even worth mentioning at all.

This of course is true; but the decision is often difficult, and it is no wonder that most American news editors have abdicated their judgment and decided that news is what is said by somebody of importance—even if it is demonstrably and even notoriously false. In the two cases I cited of discrepancies in testimony before the McCarran committee—Joe Alsop was permitted to call attention to it because he has his own column, which is a mixture of the news and of his interpretation of the news; Bill White was permitted to call attention to it because he had covered both hearings and remembered that what General Wedemeyer said at one was not quite the same as he had said at the other.

But suppose it had been not the reporter who covered the story, but the copy reader or the make-up editor who noticed that. Would he have interpolated a bracketed paragraph pointing out that this was not so—in other words, warning the reader that if he believed the quoted testimony he was buying a gold brick? In nine hundred ninety-nine cases out of a thousand, he would not. To do so would have been flying in the face of the practice of American journalism. It would have been failing in objectivity.

Well, what is objectivity? It is a praiseworthy ideal, although not as it is always practiced now; but even as it is practiced now it was in the beginning a praiseworthy ideal, since it was an endeavor to get away from the outrageous slanting of the news which characterized American journalism in what are too loosely known as its great days.

Most of you, I imagine, have had occasion to look at newspapers of the Civil War period, and of the decades just before and just after it. Their idea of objectivity, in the main, was "what helps our side." No nonsense of fairly reporting what was said on both sides, of giving the other fellow a break. What they printed was what the editor and his political backers wanted.

The New York *Times* was founded, a hundred years ago, largely in protest against that kind of news reporting—particularly on the part of Horace Greeley's *Tribune,* but also in general; and for those days it was a remarkably fair and impartial newspaper. Yet any of you who have had occasion to look into the files of the *Times* in the fifties, sixties, or seventies will have encountered a good many stories which by modern standards are conspicuously lacking in impartiality.

An instance—a mild one—is the report by Henry J. Raymond himself from the Republican national convention of 1860, after it had nominated Abraham Lincoln for president. Raymond, of course, had gone there in the hope and expectation of seeing it nominate William H. Seward and was bitterly disappointed at the outcome, and he wrote that night that endeavors were being made to find out the nominee's history but it was not yet certain that he had a history.

In due course Abraham Lincoln did have a history, and Henry J. Raymond, in a minor way, helped him make it. Even before that, the *Times* came around to his support; he was not Seward but he was the Republican candidate, and now was the time for all good men to come to the aid of the party. Still, there are very few American newspapers which would nowadays carry such a story as Raymond wrote about the nominee of the convention. And this in the most objective paper of the time.

Toward the end of the century there was a revulsion against the practice. Again the New York *Times* was out in front, but it was by no means the only paper which was trying to be objective. But newspaper editors all seemed afflicted with a certain diffidence; they knew that complete objectivity was impossible; they seemed to doubt their ability to find out the truth and tell it to the public. So they adopted the practice of reporting what everybody said about it and letting the reader make up his own mind.

Now, as a reaction against the bias and partisanship of nineteenth-century newspapers this was praiseworthy, but it put a considerable burden on the reader. The paper gave him both sides of the story; it was up to him to decide for himself where the truth lay—with this side, or that one, or in between. In theory this was admirable; in practice the reader very often did not have the information that would have enabled him to judge, or the time to look for it, and his newspaper gave him no help. A says this, B says that; either of them may be lying in his teeth, or maybe both; but the reader had to figure it out for himself, and often he simply did not have the means to do it—even assuming that he wanted to do it and did not prefer the version of the story that accorded with his own prejudices.

Of course, most newspaper editors would have an answer to that—see the editorial page, where the arguments on both sides are analyzed and evaluated, and some approximation to the truth is suggested to the reader.

That would be fine if (a) every editorial page made a conscientious effort to evaluate the arguments and arrive at the truth—some of them do, others are only concerned with that version of the truth which suits the partisan or the class interest of the owner; and if (b) everybody read the editorial page. But we all know that very few people do read it, and I have yet to see a newspaper which carried an eight-column front-page banner saying, "For the truth about what you read below, see the editorial page."

This striving for objectivity—I repeat—was in its beginnings a good thing, but it went a little too far. From holding that newspapers ought to present both sides, it went on to the position that it was all right to present only one side, if nobody happened to be talking on the other; and it was not the business of the newspaper to tell the reader if that one argument happened to be a phony.

This is not quite so bad now as it used to be; it reached its peak, I think, some twenty-five years ago—in the administration of Calvin Coolidge, when it was the opinion of the great majority of American citizens that things are what they seem. In those days, if the Hon. John P. Hoozis was important enough to be interviewed, you might see half or two-thirds of a column embodying the views of the Hon. John P. Hoozis on some topic or other, with no indication that what he said was a lie from beginning to end—even if the editor who printed the story happened to know it—and no indication that the Hon. John P. Hoozis might have a powerful personal interest, financial or otherwise, in getting that view over to the public. He had said it, and if he was important enough to be news, it would not have been objective not to print it.

We are perhaps somewhat better off in this respect than we were twenty-five years ago; too many of the respected figures of the later twenties turned out to be hollow phonies, not every man is any longer taken at his face value.

Yet those who have official positions are likely to be so taken, still. Consider Senator McCarthy; not a single one of his charges has ever been proved, most of them have been pretty conclusively disproved in public hearings—yet he can repeat those same charges and still get space in the papers, sometimes on the front page. And not always merely in papers which find him a useful stick with which to beat the political opposition; very often in papers whose editors may know that this is old stuff, may know that none of it has been proved and much of it has been refuted, yet who feel that if a United States Senator keeps on saying it, it would not be objective to refuse to print it.

The necessity for this sort of thing is not always apparent, even to people in the trade. One of the most experienced of the British correspondents in this country—Robert Waithman, who has been here fourteen years for the London *News Chronicle*—has lately written a book, not about the news business but with some incidental remarks about it.[1] I gather from a *Herald Tribune* review that he thinks it is not altogether admirable for American newspapers to be proud of giving equal space to the statements of honest men and of proven liars.

"It seems to me," he says, "that the nation would gain if it were demonstrated that you have to know what you are talking about before the newspapers will give you space."

That, however, would not be objective. You may remember the great uproar about rubber production and rubber supply early in 1942. For some time, the man who got most newspaper space in that argument was a Congressional committee expert, whose chief qualification appeared to be that he had once edited a Broadway scandal sheet. But he was the expert for a Congressional committee; therefore what he said was news.

This kind of dead-pan reporting—So-and-so said it, and if he is lying in his teeth it is not my business to say so—may salve the conscience of the reporter (or of the editor, who has the ultimate responsibility) as to his loyalty to some obscure ideal of objectivity. But what about his loyalty to the reader? The reader lays down his nickel, or whatever, for the paper, in the belief that he is going to find out what is going on in the world; and it does not seem to me that the newspaper is giving him his nickel's worth if it only gives him what somebody says is going on in the world, with no hint as to whether what that somebody says is right or wrong.

Well, what is the answer? One answer of course has been the rise of the syndicated columns. Who started them I do not know—whether Paul Mallon, or Ray Tucker (for both of whom the honor has been claimed —not by themselves), or, as I am inclined to suspect, a man now almost forgotten, Clinton Gilbert.

At any rate they first came into prominence back in the Coolidge days, when there began to be newspaper readers who were not sure that things are what they seem and who wanted somebody to try to figure things out for them; and they proliferated in the early New Deal, when government had all at once become infinitely more complex, and its problems needed more explanation than ever before. Certainly, over all, the columns have been a good thing for public enlightenment—especially in newspapers which are willing to print columns representing different opinions, instead of sticking to those that back up the editorial page.

How much influence they actually have is debatable. As most of you know, Jack Knight every Sunday writes a two-column editorial for his numerous newspapers. One Sunday when I happened to be in Miami I read one of these editorials—two columns of reasoned and powerful argument that the syndicated columns have lost their influence, that nobody believes them any more, that they have gone the way of the forgotten and disregarded editorial page. A singular argument to present on an editorial page, perhaps, but still more singular was the fact that the page opposite that editorial carried no less than twelve syndicated columns.

I ventured to ask Knight, later, about this apparent contradiction; and he said, "Well, people like to read the columns, so when they spend the winter in Miami we give them what they get at home."

So it would seem that even the readers of the Knight papers put more faith in the columns than they do in what they read on the editorial page.

Along with the columns, of course, came the radio news commentary which, like the column, is a mixture of news and interpretation—opinion, if you like—but which differs from the column in that it usually covers at least the high spots of a day's news, while the syndicated column, written as a rule a day or so in advance, is likely to deal only with a single topic. It would ill beseem me to try to estimate the influence or importance, actual or relative, of the trade in which I myself am engaged; all I can say—and this might be said of columns too—is that some radio commentaries admirably illuminate and explain the news for the customer, some seem likely to leave him in a state of total confusion.

But whatever the impact of the news broadcaster or the syndicated columnist, I doubt that either of them has materially supplanted what remains the principal source of news to the general public, the front page of the paper. And it makes a difference, a vast difference, to the health of the republic whether what is on that front page is what is so, to the best of the editor's and the reporter's capacity to ascertain it, or only what somebody falsely alleges to be so. Objectivity, a necessary and useful ideal in its day, has been carried so far that it leans over backward and often obscures the truth instead of revealing it. How can we cure that? Unfortunately, any attempt to cure it is in danger of leaning disastrously over on the other side.

The case I am about to cite is an obscure one but it illustrates the dangers. Some two or three years ago the Washington correspondent of a weekly magazine—who is its Washington correspondent no longer—decided, correctly, that this dead-pan objectivity is very apt to spread misinformation; he proposed to substitute for it what he called *Gestalt* journalism—on the analogy of the *Gestalt* psychology which attempts to present a total picture, a functioning organism which is somewhat more than the sum of all its parts.

A good idea in theory. He proceeded to build up a total picture of governmental Washington at a particular moment out of a vast number of details, but unfortunately the total picture had to be the sum of its parts, even if it was something more besides; and that total picture, the *Gestalt,* was somewhat vitiated by the fact that many of the details were wrong.

To mention just one—among the details that made up the total picture was the Chief Justice's Georgia accent. Now of course the Chief Justice comes from Kentucky; the reporter had confused Fred Vinson and Carl Vinson. I could not see myself what the Chief Justice's accent, or his provenance, had to do with the total picture; but the reporter seemed to think it had something to do with it, and in that case it would seem important to get it right.

But there were errors much more serious than that, in which the reporter—no doubt in all sincerity—had confused his own prejudices with the facts. So the end product of this *Gestalt* journalism was not the *Gestalt* of governmental Washington at a given moment in time, but only of the reporter himself.

Now this perhaps is not very important; but this man was trying to do something that it would be useful to get done, if possible, and his failure illustrated the difficulties inherent in trying to do it, even for a reporter more experienced and more judicious than he. What is now called objectivity has its great and visible shortcomings; but any attempt at interpretation has its perils too—it should be undertaken only by a man who bears always in mind that famous admonition of Oliver Cromwell: "In the bowels of Christ, think it possible you may be mistaken."

I believe the present tendency is toward more interpretation. But just how it can effectively be done—not in the columns or the radio commentary or on the editorial page, but on the front page—that is something that must still be worked out, and present American newspaper techniques offer little help. One reason we may be moving in that direction was suggested in a recent editorial in the Washington *Post,* dealing with the television reports of the San Francisco peace conference.

"Perhaps," says the *Post,* "the art of reporting, in the traditional sense of the word, is destined to disappear. The newspapers and news services may soon have to concern themselves almost exclusively with the why of things, leaving the business of who, what, when, where to the cameras."

I have never believed that television news was much of a menace to the newspapers, or to radio news either. Some things it can certainly do far better than any other medium; but you cannot be sure you are going to have a camera where the news will break. And even when you have—such a news event as a home run, a knockout punch, tells its own story; when you see it, you have got it. But even a peace conference or a crime-committee hearing is apt to need some explanation by the spoken or printed word, and there is much news that cannot be explained and cannot even be reported by pictures.

Television, however, *is* likely to increase the emphasis on the why of the news. This Washington *Post* editorial continues, "Even before the advent of television, the old-fashioned distinction between objective, or purely factual, and interpretive reporting was becoming a bit blurred; a greater proportion of newspaper space was being given over to that special mixture of news and opinion purveyed by the syndicated columnists."

Yes, but the columns are carried inside the paper; how do you get a better impression of the truth to the man who reads only the front page—or the front-page headlines? It is no good to tell him he should not be that way, that he should take time to read the rest of the paper too; if he will not do it, you owe him as good a break as you can give him.

I am not arguing against objectivity; I am all *for* the objectivity that gives the reader a real understanding of what is going on. My complaint is only that what is now called objectivity too often makes the newspaper a mere mouthpiece for pretentious phonies.

The good newspaper must walk a tight rope between two abysses—on the one side the false objectivity which takes everything at face value and lets the public be imposed upon by the charlatan with the most brazen front; on the other, the interpretive reporting which fails to draw the line between objective and subjective, between a reasonably well-established fact and what the reporter or the editor wishes were the fact. This is primary-school stuff, of course; everybody knows it, and if few people practice it, that is because practicing it is very hard. It is easier to pick out the nearest exit—to fall back on the incontrovertible fact that the Hon. John P. Hoozis said, colon quote, without going into the question whether he was lying or not.

What makes it hard to do anything else is partly the increasing complexity of the news, and partly the traditions of the trade. There is the headline; it must simplify, and simplification is often distortion; but its general pattern is fixed and it seems hopeless to try to change it now. It is permissible for the syndicated column to interpret; but if a man of enough importance to be quoted on the front pages says something that is known to be false—if Pat Hurley, for instance, blames the Atomic Energy Commission for something that happened before the Commission was created or even thought of—it would be an outrageous innovation to interrupt his reported discourse with a bracketed paragraph pointing out that this is not true. I believe I have seen that done, during the war, with some speeches of Hitler; it may have been done since the war with some statements by Stalin; but I cannot recall that I have ever seen it done with one of our own people. If it was ever done, any time, anywhere, it has certainly been done very seldom indeed.

Interpretive and corrective journalism not only entails the risk of confusing opinion with fact—a statement which could easily be documented out of certain newspaper columns, and certain radio commentaries. It is also extremely hard work—increasingly hard these days in Washington, when we get the same old subjects gone over, again and again, with the same old witnesses coming up and telling stories something like, but not exactly like, what they told before.

Few papers can afford a McCarthy specialist, a Budenz specialist, to check what they say today against what they said last year; it is practically a full-time job.

It is an attractive idea that there might be more exchange of information among reporters on the same paper—the diplomatic expert, for instance, telling the man who covered the MacArthur hearings that there really was practically no chance of peace being wrecked by MacArthur's interposition. But both of those men have plenty of work to do; they might not have time to exchange information—indeed normally they might not even know that there was any occasion for information to be exchanged.

For that matter, few reporters who covered the MacArthur hearings— with the interminable repetitions, the same question asked by successive senators of the same witness, and then asked of each succeeding witness, over and over—few people were able to remember, by the end of that ordeal, just who had said what when. We have the printed record now, of course, and it is pretty well indexed; still it takes time to find what you are looking for—more time than a reporter with today's story to write may always have.

With good luck, and a good memory, he may hit on the right road from Athens to Thebes, but he is likely to have missed a good many landmarks along the way.

To sum up—objectivity is all right if it is really objective, if it conveys as accurate an impression of the truth as can be obtained. But to let demonstrably false statements stand with no warning of their falsity is not what I would call objectivity.

I happen to work in a field of the news whose traditions and standards permit calling attention to false statements; and I think we might have better newspapers if their traditions and standards permitted it too, in some spot more generally noticeable than the editorial page. But it entails great danger; it requires conscientious care to make sure that you do not substitute your own hopes or opinions for demonstrable fact.

A couple of years ago, at the University of Missouri, I remarked that one of the qualities needed by a good reporter is humility; for which I was taken to task by Westbrook Pegler—very naturally, since humility is one of several things that Pegler has not got much of, and seems to get along all right without.

Nevertheless it seems to me an essential piece of a reporter's equipment. To be aware of his own fallibility, to make just as sure as he can that he is right, and then to have the confidence to go ahead when he has done the best he can—always conscious of his responsibility, not merely to his own conscience but above all to the customer who relies on him to give the truth; whether it be the customer who lays down his nickel for the newspaper, or the customer who only turns on the radio for free.

The Government

and the Press

There are, I think, two outstanding influences which have contributed fresh strength and vitality to the American press during the past quarter of a century.* One of these influences—perhaps the most important in raising the standards of American journalism—has been the growth of the American Newspaper Guild. The guild may have been less eloquent than some of the associations of publishers and editors in adopting resolutions and formulating canons of conduct for newspapers. But in its own mundane, bread-and-butter way, it has managed to lift the wages and working conditions of newspapermen, so that newspapering has become a respectable, if not yet a highly remunerative, livelihood.

In the good old days before Heywood Broun propounded his radical notion of a decent wage scale, the newspaper game (as we all loved to call it then) employed a distressingly high proportion of beaten-down hacks or juvenile romantics. The movies gave currency to a not altogether unwarranted caricature of the American journalist as a happy-go-lucky, carefree daredevil, boozily indifferent to the deficiencies of his weekly paycheck.

The American Newspaper Guild, by virtue of some pretty stern and stubborn effort, has managed to improve that weekly paycheck to a

---

* This lecture was delivered December 5, 1952.

68

point at which men could begin to think of newspaper work as a career rather than as an escape from reality. Hollywood's loss was journalism's gain. By making journalism a calling in which men of competence and conscience could hope to support themselves and even to raise families —could hope indeed to take a responsible place in the life of their communities—the guild made it possible for men of first-rate capacities to enter the calling and to stay in it beyond their salad days. I can think of nothing that has done so much to improve the caliber of the American press as this improvement in the caliber of the men serving it.

The second major influence upon the contemporary American press, it seems to me, has been wrought by the schools of journalism. And I trust that, in this room at least, I shall arouse no serious contention if I say what is obvious and generally acknowledged: that among these, the University of Minnesota's school of journalism has assumed a position of pre-eminent leadership.

The press has responsibilities which go beyond that of any other private enterprise. And it is with the discharge of these responsibilities that the schools of journalism must be primarily concerned. They set standards of performance for the working press. They are the keepers of the conscience of our calling.

It is because the joint sponsors of this memorial lecture have a common concern about the performance of the American press that I take it to be the obligation of anyone speaking under their auspices to speak candidly and critically. A great deal can be said, and said honestly, about the virtues of American newspapers. Perhaps it can fairly be said that, with all their faults, they remain the best that men have yet developed. I have a strong feeling, however, that it would be well to let others, outside the craft, give us such applause as they may think that we deserve; and that for us who are members of the fourth estate, the need at present is to concentrate on our shortcomings and to look at them unflinchingly and realistically.

American newspapers have just won an election. They have won this election after a number of unsuccessful tries, and they have won it, I think, at a very considerable cost to their own prestige and independence.

The president of the American Newspaper Publishers Association, Charles F. McCahill, said a great deal more than he meant to say, I suspect, when he told the board of the Bureau of Advertising of the ANPA at a recent meeting that the press exerted great influence in the election of General Dwight Eisenhower. "When the merchandise is good," he said, "the press can sell it. I think the newspapers exerted great influence in this election. They had a great product to sell. They presented it factually and forcefully to the American people, and the people accepted it."

I intend no partisanship, and certainly I intend no disparagement of a great American who is soon to assume the awful burdens of the Presidency, when I say that General Eisenhower, as a political figure, was to a large extent the creation of the American press. Newspaper publishers had a good deal to do with initiating and promoting his "draft" for the Republican nomination. They took part in a common if not concerted publicity campaign to transform the general from a military hero into a civilian leader. An extraordinary number of them pledged him their support and endorsed him without qualification before he became a candidate—and before they knew anything at all about his political outlook. They packaged the product which McCahill says they sold.

It goes without saying that they had every right to do this. And perhaps their preference for General Eisenhower over Governor Adlai Stevenson stemmed from the perspective of their professional position, reflecting only their disinterested, objective, unprejudiced appraisal of the two men and the two major political parties. I am inclined to think, however, that it was more reflective of a natural propensity on the part of newspaper publishers to behave like newspaper publishers—which is to say, like conservative businessmen.

Let me offer you a couple of inconclusive but not altogether insignificant considerations which lead me to put more stock in the latter explanation than in the former. The first of these is the striking divergence between the views of the publishers and their professional employees. Eric Sevareid observed in a mid-October broadcast that "a most bizarre situation has developed in this campaign, worthy of attention at least as a footnote to history. Never before has such a high percentage of American publishers come out personally for a candidate; and what *makes* it bizarre is that the working journalists appear just as overwhelmingly for Stevenson as their publishers are for Eisenhower. In political sentiment at least, publishers are drawing closer to other publishers, and farther away from their own staffs."

The second consideration which I think deserves to be taken into account may be a mere coincidence—although it does not seem so to me and, I fancy, does not seem so to most Americans—the fact that General Eisenhower happened to be the candidate of the Republican party, and that the Republican party is the party of the conservatives and of the businessmen.

Editor & Publisher reported in its issue of November 1,[1] just prior to the election, that the General had the editorial support of 67 per cent of the daily newspapers published in the United States and that these newspapers represented 80 per cent of the total daily circulation in the country. The governor, on the other hand, was endorsed editorially by only 14 per cent of the dailies, and these comprised only 11 per cent of the total circulation. The rest of the press was not formally committed. While Eisenhower had the backing of at least one newspaper in every state of the Union, there were nine states in which Stevenson had no editorial support whatever.

In Governor Stevenson's home state of Illinois, according to the *Editor & Publisher* survey, fifty-two newspapers backed the General while only four backed the governor. And it seems worth noting that the combined circulation of the Eisenhower backers was 3,488,969, while the combined circulation of the Stevenson backers was 35,420—a ratio of almost precisely 100 to 1.

In Michigan, a key state, the newspaper line-up was 35 to 1, the circulation line-up two million as compared with thirty-three hundred. In Pennsylvania, it was 83 to 5, or three and one-third million against a combined circulation slightly under one hundred thousand.

It seems to me that the most newsworthy aspect of this striking disparity is—that there was no news in it. It contained no element of novelty whatever. The division in 1948 was 65 per cent of the dailies against 15 per cent. In 1944, it was 60 against 22. In 1940, 66 against 20. In 1936, 60 against 35. Need I say that in each of these divisions the preponderance was on the Republican side?

"In my new role in life," Governor Stevenson observed in a talk to newspaper editors at the very beginning of the campaign, "I can't help noticing from time to time—I want to put it as delicately as I can—that the overwhelming majority of the newspapers of the country are supporting the opposition candidate. This is something, I find, that even my best friends will tell me! And I certainly don't take it personally."

He was quite right not to take it personally. It had nothing whatever to do with him or with the merits of his candidacy. It would have remained just about the same in all probability, no matter what he said or how he conducted his campaign. "It would seem," he said philosophically, "that the overwhelming majority of the press is just against Democrats. And it is against Democrats, so far as I can see, not after a sober and considered review of the alternatives, but automatically, as dogs are against cats. As soon as a newspaper—I speak of the great majority, not the enlightened 10 per cent—sees a Democratic candidate, it is filled with an unconquerable yen to chase him up an alley."

It was in this sense that Governor Stevenson expressed concern over "the extent to which we are developing a one-party press in a two-party country." All of us who are members of the press need, I think, to share in his concern.

It has been possible in the past to gloss over the bias of the press on the ground that it has not seemed to be very influential. In five successive national elections, the American public managed to ignore the editorial importunities of the newspapers. But those who disparage the influence of the press sometimes tend to confuse the influence of the editorial page with the influence of the news pages.

Any generalization about the 1,700-odd daily newspapers in the United States—even perhaps, the generalization I am now indulging in—has very doubtful validity. And a generalization drawn from isolated, random incidents—especially those selected to show the worst instead of the best aspects of an institution—is bound to be misleading and unjust. For my own part, however, I find extremely disquieting some of the "atrocity stories" which have come out of the campaign.

Let me quote once more Eric Sevareid, a sober and balanced analyst. "Nearly all the great weekly publications, such as *Time* and *Life,*" he said, "are not only for Eisenhower in their editorials but some are unabashedly using their news and picture space as well to help his cause, by giving him the predominant play, week after week. But they are fairness itself, compared to some big Midwest and Western dailies where Stevenson is reported as if he were a candidate for county clerk. Little wonder that Stevenson is concentrating on radio and television to get his arguments across."

Another experienced and thoroughly dependable witness on the campaign performance of the press is Roscoe Drummond of the *Christian Science Monitor*. "The Democratic nominee," Mr. Drummond said, "is getting considerably less than an even break in the news columns of the daily newspapers across the country. . . . My own daily observations on this matter lead me to the conclusion that much of the daily press is committing a serious offense against its readers—and against the canons of responsible journalism—in showing marked one-sidedness in covering the news of this campaign and in slanting much of the news it does cover."

Add to such estimates as these the isolated instances of unfair play, which seem to have been pretty widespread, and you have a very disagreeable picture of what might be called, in the editorial jargon so popular a few weeks ago, "a captive press." There are the numerous stories—to suggest only a single example—of newspapers which chronicled the General's arrival to make a speech with banner headlines but seemed to regard a visit from the governor as a military secret.

But such stories, whether or not they are typical and true, do not go to the heart of the influence which the press has exerted, and will continue to exert, on American opinion. It may be doubted whether the outcome of the election could have been determined by any amount of distortion in the reporting of the campaign. There is no room for doubt, however, that the thinking of the American people—the attitude with which they approach an election—is shaped and conditioned to a major degree by what they read in their newspapers.

The values by which people appraise individuals and issues are immeasurably affected by the values which their newspapers set before them —in news pages even more than in editorial pages, in advertising, in comics, and in the other syndicated material that is more and more reducing the diversity and individuality of the American press. The public's emotional temperature may be governed by the heat of the headlines, much as the temperature of a living room may be governed by a thermostat.

For some time past the press has been conveying to the American people some fantastically misshapen pictures of their country and their fellow-citizens. It has allowed itself to be used by demagogues as a vehicle for the exploitation of anxiety. Day after day it has reported— with an "objectivity" that treats with perfect evenhandedness the character assassin and his victim—allegations that the government of the United States is overrun with Communists and subversives. Week after week it has conveyed from Congressional committees and from supposedly sober senators an impression that the Communist party is a powerful octopus extending its tentacles into every aspect of American life—our homes, our churches, our schools, our labor unions, our arts and our professions. Month after month it has made the public flesh creep with hints of saboteurs and spies who have penetrated into every sanctum of security. Quadrennially, these accusations have grown increasingly shrill and insistent. They reached a crescendo a couple of years ago and have maintained that pitch, like a stuck whistle, ever since.

It is not easy in such an atmosphere to make rational judgments. An atmosphere in which the newspapers report straight-facedly the assertions of a United States Senator that the Secretary of State is a Soviet agent, that the Chief of Staff who guided the United States Army to victory in the greatest of world wars is the leader of a treasonable conspiracy, that one of the country's principal spokesmen at the United

Nations is not to be trusted—this is an atmosphere more conducive to lynching than to the operation of the democratic process.

The constant repetition of such charges, the incessant sowing of suspicion and distrust, could not fail to affect men's minds in a time of tightening international tension—and in a world waiting apprehensively for atomic extinction. I am not saying that the newspapers originated these charges or that they are responsible for them. But they have been the carriers of hysteria in much the same way that the mosquito has been the carrier of malaria. When men have been led long enough to believe that they are teetering on the edge of an abyss, it is small wonder if they lose their balance. When the news pages have created a panic, the editorial pages are likely to be powerless to quell it.

It is upon this larger problem, rather than upon coverage of the campaign itself, that I would urge the focusing of the post-election inquest into the performance of the press which has already been suggested by a number of thoughtful commentators. The inquest will not serve much useful purpose if it is conducted by counting the linage devoted to the Democrats and the linage devoted to the Republicans in the brief period between Labor Day and Election Day. More subtle matters of content will have to be weighed; and the weighing, if it is to have much meaning, will have to deal with the larger question whether the press is, in fact, conveying to its readers a focused picture of the world around them.

The study ought to be a tough and searching one. And it ought not to be dismissed cavalierly by the press—as the study made by the Commission on Freedom of the Press, a group of distinguished scholars under the chairmanship of Dr. Robert M. Hutchins, was dismissed five years ago. The warning expressed by that commission is worth remembering today. "The press must know," it declared, "that its faults and errors have ceased to be private vagaries and have become public dangers. Its inadequacies menace the balance of public opinion. It has lost the common and ancient human liberty to be deficient in its function or to offer half-truth for the whole."

The press must make itself, and keep itself, genuinely independent if it is to retain its freedom. The two go inescapably hand in hand. If the press becomes the captive—or, equally, if it becomes the captor—of any political party, it will eventually arouse in the opposition a demand that it be brought under some sort of governmental regulation. And if that demand should ever prevail, the indispensable condition of press freedom will be destroyed. A free press must be an independent press.

A one-party press is dangerous enough, as I have tried to suggest, when its party is out of office. It becomes intolerable when its party is in power.

For the paramount function of the press in the American social system is censorship of the government. It was primarily in order to enable it to fulfill this function that the founders of the Republic insisted upon adding to the Constitution as its first amendment—and as the first article in its Bill of Rights—a flat, absolute prohibition against any governmental regulation of the press.

The men who wrote the Bill of Rights were not sentimentalists. They valued freedom of the press not as an abstract ideal but for utilitarian purposes. They granted to newspapers—despite the fact that these were private enterprises operated for private profit—a uniquely privileged position because they looked upon them as one of the essential elements in the elaborate system of checks and balances they had contrived to keep governmental authority within appropriate bounds. So far from conceiving of the press as subject to censorship by the government—as it had been in the England from which they declared their independence —they aimed to establish censorship of the government by the press.

This view of the fourth estate as distinct from, and as an offset to, all the other estates of the realm was an axiom among the libertarian political thinkers of the late eighteenth century. The First Continental Congress sent a memorial to the inhabitants of the Province of Quebec in 1774, referring to liberty of the press as a means "whereby oppressive officers are shamed or intimidated into more honorable or just modes of conducting affairs."

The idea that the press ought to serve as a censor of the government was explicitly stated by Thomas Jefferson. He wrote to President Washington in 1792: "No government ought to be without censors, and while the press is free, no one will."

It was precisely in order to enable the press to discharge this indispensable censorial function that the American people have tolerated a great deal of newspaper irresponsibility. For it is a central principle of the American political faith that total divorcement of the press from the government is a condition of freedom. Indeed, nothing more sharply differentiates the Russian system from the American system—or any totalitarian from any free society—than the contrasting relationships they maintain between the government and the press.

It happens that the bias of the press has been on the side of its censorial function during the past two decades when the political party it predominantly supported was out of office. And it must certainly be admitted that the press has been vigorous enough in exposing venality in the Bureau of Internal Revenue and the Reconstruction Finance Corporation and other federal agencies.

I am convinced, however, that the government has been engaged in something much worse and much more dangerous then venality, and the press, I think, has almost entirely ignored it. There has been taking place an expansion of governmental power and an encroachment of that power upon traditional civil liberties of a sort that the authors of the Bill of Rights would have considered intolerable—and which they relied upon a free press to prevent.

Think, for example, of the prevalence of the political test oath today. Our forefathers considered it an abomination. But now almost everyone who accepts any kind of public employment, and many who are engaged in private industry, are required to go through the mumbo-jumbo of disclaiming disloyalty—as though, somehow, the safety of the nation could be assured by this ritual of expurgation.

Think of the extent to which we have whittled down the great safeguards of individual rights which we customarily refer to as due process of law. Men are condemned and punished in these times for the undefined offense of disloyalty—on the basis of information from anonymous sources—information the source of which is often unknown even to the judges in these strange, un-American proceedings.

Think, if you will, of the ways in which Congressional committees, in the guise of investigation, have usurped the functions of courts of law, placing men on trial as it were—although without any of the protections which a court of law would provide, probing into their private political beliefs (and sometimes even into their religious faith), forcing them to profess their patriotism, and punishing them by publicity for conduct which the Constitution forbids Congress to make punishable by law.

Think of the extent to which we have permitted petty officials to make arbitrary decisions affecting the rights of American citizens—the right to travel abroad, for instance—and this in a country whose citizens have always proudly asserted that they lived under a government of laws, not a government of men.

Think how far we have allowed the federal police to invade our vaunted rights of privacy. Wiretapping, for example, has become an accepted practice, despite the fact that a federal statute expressly prohibits it.

Think how flagrantly members of the United States Senate have abused the immunity from suits for slander which their office confers upon them —to vilify and destroy innocent men for personal or political purposes.

All this extension of governmental power—all these violations of the individual rights traditionally claimed by Americans—are justified in the name of national security. Yet I am convinced that they operate, in fact, to impair the security they are supposed to protect—that by diminishing the freedom of American citizens, they diminish the real sources of American strength. They are aimed, like the Japanese thought-control system of which we used to make so much fun during the war, at the elimination of "dangerous thoughts" and the enforcement of a rigid and sterile conformity.

The worst and the most frightening aspect of this invasion of individual rights is that the newspapers, with few exceptions, have not cried out against it. Many, indeed, have applauded it and have let themselves be used, for the most part unwittingly, as instruments for the execution of sentences arbitrarily imposed by Congressional committees or by senatorial demagogues.

It does not matter that the extension of government authority and the invasion of what were once deemed inalienable rights have taken place in the name of national security. It does not matter that the men responsible for this corruption of basic American principles were patriotic and well-intentioned. Dictatorship always has its origin in the assumption that men supposed to be benevolent may be entrusted with arbitrary authority. The American Republic was born in rebellion against such authority; it was nurtured on the doctrine that governmental power must be jealously circumscribed and kept, in particular, from interference with individual freedom of expression and association.

The press was meant to serve as a sentinel of this freedom. It ought always to remember the warning uttered by Justice Louis Brandeis. "Experience should teach us to be most on our guard to protect liberty," he said, "when the government's purposes are beneficent. Men born to freedom are naturally alert to repel invasion of their liberty by evil-minded rulers. The greatest dangers to liberty lurk in insidious encroachment by men of zeal, well-meaning but without understanding."

The American press is going to face a crucial test when the party it has so long supported assumes office in January. It will have to prove that it deserves its freedom by reaffirming its independence. It will have to resume its ancient role as a censor of the government.

Its commitment must be, not to any party, but to the public. Freedom of the press, as Justice Felix Frankfurter has pointed out, "is not an end in itself but a means to the end of a free society." A free press can exist only in a society that is free. If the press fails in its championship of freedom for the society as a whole, it will lose its own freedom. If it fails in its censorship *of* the government, it will succumb in the end to censorship *by* the government.

Americans look to their armed forces to protect their liberties from totalitarian assault from abroad. They look to their newspapers to protect their liberties from the assault of demagogues at home. This is the first function of a free press.

In the long, bitter and titanic struggle now in progress between totalitarianism and democracy, the real superiority of the democratic system lies fundamentally not in the number and power of its machines, not in its capacity to produce steel or to manufacture weapons, not even in its supremacy in the field of atomic energy—important as these assets may be; it lies, rather, in the techniques and the resources of freedom—in the loyalty and unity and spirit which can be forged only among free men.

Freedom has been, from the beginning of our history, the real secret of America's growth to greatness and the most vital source of American security. Freedom is the special symbol of America. In the harbor of our greatest city stands a heroic statue of Liberty, holding aloft a blazing torch. We must never allow that torch to be extinguished, either by dictators abroad or by demagogues at home. It has always given us the light to see our way.

ERIC SEVAREID

The Big Truth

My own state of mind about American journalism in this year of our Lord, I am afraid, is somewhat schizophrenic.* You cannot live around the world without marveling at the superiorities of American press and radio news—its speed, the vigorous enterprise of its reporters, the enormous flood of facts it provides every day; you cannot doubt that in these respects no other people is so well provided; and you cannot doubt that in very few countries does the journalist enjoy the prestige he enjoys with us. But you cannot move around the world, or around your own country, for that matter, sense the prodigious, rapid changes that are remaking the world, shaking all the familiar forms and values out of joint, without a hollow feeling in the pit of the stomach that we are not really getting it across, not really preparing the American mind to cope with a fierce test of the American civilization—indeed, what is almost surely the supreme test of the Christian era.

We are showing our people who, what, where, and how; we are not sufficiently showing them *why*. The journalism we throw on our daily screen is still two-D journalism, the flat fact accompanied by the flat opinion. That never was good enough, and it is perilously inadequate now. We have not really moved into the era of three-D journalism, al-

---

* This lecture was delivered October 23, 1953.

though some are trying; we are not providing the depth, not illuminating the background, making it a living part of the picture with the third dimension, which is Meaning.

There are no obstacles save those we impose upon ourselves. We are our own self-censors of our own much greater capacities. All honor to those editors who continue to fight the classic fight to free the news from government censorship or suppression at source. It is a continuing task in this country, the first and basic task in many countries; but it is not, to my mind, the supreme challenge of American journalism today, the many resolutions of editors' conventions to the contrary notwithstanding. The real struggle is within ourselves, within our own industry.

Before dealing with this internal challenge, which will be the burden of my speech tonight, I would like to say something about government, about the new federal administration, vis-à-vis the press. At times, some of us—myself included—have expressed apprehensions, but I think now it has given a pretty fair performance, and where it has given a bad performance, that has been mostly due to the defensiveness—not really the aggressiveness, though it sometimes looked like it—of new men not quite sure of themselves. The chief example of this was the Secretary of Defense [1] in the winter months. He is now much more accessible to reporters, his department is opening up. The present Secretary of State is even more accessible than his predecessor; [2] curiously, the present Secretary has more respect for the press than his predecessor had, yet the press covering his department had more respect for the predecessor than it has for the incumbent.

By happenstance, I did the first personal interviews, last winter, with most of the new cabinet officers, via television. Cooperation was excellent, save in two instances, Defense and Justice, where I was totally blocked. It seemed to me there was a certain air of defensive arrogance toward the journalists in the Justice Department; and it was not greatly surprising that the Attorney General [3] presumed to give out the news of the new Chief Justice to four hand-picked and friendly news organs, a news leak of a peculiarly crude and arrogant nature considering the august quality of the subject matter. But judging by the Attorney General's contrite and friendly manner before the National Press Club two weeks ago, I gather that he, like the Defense Secretary, is now trying to establish his press relations on a sounder footing.

At the White House, things have changed. The President's relations with the reporters are—tentative. That is the most fitting word I can think of. This President feels personally more comfortable with publishers than with the working press; for twenty years it had been the other way around. There is no question that, before inauguration, the President was doubtful that he should hold regular news conferences. One of the men who persuaded him he must was J. Russell Wiggins of Saint Paul and Washington. He has not always enjoyed the conferences, and he has not known how to *use* them, as a positive technique in governing, as did his two immediate predecessors; but he has not done too badly. He is scrupulously fair, never resorts to any deviousness, and he tries to answer every question. The problem of the reporters in writing their accounts is not that two-word remark, "no comment"; it is the well-intended remark which too often amounts to "no comment" expressed in several hundred words. There are times, even with the stenographic transcript before them, when no two reporters will agree on just what the President meant, and this confusion, of course, is reflected in subsequent accounts the people read and hear.

Last winter's well-publicized White House plan for enlarging the news conference, by having cabinet members present, and by occasionally televising the proceedings, has not been carried out. The procedure is the same as under Truman and Roosevelt, but the frequency of the meetings has seriously declined. The number of Eisenhower meetings with reporters is running about one-half the Truman rate, and one-fourth the Roosevelt rate. I do not believe, myself, that the rate will be increased. At least, not until and unless the President develops a greater mastery of his material and consequently a greater sense of ease in meeting the questions.

Some Republican leaders, notably the late Senator Robert Taft, were quick to charge, last winter, that Washington writers and broadcasters were overly critical of the new regime, because, they said, we were nearly all Democrats. This criticism, I thought, reflected an oversimplified evaluation of the Washington writing corps and its motivations, and it was another example of the strangely sensitive, defensive attitude of the new administration—strange in view of the enormous public backing the election revealed it had. A more pertinent criticism of the Washington writers was made by the *Wall Street Journal*. It found fault with us, not because of our views regarding a Republican President in the White House, but because of our views regarding the Presidency. That is, so the *Journal* argued, we now have a President who, out of constitutional conviction, is trying to reduce the dominance of the executive branch, end twenty years of executive legislation, and restore the Congress to a coequal status; and, this argument runs, the writers, accustomed to two decades of aggressive chief executives, are wrongly interpreting a traditional, legitimate policy as weakness.

There is a certain truth in this criticism; I think we working writers, who are—let's face it—in our own way almost as resentful of criticism as publishers, must take a long look at ourselves within this framework. The intellectually dull and prosaic atmosphere of the present White House ought not to affect our judgment on this point. I still feel, however, that the *Journal*'s answer begs the greater question: Whether this limited executive function can really deal with the times we live in; whether this limited conception does not result in *congressional* government; whether, in fact, this modern, world-sprawled America can exercise the leadership history imposes upon it except by executive dominance. For myself, I do not believe it can. We who write the first draft of history each day cannot really write it against the perspective of the past, as an academic historian can; we are compelled to judge present actions against present conditions and the probable future.

Altogether, I am not very worried about the attitude of the journalists toward the government, and I am not very worried about the attitude of the government in terms of news suppression. So long as our press and radio and our parliament remain free, no administration can suppress important news for long.

I am *more* concerned about the *positive,* news-*projecting* attitudes of the administration. For something new has been added. The huckster has moved into Washington, in a force and with an official acquiescence never seen before. We are witnessing not the death of the salesman, but his apotheosis. I do not object to the mass-suggestion technique, the single-thought technique, the saturation and hammer-hammer repetition technique in the merchandising of cars or cigarettes. The competition equalizes the effect and is probably a positive force for economic development. I am frightened about these techniques when applied to the merchandising of ideas, to truth which is never simple, to national policies which involve the hearts and lives of a great, free people. All the instincts and social principles I thought I acquired under the severe refining process of the university are disturbed by this development. I object to the presence of the quick-result, Hooper rating, box office mentality around the temple of the White House and the hallowed corridors of diplomacy. I object to the guile behind this approach, to the basic contempt inherent in its mass-market concept of American citizens; I am appalled by this confusion of technique with substance, of means with end, this tendency for matter to triumph over mind.

This technique is toward oversimplification at a time when the substance, the truth, has become more and more complex and must be understood in all its complexity. The apotheosis of mass salesmanship in the realm of political affairs could lead to the death of responsible citizenship. The responsible journalists of America have got to watch this, very closely, and make sure it remains within its proper bounds.

But now I have talked about government much more than I had intended. Let me return to my premise that the supreme challenge of American journalism lies within it. There are three prongs to this challenge: The commercial compulsions, the rut of news handling formulae, and news dishonesty.

Let me take the last one first, because, however strange it may sound, I believe this is probably the least of these evils. The news is played more fairly in this country than in any other and infinitely more fairly than it was a couple of generations ago. I am not unmindful of such examples as the McCormick papers [4] or a few nightly voices on the radio which distort the news to suit their destructive purposes. Yet I think we fairly well take the measure of those and counter them. I am more disturbed about the far more subtle technique and unmeasurable effect of a brilliant mass-circulation news vehicle like *Time* magazine which frequently does a real public service, but in which a policy-line, handed down from the top, governs the writing of its major news stories.

But my reason for including news distortion in my list is that the country experienced, one year ago in the election campaign, a sudden rash of news cheating such as we have not known for years. The last speaker in this series, Alan Barth, went into this in some detail, and I shall not repeat his words, with which I agreed. The truth must be faced: Dozens of excellent newspapers, with a record of honorable news handling, cheated in their allotment of news and picture space between the two candidates. I do not believe the election result would have been any different, even had absolute fairness ruled, but that does not erase this blot on the record. I wish American editors had gone ahead with the self-investigation of that performance that Sigma Delta Chi and others urged; but I knew they would not, because the general finding, if sought with ruthless honesty, was a foregone conclusion and would have been too painful.

I have called this evil the least of the three because I have an idea we shall not again see such a manifestation of it any time soon. I may be wrong, but I have a feeling that many American editors and publishers are trying, subconsciously if you will, to make atonement now. Robert Estabrook of the Washington *Post* warned, at the Nebraska School of Journalism, that a press so heavily committed to one party might find itself apologizing for that party's stewardship now that it controls the government, rather than give it the independent, constructive criticism any administration needs. It is here that I feel reassured in the basic steadiness and fairness of the American press. Despite the opinions of some in the profession, I think editors are *not* falling into this self-opened trap. Their habits of independent editorial judgment are reasserting themselves already; as proof of this, note that the new *Democratic Digest* is relying on comments and cartoons critical of the administration which are taken from Republican papers. Habits of political fairness in the news column are being reasserted, as witness the very great play given the opposition party meeting in Chicago last month. I choose to believe last year's performance was an aberration; I choose to believe the people can still trust the honest intent of the overwhelming bulk of news columns and news broadcasts.

But honest intent is not enough in a time when new wars and revolutions and new threats of human extinction seem to assail our minds with every fresh edition.

And this brings me to the second hazard and handicap, our rut of routine and formulae in defining, writing, and displaying the news. They were our tools and they have all but become our masters. Our rigid formulae of so-called objectivity, beginning with the wire agency bulletins and reports—the warp and woof of what the papers print and the broadcasters voice—our flat, one-dimensional handling of the news, have given the lie the same prominence and impact that truth is given; they have elevated the influence of fools to that of wise men; the ignorant to the level of the learned; the evil to the level of the good.

At times, the lie has overmastered the truth simply by using our own rigid techniques against us. I am thinking chiefly of the simple, headlineable accusations of disloyalty in those cases where the accusation was false, yet where the truth was overmastered because the defense was *complex;* this has happened, time after time, simply because our hour-to-hour news techniques cannot handle complexity; they cannot handle it because we do not add the third dimension, Meaning. I do not suggest that we add the second dimension, Opinion, in our running news file; I suggest only that we add the meaning, that is, the background, to give perspective. It means a great change in handling certain categories of news; it means the hiring of better men in some places; it means a slowing down, on these stories, of the senseless minute-to-minute rat-race for headline space, beginning with the news agencies.

This is a large order; I believe we have to meet it, somehow. We cannot go on, witlessly, helplessly aiding in the destruction of men we know to be honorable; we cannot go on helplessly aiding in the creation of giant public myths, knowing at the time that they are myths. We cannot permit ourselves any longer to be hoist with our own petard by ugly and antidemocratic men who try to intimidate us by stirring up the know-nothing fringe of our readers and listeners, who are not a majority, who are only a minority within a minority.

What sort of trap have our news techniques led us into when Palmer Hoyt of the Denver *Post* must instruct his staff to evaluate accusations in the news, even those made by official agencies? to hold back publication until proof or qualification may be at hand, to apply the headline with an eye to importance, and not to circulation? What sort of trap have we fallen in, when one of the most respected journalists—and a conservative one—of the country is trying to set up a national clearing house of immediate information on these loyalty cases from which editors and writers can quickly obtain the facts that the accusation does not mention?

These episodes amount to severe indictments of our handling of the news. The concrete examples are legion. One of the ablest, most devoted Secretaries of State America has ever had lives today in infamy, in the minds of millions, largely because of our news techniques. Millions recall that he said "I will not turn my back on Alger Hiss," and millions believe that he was defying American justice and asserting belief in the convicted man's innocence. Millions so believe because we did not provide them with the meaning of the remark at the time we wrote the story. Acheson pointed to his meaning at the time. He was overly subtle, but we should not have missed it. He pointed to it by mentioning certain verses in the Bible. The story was blared around the world by hurried reporters who did not bother to look up the verses, or to ponder their meaning if they did. His meaning was *not* that he considered Hiss innocent, but that he considered him guilty. His meaning was that he himself would apply the basic tenet of Christianity—the forgiveness of sin.

McCarthy is not the only current demagogue who has detected our weakness of formulae and turned it to his uses. But he is the shrewdest at this subtle art. With our help, he and others have weakened security against internal subversion. They have weakened it because they have complicated the basic strategy, which must be to *isolate* the real subversives. It is harder to isolate them because so many innocents, so many former but not present Communists, so many plain liberals have been dragged across the screen, and for so long that the viewing public is now totally confused as to who is who and what is what. And what wonderful camouflage this is for present or potential subversives of serious menace!

For the uninitiated, let me give a couple of small but typical examples of how the McCarthys can use even the best of the daily press to do their work. When, during McCarthy's assault of innuendo against Ambassador Charles Bohlen,[5] the press play began to go against him, he reached into his bag of tricks. He demanded—the headline word is always "demanded," somehow—that Bohlen be subjected to a lie detector test. Now it was preposterously impossible that the administration, having nominated Bohlen, would subject its distinguished diplomat to any such indignity or that Bohlen would accept the indignity. Every sensible reporter and editor in town knew this was just a McCarthy straw man, for headline purposes. Yet so sober a paper as the Washington *Star* gave an eight-column streamer to this so-called "demand," which of course spread the notion among those who read as they run that Charles Bohlen might be a liar.

Again in difficulties, McCarthy disappeared and his office carefully leaked out the news that he was on his way to consult with Whittaker Chambers. This was entirely a stunt, yet so responsible a paper as the Washington *Post* gave it an eight-column streamer, which of course spread the notion among those who read as they run that somehow Bohlen was mixed up with Hiss and pumpkin papers and treason.[6] And McCarthy stayed in the headlines that much longer, prolonged the agony for Bohlen and the President that much more, spread, through innuendo, an evil lie that much further.

Where this one demagogue is concerned, press and radio are caught in what the *Wall Street Journal* calls a compulsion neurosis. And it is no wonder, as the *Journal* goes on, that our foreign friends think we have gone mad and are about to be taken over by this man. I agree with the *Journal* when it concludes that this is one obsession, one distortion for which we of press and radio are responsible, not the senator himself.

Our rigid news techniques have not only helped to dishonor some honorable men; they have helped, in a sense, in the deliberate rewriting of history, almost in the manner of George Orwell's *1984*. They have installed giant myths in the minds of millions of citizens, imbedded them so deeply that the government today, even against its best instincts, is caught in the confines of these myths, its maneuverability in foreign and domestic policy and in personnel policy thereby dangerously restricted. One is the myth that the containment policy of the former administration was somehow appeasement or soft toward Russia. You may notice that the man identified with that word containment, George Kennan, is not used by the present Department of State, despite his unmatched understanding of our Soviet enemy.

Another is the myth that a group of pro-Reds in the State Department sent Nationalist China down the skids. You may notice that our real diplomatic experts on China are now scattered to the four winds, replaced in large part by amateurs. Because the influence of the professionals was destroyed by this political and popular myth, their insistence that China would attack if we sent our troops to the Yalu River was ignored.[7] Partly because of the myth that Yalta was a conspiratorial sellout of national interests, our present diplomats are frightened to death of even trying confidential diplomacy with Russia of the kind Churchill advocates, which just conceivably might do some good.

Because of the myth that the former administration was reeking with Communism and corruption, political patronage has had free rein to tear at the career, civil service structure at serious cost in talent; the cop mentality has had free rein to prowl the corridors of some departments, destroying morale, terrorizing the weak and insecure, driving out many of the able and strong who refuse to abide it; because of these myths, politically created and innocently propagated by ourselves—including the notion that anybody who can read without moving his lips is an egghead and therefore suspect—because of these myths, the new administration is having a severe time of it, trying to attract the best brains in many fields (we do not even yet have a solicitor general); and I will go out on the limb and make here the unprovable assertion that in the crucial *secondary* levels of policy-making and administration, the country is being run by a team inferior to the last one. Years of myths, based on quarter-truths or less, have badly bent if not broken the moral *continuity* of government, so to speak.

We have traded some small risk of government by the corrupt for the large risk of government by stuffed shirt. The transfer to new men and a new philosophy could have been normal and efficient; it has been abnormal and wasteful largely because of the myths that you and I, caught in our routines, did not prevent. And this is too high a price the country is paying.

Journalism's challenge—indeed, its plain duty—is to see the world steady and see it whole, and to so portray it. The third great hazard to fulfillment of our duty is the commercial compulsions that beat upon us. Obviously, news distortion and the quick, thoughtless news techniques are not unconnected with these compulsions.

Unless papers and radio stations can flourish economically, they cannot do anything; and, in the long haul the stronger they are economically, the stronger and freer they are editorially. But not always in the short haul. I am sometimes depressingly impressed with how timid a million dollars profit can make a publisher or a radio executive, instead of how

88 ERIC SEVAREID

bold it makes him. I have always been discouraged at the fear and reluctance of individual radio station owners to assert the right of editorial expression that individual publishers have always asserted. I wonder at the phenomenon of the biggest mass circulation media, such as films, networks, and slick paper magazines, showing the least editorial boldness and sense of intellectual freedom, while the small business, low box-office media of books and legitimate theater remain the freest, boldest, most intellectually challenging and experimental media that we have. I see little evidence that moral size is in direct ratio to economic size, and it may well be that the present shrinkage of films and radio because of television will prove a boon, will make both films and radio, having less hostage to commercial fortune, braver and more original than they have ever been.

None of us can be very happy at the phenomenon of daily newspapers decreasing in numbers, while the population itself increases rapidly. Nobody bred in the editorial side of this business is easy in his mind as he sees great papers fail or merge and great communities become more and more one-paper-ownership cities. With some foreboding we watch new ventures with opinion magazines struggle and falter, while the smooth, slick, conformity-ridden, intellectually empty magazines grow bigger and bigger. We feel this foreboding because we know in our hearts that the need for rigorous thinking and new understanding of our country and world is desperately pressing. We are disturbed to see that for every new and responsible publication, concerned with our fate, five new publications concerned only with sex and violence take their places in the already mindless, visceral, ghastly array on the corner newsstand. I am disturbed at the spread of Broadway and crackpot columnists masquerading as monitors of political thought, printed because the box office fight has become so fierce.

It is not reassuring to see the breakup of once-great foreign staffs, as happened with the Chicago *Daily News,* in the interest of "color" and "brightness" and newsstand sale. It is not reassuring to see the respected *Herald Tribune* of New York abandon the effort to be a paper of record and slide in the direction of the tabloids; not reassuring to learn that even the great St. Louis *Post-Dispatch* has decided it can get along without a full-time diplomatic correspondent.

I am reassured, if I may appropriately say so here, at the growth in news source coverage and responsibility of radio over these last twenty years; but I am not too happy about television, now taking over much radio audience, and which, save for a documentary program here and there of rare quality, has not yet found a satisfying way to handle news; which, in fact, shows a retrogression from radio news techniques, as television finds itself limited by its visual material, giving us little better than the picture-page treatment, or the slapdash treatment of the newsreel, perhaps the most moribund of all journalistic media. And, while most radio stations gradually lost the fight to keep their own control of news broadcast content and broadcasting personnel—to keep it away from agency or sponsor—most television stations seem to have abandoned that fight without even trying. So fierce are the commercial compulsions.

"Box office." Carried to its logical if not inevitable extreme, the search for the common denominator will find it. And the common denominator is what? It is commonness.

I wish to quote a few lines taken from a strange short story of fantasy by Ray Bradbury called "Fahrenheit 451." [8] The scene is New York City; the time, many generations in the future. A young fireman lies abed, sick, and troubled in his mind. He has heard a rumor that there was once a time when all buildings were *not* 100 per cent fireproof. A time when firemen existed to put *out* fires, not to *start* fires. A time when they used water in their hoses, not kerosene. A time when their duty was to save objects, including books, instead of destroying them.

His elderly chief, knowing the trouble, comes to talk with the young man at his bedside, to fill him in on the history and meaning of his trade:

> I'd say it really got started around about a thing called the Civil War, . . . We didn't get along well until photography came into its own. Then —motion pictures in the early twentieth century. Radio. Television. Things began to have *mass*.
> And because they had mass, they became simpler . . . once, books appealed to a few people, here, there, everywhere. They could afford to be different. The world was roomy. But then the world got full of eyes and elbows and mouths. Double, triple, quadruple population. Films and radios, magazines, books leveled down to a sort of paste pudding norm. . . . Picture it. Nineteenth-century man with his horses, dogs, carts, slow motion. Then in the Twentieth Century, speed up your camera. Books cut shorter. Condensations. Digests. Tabloids. Everything boils down to the gag, the snap ending. . . . Classics cut to fit fifteen-minute radio shows, then cut again to fill a two-minute book column, winding up last as a ten or twelve line dictionary résumé. . . .
> Speed up the film . . . *Click, Pic, Look, Eye, Now, Flick, Here, There, Pace, Up, Down, In, Out, Who, What, Bang, Smack, Wallop.* Digest-digests, digest-digest-digests. Politics? One column, two sentences, a headline. Then, in mid-air, all vanishes. Whirl man's mind around about so fast under the pumping hands of publishers, exploiters, broadcasters, that the centrifuge flings off all unnecessary, time-wasting thought! . . .

School is shortened, discipline relaxed, philosophies, histories, languages dropped, English and spelling gradually, gradually neglected. . . . Life is immediate, the job counts, pleasure lies all about after work. . . .

Bigger the population, the more minorities. Don't step on the toes of the dog-lovers, the cat-lovers, doctors, lawyers, merchants, chiefs, Mormons, Baptists, Unitarians, second-generation Chinese . . . people from Oregon or Mexico. The people in this book, this play, this TV serial are not meant to represent any actual painters, cartographers, mechanics anywhere. The bigger your market, the less you handle controversy. . . . No wonder books stopped selling. But the public, knowing what it wanted, spinning happily, let the comic books survive. And the three dimensional sex magazines, of course. There you have it.[9]

Fantasy? Yes. Impossible? We have to believe so. But it is not without a certain seed of warning.

It reminds us of George Orwell's *1984*. But there is a fundamental difference in the two, and that difference is my whole point in reading these lines. It was *government,* authoritarian government that brought Winston, the writer, and his imagined generation to the level of yapping beasts. But it was *not* government that brought Montag, the fireman, and his imagined generation to the level of mindless ciphers. Government had nothing much to do with it. Technology did it; mass exploitation and gutless unresistance to minority pressures did it. In sum, *we* did it.

God and our own common sense willing, the fiction story will remain a fiction, and not become a prophecy.

You and I cannot usefully project even our telescopic sights *beyond* the horizon as the fiction writer can. We have got to deal with what we see before us. What we see now is not a fantasy, but a living reality. It is the question of whether our civilization will have *any* kind of future, with or without firemen; whether we shall get through the next decade intact, let alone the next century. I do not have to tell you that half the world is bursting with revolution; I do not have to tell you that the Orient has leaped from its ancient sleep to challenge the Occident; that the two mightiest powers history has known, each incredibly, brutally, and perilously ignorant of the other, are locked in a psychological death-cycle of hate and fear which has not been arrested. I do not have to tell you that the process of arresting it must begin with the minds of men, with their attitudes, and that their attitudes can be no sounder than their information.

There is not much we can do to inform the Russian and Chinese peoples about ourselves. There is an enormous job we can do to inform our own people about them. We do not have to *accept* one particle of their philosophy or aspirations in order to understand them. But understand them we must. And what a failure is here! Our economic moves in the world, our diplomatic policies, the forms and scope of our military strategy, probably our very survival, depend upon the fullest, most continuous flow of sound information and explanation about the very countries and societies of which we have the *least* information. Show me the daily paper that makes a systematic, continued effort to explain to its readers just what Marxism really is, how it started, and the forms it has taken. Show me more than a handful of editors who make a sustained effort to get, translate, and interpret Russian documents and publications. Show me the magazine that braves the current head-in-the-sand atmosphere of fear about subversion and tries to understand and explain the domestic Communists and how they got that way. Show me the radio or television program that attempts to trace and bring alive the mysterious story of how Communism started and then succeeded in the highly individualized Chinese society. Show me more than a handful of papers, syndicates, and agencies that even try to get men into Russia or the satellite countries, or even to get them stationed in Hong Kong, India, Vienna and other listening posts around the fringes of the Iron Curtain.

Let us, to borrow a cliché from the editorial writers, view ourselves, at last, with a little alarm.

I would like to end this inadequate communication by quoting some words that I heard last spring. I heard them at the Overseas Press Club dinner in New York. I cannot get them out of my mind.

They were spoken by a big, shaggy man who sits in Washington and broods a good deal about this world. A man whose own mind has bridged Occident and Orient. Dr. Charles Malik, ambassador of Lebanon, where the two worlds of the mind come together.

The truth of the world, he told us, the *big truth,* is dangerously hidden, and in our time only a man of profound spiritual crisis is qualified for the noble profession of explaining it. He said:

> For every age, there is one unpardonable sin. I mean a sin whose commission spells absolute moral death. Do you know what is the unpardonable sin of the present age? It is superficiality, lack of depth, absence of perspective—a happy skimming over the surface of things.
>
> And, these are not ordinary times when so-called "factual" reporting can tell the story of what is really happening. The real "facts" are the hidden clashes of will and outlook and culture whereby whole civilizations are today in the balance. To convey this critical sense of destiny—which is the "truth" that must be reported behind every manifestation—the foreign correspondent cannot be satisfied with the knowledge of economics, politics, statistics and sociology; he must be grounded, as never

before, in history, philosophy, religion, fundamental literature: in a word, in the great tradition of the liberal arts. . . .

But it "so happens" that precisely at the moment when they are most desperately needed, the liberal arts are themselves in a state of crisis. Do you think the coincidence of these two crises—the special crisis of the liberal arts and the general crisis of the world—is purely accidental? May there not be some connection between the absence of peace and rest in the world today and the neglect of those pursuits whose very presupposition is that there is a real, transcendent sphere, whose loving vision alone can impart peace and assurance to the soul?

American public opinion is crucial in the determination of history today. Never perhaps did the public opinion of a single country count so much in the scale of things. I think, therefore, that I am right in holding that no greater responsibility falls upon any group of men today than that which is your honour and duty—you members of the American press—to discharge. . . .

If you aim at the real truth in your mediation, not the obvious truth, not the superficial truth, but the deep, hidden, tragic truth; if you always faithfully bring out what is ultimately at stake today, namely that there is a rebellion of the elements against all that you have held true and holy and sacred for thousands of years—then I believe you will put the entire world in your debt.

VIII   GEORGE V. FERGUSON

Foreign News:

Weapon for World Peace?

If there is one thing lacking in this curious trade
of ours, it is a sense of continuity, of the flow of events out of the past
into the present, and, beyond the present, into the future.* We play our
notes *staccato,* and our themes *allegro* or even *presto.* I would prefer our
chords *arpeggio,* and our melodies and themes *andante,* even *lento,* or at
least *rallentando.*

You will note, if you can fight your way through these musical
metaphors which I now abandon, that I am playing the same tune as
that played to you in years gone by by such men as Elmer Davis and
Eric Sevareid. I am not happy about the techniques of the press—or
indeed of radio and television—of the mid-twentieth century. There is
something wrong about them. Having passed through a period of frankly
biased presentation of the news into one which we call objective, we find
that the rigidities of our techniques are now biasing the news in another
way. In an attempt to be absolutely fair we have wound up by being often
obviously very unfair indeed; and although our news stories are much
better than once they were, our technique of headlines and our determination of news values lead us astray perhaps just as much.

As a foreigner here, I am determined, if I can, to avoid getting mixed

---

* This lecture was delivered October 22, 1954.

up in your domestic issues. But let me give you just one illustration of what I mean. I happened to be in this country four years ago, when Senator Joseph R. McCarthy denounced Owen Lattimore as the chief Russian agent in the United States.[1] In one of the best dailies in this country, the report was given an eight-column banner line on the front page. Next day, when Lattimore denied the story, the denial was published under a one-column head on page 11. Lattimore's actual position has not yet been completely clarified. But no one today would suggest that he is, or was, the Soviet Union's chief espionage agent. Yet the damage of the headline remains—the object of much criticism among critics of the press; and, among the distinguished lecturers under this foundation, the subject of learned comment on our sins of both commission and omission.

Beyond saying that I agree broadly with the criticism, I will go no further. Enough has been said on that point. I will say only that the criticism applies not only to the American press, but to the Canadian press as well, and to all the other organs of the press, the radio and television in any other part of the world where these media of communication are free. We are all enslaved by the god of speed, by getting there "fustest with the mostest," to quote a Civil War general; and since we are writing for the Kansas City milkman or his local equivalent, who is, like ourselves, in a vast hurry, we simplify, we condense, we pare things down to bare essentials. The results are often disconnected and unhappy, but if we recall, and ask ourselves again, the question which formed the subject of Elmer Davis' address—"Must We Mislead the Public?"—I think the honest answer is, "Yes, we must. But we can go on trying to keep the degree of error just as low as we possibly can." We can, I think and I hope, narrow that margin from its present level. But I wonder if it can be done if we maintain, without some relaxation, the present rule of speed.

It is here, it seems to me, that we have allowed our technology to become our master. We who, in our own private affairs, take days, weeks, or even months to come to the wisest possible decisions, are driven by the fierce exigencies of our craft to make news decisions in a matter of moments. What school or what church should our youngsters go to? Over such decisions we take our time. But, as deadlines approach at the office, we apply very different standards. What is the best lead? What is the best angle? What will most effectively catch the reader's eye? And away we go. Our test is not the test we apply to the decision of the child's school—which is the best school for him? Our test in the office too often is not even what is the most important news, but—what will sell most papers? What will make the passer-by stop and buy? The new angle and the hottest angle are what get the play. Very often, as we go to press with only a half a story properly told, we make up our minds to correct the balance in the next edition. But we all know very well that, very often, the next edition is absorbed in something quite different.

I began newspaper life with the very dignified London *Times* in England. In London, newsboys are not allowed to yell about their featured stories. They cry out the names of the papers they sell. Posters are put up beside them which declare the chief contents of the papers. The *Times,* I recall, made a continuing and gallant effort to keep on its poster the most significant news of the day. The Dawes plan to whittle down German reparations after the First World War was being worked out.[2] Day after day, the rather cynical circulation manager of the *Times* would come to the room where I worked and ask what the news was. Day after day he would be told "The Reparations Conference," which would duly appear on next day's posters.

And every day he would snort and curse and leave the room remarking, "That'll sell a hell of a lot of papers." For he knew he would be in competition with the rest of Fleet Street showing posters such as "Ax Slayer Tells All," or, if a cricket match was on, "Australia's First Inning—England's Crisis."

Quite apart from the business of selling papers, however, there is another consideration involved. It seems to me that our technology has long since surpassed the capacity of the reader to take in, to fully absorb, the meaning of the news he reads. It comes at him too fast and at too frequent intervals. Technology has advanced far faster than the ability of man to adjust himself to its achievements. In days gone by, this country got its news at irregular but infrequent intervals by sailing ship or stage coach. The budgets of news when they arrived would be printed and distributed reasonably fast, but days would then elapse before another budget would arrive. Man's mind had some kind of chance to get the news and its meaning into perspective.

But the man of today, with no better mental equipment, now has the news—and often contradictory news—hurled at him every hour, on the hour. We are drenched in it, and our readers are drenched in it too, and if they get neurotic and unstable in consequence, it is neither their fault nor our fault. We are, all alike, slaves to technology and technological change which neither they nor we can change or wipe out. The instruments are there, and they are going to be used by somebody. It might as well be us as somebody else, and I can name you worse persons than ourselves.

I make this self-flattering remark in the light of a great deal of the criticism I have read of the modern press and its practices. You are familiar both in theory and in practice with the shortcomings I have mentioned. Many of you, I am sure, would agree that they have at least some validity. But, as the critics continue their denunciations, I confess to a feeling of restlessness. They have no concrete suggestions for a remedy. They are lucid and analytic in their exposure of our weak points, but they begin to flounder when it comes to offering remedies. The easy remedy is one found by dictators in totalitarian states. They take over the function of news presentation themselves, and that remedy, in a short space of time, becomes worse than the disease it is designed to cure. The critics often edge up to some ideas of restriction or control, yet they know full well that this is worse than what we have. There is, it seems to me, a definite limit to be placed on criticism when criticism is not coupled with a practical realism; and I see no quick way out of the impasse into which our traditions and our techniques have led us. The whole field of mass communications—press, radio, and television— is involved in violent competition, complicated and rendered more unmanageable by the impact of the continuing technological revolution.

Let me emphasize that there is no *quick* way out, a point to which I will return; meanwhile I will continue discussing briefly what is happening to us all now. The realization and the acceptance of this revolution and resulting competition are vital, for the consequences are both many and inevitable. It means in the first place a great intensification of the struggle to capture and to hold the mass audience. It does not matter if this effort is between newspaper and newspaper, as it used solely to be, or between newspaper and radio, or radio and television, or television and newspaper. Failure to effect that capture means extinction. The struggle to attain it involves an unending search for the largest common factor in reader interest, and it is an obvious fact that that factor is pretty low. It means focusing every available effort on an attempt to catch and to hold the interest, the attention and the money of the most people. In such circumstances it is talking pretty well through one's hat to discuss the ideal of higher standards and the patient study of the infinite complexities of important events.

It is, I suppose, in the experience of every newspaperman that, when competition breaks out in violent form, the first part of the content of a newspaper to suffer is its serious news. We expand features, comic strips, and entertainment at once. We redouble our search for the neurotics, the psychopaths, and the ill-adjusted members of society who are the source of so much sensational news. This is what takes with the mass audience which wants either to be thrilled or amused, and the space it takes in our columns leaves not too much room for the dull and distant events upon which the fate of our civilization and our culture literally depends.

This state of competition increases the emphasis on speed, the consequences of which I have tried to outline. There is another aspect to be considered. What interests our readers and our audiences is conflict. Mankind is a pugnacious animal, always on the lookout for a fight. Events can thus be most effectively and attractively described if they are set in a background of strife. Marciano is fighting Ezzard Charles. Cleveland is fighting the Giants. Roosevelt is fighting the Supreme Court. Senator Flanders is fighting Senator McCarthy. Eisenhower is fighting Malenkov. Dulles is fighting Molotov, and taking on Eden and Mendes-France on the side. The Catholics are fighting the Protestants, and the Witnesses of Jehovah are taking on both of them. Tommy Manville is fighting his forty-seventh wife, and Herbert Hoover is still fighting the depression of 1930.

So far as I know the only man who escaped from this continent without a fight in 1954 was the Archbishop of Canterbury and that was only because the Chicago *Tribune* did not realize he was in town until he had left it.

We spend a good deal of our time in the search for a hot angle, for the creation of a state of crisis and dire emergency. We do, from day to day, a lot of breathless panting in our business, and what it leads to is to increase that sense of insecurity and instability which, in the first place, flows from technological change and competition, and, in the second place, reacts upon society itself, rendering it more unstable than it otherwise would be.

I know, and I have read, that some newspapermen regard themselves as passive instruments—holding up a mirror to the community or the society which they serve, trying to act only as an accurate and honest mirror. The truth, I think, is otherwise. We are, all of us, positive and active agents. As the Commission on Freedom of the Press pointed out, "The owners and managers of the press determine which persons, which facts, which versions of facts and which ideas shall reach the public"; this is the plain truth, as anyone who has ever worked on a copy-desk knows. It is neither creditable nor discreditable that this is so. It is simply a fact.

What is less well recognized is that the performance of this function with the techniques which we employ acts, reacts, and interacts on the society which it serves and on ourselves as well. I do not mean

that we are a Frankenstein. I do mean that we are not always under
complete control, and I believe further that the circumstances in which
the whole field of mass communications today finds itself is not likely
to lead to any very profound improvement in what we now have in the
way of newspaper news content and presentation, or radio and television
programming.

There remain the editorial page and its frequent adjunct, the
opposite-editorial page. I will come back to them later. Meanwhile, after
these introductory remarks, I want to move one stage nearer my real
subject. In this stage I want to discuss briefly another plain and obvious
fact which is, I think, much more plain and obvious to outsiders than
it is to yourselves. This simply is that the American democracy not
only differs markedly from every other nation in the world but that it
differs markedly from every other democracy in certain very important
respects.

For the purposes of this talk, I will discuss only one of those respects: the process by which public opinion is formed and is changed
into policy. In one of his brilliant spectacular essays, the English historian Arnold Toynbee describes his belief that the most vigorous societies are those which have to struggle against physical obstacles and
difficulties. He suggests that an observer of the early American colonies
would have predicted that a colony like Virginia, blessed with rich
natural resources and an easy climate, would have laid its mark most
deeply upon the growing American society. Instead, he declares that
New England assumed that role, although the New England states were
in many respects poor in resources and had, additionally, a severe and
difficult struggle against Nature. For those very reasons, however, he
believes that the New Englander, rather than any other type, laid his
mark most deeply upon American society.

I depart now from Toynbee to suggest that among the manifestations
of that fact is the transplantation of the New England town meeting into
a national institution. It may no longer be possible for every citizen to
gather on the village green and decide the policies of the group. But
in no other country in the whole world is there more prolonged and more
vigorous and more sustained public debate of every aspect of public
affairs.

To the outside eye the first impression is one of unending confusion
and disorder. Discordant voices are raised on every side. The debates
seem to proceed in a series of vast and unregulated explosions. It is a
process which encourages extremes, and, as public opinion slowly
forms, the extreme voices are those most loudly and most frequently

heard. The impression is one of Babel in its more inchoate moments, and, from day to day, as one voice and then another makes itself most clearly heard in the tumult, the untrained outsider is likely to conclude that a people so inherently confused and unstable has only itself to blame for the disasters that are bound to pursue it.

Yet those who follow the process patiently learn quickly to make the necessary discounts. They realize that the prophesied disasters seldom occur, and that, when the smoke and steam and noise have died away, the great nationwide town meeting has come up with some very reasonable and moderate conclusions. But it is worth pointing out that this process—so easy, so natural, and so traditional to you—is one which leads to a very great degree of misunderstanding abroad, and this is a fact which should be always remembered by thoughtful Americans. The process I have described, moreover, by its very violence is likely to leave scars behind it. I was once told by one of your greatest authorities on civil liberties that the hysterical witch-hunting which followed World War I—the Palmer-led campaign [3] against Reds—led to the loss of ground in the cause of liberty. It was ground, he said, which, when the excitement died down, was never regained. An absolute loss was recorded, and he speculated sadly that the similar state of affairs in these postwar years would leave similar scars. As to that, you would be a better judge than I. I am merely quoting.

I am not, however, concerned with whatever internal effects there may be as a result of this unique opinion-making process. That is strictly your business. I am, however, very much concerned by its consequences on the world outside your borders. Two facts about your country have confused that world very much. One is the form of the United States Constitution and its mode of operation. Nowhere else in the free world, so far as I know, is there the marked separation of powers which exists here. Elsewhere, freedom-loving countries, among them the democracies, operate almost entirely under a system of parliamentary democracy—what we call responsible government, in which the executive is at all times directly responsible to the legislative branch. The impression given abroad by the operation at Washington is one of competing sovereignties. The foreigner therefore often mistakes the objectives of policy in his confusion over whose right it is to announce it.

The kind of example I have in mind is when the President makes one announcement on foreign policy, while the chairman of the Senate Foreign Relations Committee makes another and conflicting one. Now, this again is strictly your domestic business. You have this constitution, you are used to it and you like it, and no one in his senses could ask you to change it for his sake. The outside world recognizes this fact, and I have been pleased to note that outside observers of your domestic scene have been making steady progress in comprehension, and, since many of them are writers or commentators, it may be assumed that the area of knowledge is widening steadily.

Up to fifteen years or so ago, whether they understood or not was of relatively slight importance. It had been up to that point an American tradition to interpose neither its policies nor its strength into international affairs. When it did so as in World War I, its intervention was decisive, but the American people had not at that time made up its mind that intervention, to be effective, had to be continuous. That decision, I take it, has now been made.

In a lesser, but also very important, respect, there is confusion on another point. (You will remember that I said there were two.) That is the nature of the opinion-making process, and what is, to outside minds, its extreme violence. I previously tried to describe it and its origins. In this context I want to discuss it in terms of its impact on foreign policy, or rather on foreign opinion as it is brought to bear on the creation of common policies throughout the free world.

It is, I suppose, one of the more widespread errors of nations to believe not only that their own particular way of doing things is the best way, but also that other friendly nations with whom they have certain common objectives do things in precisely the same way. They are, therefore, likely to assume a much wider area of common understanding than does, in actual fact, exist.

Let me illustrate this by a comparison, in this single respect, of the United States and Great Britain, with the purpose of illustrating the problems that arise to confront us in our daily tasks of publishing and interpreting foreign news. In Europe, for some centuries—indeed until fairly recent times—diplomacy was the closed preserve either of a monarch or of the handful of noblemen who formed his council of state. Even when the absolute power of kings gave way to constitutional monarchies, the tradition of foreign policy as a specialized craft into which the common man could venture only at his peril persisted. In England, universal suffrage was introduced in three great steps in the nineteenth century, the last of which came in 1885, yet, even at the turn of the century the tradition and prestige of a governing class persisted. In effective terms the old Whig and Tory aristocracy still ruled the land, accepting new figures into their midst only as outstanding ability and a certain amount of slowly growing pressure from below asserted themselves.

The cheap, popular press—papers sold at low prices to a mass circulation—was an innovation of the 1880's and 1890's, for popular education was introduced only in 1870, by a member of a Liberal government who remarked, "We must educate our masters," and literacy of a kind is needed even for the reading of a newspaper. Gradually the popular pressures of public opinion asserted themselves on government, but the last stronghold of the educated, and usually aristocratic, few was the foreign office. Within its stately confines, peers, the sons of peers, and their friends conducted the day-to-day negotiations with foreign capitals; and incidentally, conducted them so well that Great Britain was involved in no major war for a period of ninety-nine years—from 1815 until 1914—a period of peace seldom interrupted or broken by serious conflicts.

One of the last and one of the greatest of these moguls of diplomacy was the Marquess of Salisbury who, about 1900, predicted with ill-concealed loathing that this long period of prosperous stability would come to an end as soon as the general public became deeply interested, or involved, in the conduct of foreign policy.

I am not attempting in any way to defend this state of affairs which is of course deeply repugnant to the instincts and practice of modern democracy. All I am doing is to try and set out the facts as they existed in Europe a very short time ago, for this state of affairs was paralleled practically everywhere on that continent. An excellent example of the kind of thing that could happen in circumstances of this kind is that Sir Edward Grey, the British foreign secretary, could conduct negotiations to the very eve of the declaration of war against Germany in 1914 without even informing all his Cabinet colleagues of the full implications of the commitments he had made on his country's behalf.

As a consequence both of this secret, but very stable, diplomacy, and of the long period of nineteenth-century peace, foreign policy was to no very important extent invaded by the merchants of news and their representatives. Even when they did force their way in, they ran into an all but inviolate tradition of secrecy. In addition, they shared a quite general feeling in the community as a whole that such sacred matters were not either suitable, or indeed, very interesting for the run of their readers. There were, of course, notable exceptions to this state of affairs, but, as a general rule, it represents something like the truth.

Contrast this, now, with the very different tradition both of democracy and of journalism in this republic. The rupture with the ties of the past which began in 1776 went very far indeed. It was accompanied, indeed it was perhaps caused by, the development of a form of social, as distinct from political, democracy quite new in the story of the world. It was compounded of many things such as the philosophic thinking of France before the revolution, and the existence of an expanding frontier which kept power out of the hands of a privileged few who, in Europe, had long since corralled all the land in sight in an era when land, rather than stocks and shares, was the chief symbol of wealth. The young American democracy had no counterpart elsewhere. It was, putting it mildly, rambunctious, and among its most rambunctious representatives were the gentlemen who edited and sold the daily newspapers of the land.

The result was that the conduct of foreign policy was subject, in the two countries I am discussing, to completely different pressures and, consequently, to developments of entirely different kinds. One could afford to be quiet, unobtrusive, even secret; the other was bound to be better known, more obtrusive and subject to publicity which, particularly under your form of government, leads in certain aspects toward distortion. By this I mean that in no other country in the world is foreign policy so susceptible to vagaries of a legislature not amenable, as most legislatures are, to the disciplines imposed on it by an executive. This difference, of course, leads back to, or stems from, your form of government.

I do not by this mean that American foreign policy is less stable than that of the allies of the United States abroad. On the other hand, over any length of time, it displays admirable characteristics of steadiness in its movement toward objectives which are dictated by the major influences in world politics. But I do mean that, in the short run, it displays the familiar ups and downs, the extremities of view which are part and parcel of the conduct of your own internal domestic affairs.

Foreign observers note these developments with disquiet. They grow anxious and nervous; for they forget Chief Justice Harlan Fiske Stone's famous dictum about the sober second thought of the American people, and they fear that the expression of some extreme opinion, even if it does not emanate either from the White House or the State Department, may, and possibly does, throw a penetrating light on what is really going on behind the scenes. This very fact is one which increases whatever tendencies toward instability there may be in world politics as a whole.

Let me expand this point briefly. Very few countries in the world outside the United States have both press and radio completely in private hands. Most of them employ at least some measure of government control or government operation. The people who read the press and listen to the radio of these countries are accustomed to believe that there is some government interference in the dissemination of information. When they turn to the United States, read its papers and listen to its radio, they find it almost impossible to believe that government is not, somehow or other, taking a hand in it. Here lies the seed of some very real misunderstanding, for many of these people, when they read or listen to extreme opinion, come to the decision that the government, if it is not actually showing its true hand, is flying a kite or two in order to ascertain the effect abroad.

It is difficult to explain to them, or to make them understand that, because of this complete freedom, representatives of press, radio, and television have a status in the United States which surpasses that of the profession elsewhere. They are important elements in this inchoate and endless process of opinion-making; and because they are, as an English observer pointed out recently, the profession attracts in this country more ability and more intelligence than it attracts elsewhere.

It may be, as a shrewd Washington correspondent has pointed out, that the utterances of the United States Secretary of State are in normal times directed 80 per cent toward Congress and only 20 per cent to the foreign powers most nearly concerned with what he says. It is also true that this ranking Cabinet official is also addressing himself to those men and women who, by their professional standing, may be in a position to influence Congress or public opinion.

This is true, to the same extent, in no other country of the world. Every democratic government does, of course, take public opinion into account in its policies and declaration of policy. But the continuing need of the executive in the United States to surmount the hurdles and obstacles which face it in Congress has no counterpart elsewhere, at least so far as I know.

I am talking both about your history, your national characteristics, and your form of government in a set of sweeping generalities which you may well resent, being well aware of all the many exceptions each one of you can set against the generalities I present. Yet the formation of foreign policy by the greatest nation in the world, a nation which is moreover the leader of a world-wide coalition (of which my own country is a member), is a matter of grave concern to all; and I am trying to tell you, rightly or wrongly, what foreign countries think of the process, its advantages, and its disadvantages to them.

You would please me if you would put these suggestions about the distinctive features of your own situation into their perspective in relation to the general analysis of the technology of the newspaper business in free countries, and the techniques which are in common use not only in this country but in all lands which possess a free press. That technology, as I have said, lays every emphasis upon speed and upon the immediate impact of the presentation of facts or opinions upon readers and listeners. When it has achieved this, technology has accomplished its main function. What happened the day before, or what is likely to happen tomorrow, takes very much of a back seat.

The sense of continuity, of the steady, implacable flow of history from the past into the present and on into the future, is largely forgotten. What stands in first place are the hot angle, the presentation of conflict, the headline or the arresting sentence which will hold the reader or the listener long enough for him to buy the day's paper, to go on listening, and to attract him toward the idea that this particular source of news is worth while at least taking a look at next day before he makes up his mind what to buy or what to listen to. The result is a form of breathlessness, a panting sense of excitement which we build up almost subconsciously because that is the way, and the only way, in which we have been taught to play our roles. The teacher is not the greedy owner or the unscrupulous publisher. It is the god of applied science which has put instruments and techniques into the hands of mankind which can be effectively used only in that way. In that sense we are slaves of the lamp.

I belong to that already half-forgotten era when the production of newspaper extras was an important factor in newspaper life. We did not produce extras only because some boss told us to do so, or because competition impelled us. A real reason was because the publisher, the editor, the news desk and the reporter were all fully conscious of the fact that technologists had given us the means to rush the news out on to the street, and it was a betrayal of our trusteeship not to use them whenever we could.

The fact is that real, hard news is very often neither exciting nor unexpected. When it appears so, it is often either because we do not know enough about the past, or because we have forgotten it; and if we do not know or have forgotten, we can be reasonably sure that most of our readers are in the same plight. The result is that all of us get unduly excited about the progress of events, and the pressure of our technology drives us to produce big headlines and flaming leads. It drives us, quite apart from the other pressure, the commercial one, which in a field of violent competition makes us spend a large part of time trying to hold, or to improve, our relative position.

The whole atmosphere of the society in which we live is one filled with uneasiness, with fear and with instabilities and insecurities. Of these, only one is the cold war, and that phenomenon which occupies so much of our professional time and effort is not the most important of them. Far more important in the creation of these basic conditions are such factors as the continuing industrial revolution. The technologists have done far more than to swamp us with facts which the individual is unable to assimilate. They have torn up and destroyed the kind of life which mankind lived on this planet, with little interruption or change for thousands and thousands of years. Most of us may be one, two, or even three generations removed from the farm. But our heritage is the heritage of the peasant, rooted in his land and watchful mainly only of the seasons. No wonder we get a bit neurotic.

With that cataclysmic change has come, too, the widespread loss of real religious faith. Here too, note that it is loss of roots that counts, the weakening of an instinct which has been fundamental to all our ancestors, the deep sense of the continuity of existence of the human soul, the recognition of the belief that our life on earth is only a part, and not the major part, of the spirit's immortality. This contributes to the kind of newspapers we have and to the kind of effect our newspapers have upon those who read them.

Because I believe that most of these facts are ineluctable, I am driven to a major conclusion. The first is that, by the nature of the society in which we live, certainly in that society's present stage of development, the media of mass communications cannot be very different from what they now are. Those who urge reform and better practices on the part of press, radio, and television overlook the fundamental strength of the causes which make them what they now are. I am not, of course, talking about the handful of deliberately dishonest and unscrupulous men and women who from time to time entrench themselves in the newspaper and electronic fields. Bad as they are, I am not really interested in them, because even if the industry as a whole were open for sweeping reform and betterment, they would exempt themselves from all reformist tendencies. You put up with them just as you necessarily put up with some incurable type of nonfatal disease. You learn to live with it.

What I am talking about is the huge majority of decent newspapers, radio and television stations, staffed by decent men and women who yet find themselves applying to the work they do standards of judgment which would not for an instant apply to their own private affairs or to their relations with their families and friends. Because of this fact I go on the assumption that they act as they do professionally because there is, under the circumstances, no other way to act. There is no escaping it. One may as well ask a monkey to turn himself overnight into an elephant as to ask for an overnight, or indeed an overyear, change in present practices.

In the present state of society, then, I do not believe that what we have can be made much better. If we believe in progress and in a basic human will to improvement, we are bound to believe that newspapers and their companions in the news field will get better too. There are signs of it, although perhaps not as many as many of us think. We are in what we call the objective era of reporting, and we regard this rightly as a vast improvement over the old days when no editor consciously gave any political opponent, for instance, a break. Newspapers, largely dedicated in their news and comment to public affairs, were consciously unfair. To a vastly increased degree they do so no longer. But of course it is also true that newspapers are no longer so dedicated. They have at the same time become vast entertainment media, and entertainment, valuable though it is, is not information. It would be interesting to learn if expenditures on hard news have kept pace with the expenditures on entertainment features. One of the most "successful" newspapers in the world today, the London *Daily Mirror,* hardly publishes any real news at all, although its daily sales outstrip any other newspaper in England.

In still another respect I would be critical. It is that, while fair reporting now dominates the writing of domestic news, the same standard of reporting has not spread as yet anything like so fully into the field of international affairs. The basic reason for this is, I think, the almost unconscious operation of nationalism. We interpret news in terms of conflict; and this is, of course, particularly easy to do under the pressure of the cold war when almost the whole world, with one or two notable exceptions, is lined up with the United States or with the Soviet Union, more or less like the crowd at a football game. In such circumstances it is almost inevitable that a good deal of the reporting follows the line of the sports pages which so often explain that, while the home team lost, the score did not fairly represent the real quality of the teams.

This is a dangerous extension of a sports page tendency; for if there is ever to be a positive improvement in world affairs, it will have to be by some process of negotiation and compromise, and a tie game is never very interesting or satisfying. I know how futile and how wearisome it has been this past number of years to try to look fairly and impartially at the various Soviet proposals which have come forward; but you know as well as I do how easy it is not only for newspapers but for state departments and foreign offices to begin by instant denunciation and condemnation of whatever emerges from a Red capital. Sometimes the official blow is struck even before the reception of the official text, and our newspapers faithfully and objectively report the rejection with appropriate headlines. Days or weeks later, they learn that very serious attention is being paid to some new and conceivably fruitful proposal. We might all just as well look before we leap.

There is another tendency which can be noted, and which applies chiefly to the press of the United States. This is a tendency to report events, negotiations, or discussions in terms almost wholly of what is said by the Americans and by the Russians. The contributions of lesser states very often indeed get no attention from the news agencies and no space in the papers of this country. I have no objection to failure to report what the representatives of Red satellites, for instance, say at the United Nations. They play the sedulous ape to their masters, and the party line is imposed on them down to the dotting of every "i" and the crossing of every "t." But this is not true of the lesser members of the great, free coalition which the United States leads today.

I hope you will not think I am talking now with the hurt pride of an ignored Canadian. I do not believe I am. I sat, some seven years ago on a United Nations Sub-Commission for the better part of six weeks, and I think I can honestly remark of my performance there that I never said anything worth reporting at any time. I did, let me say modestly, do some useful drafting, but I never said anything that was worth an inch of, or even a line of type. But this was not true of certain others of my colleagues, men from lands like Holland, Uruguay, and France; and I noted that once the agencies had reported what the Russian had said and what the American had said, they felt they had done plenty. Certainly if they reported the often useful arguments and suggestions of the lesser lights, the news desks of the papers I read had eliminated them all, or nearly all.

The reason I regard this as a matter of some importance is not because some friend's *amour propre* has been hurt. The reason lies deeper. It lies in the fact that there is never unanimity in any coalition that ever exists. The leader of that coalition, if it is to be a successful leader, must take these various differences of opinion into account, particularly when they flow from the different traditions or geographical position of its allies. They cannot be regarded as mere yes-men.

It follows from this that, when the leader of a coalition is the United States, whose government is so singularly susceptible to public opinion as Washington is bound to be, those who make public opinion must, as much as the State Department, although not of course in such detail, be made conscious of all these varying currents of opinion, and all these diverse trends. If they are not, the people of the United States are in for an endless series of shocks and rude surprises; and, if you extend such a series indefinitely it will result in a serious, indeed a desperate, weakening of the strength of the coalition upon which both the free world and the United States depend.

Let me illustrate this in two ways. When the French National Assembly rejected the proposal for a European Defense Community, it was soberly reported by foreign correspondents in Washington that never in their experience there had they witnessed such alarm and real anger in the country. Now, this was an eventuality which could have been, and should have been, discounted, if not predicted, weeks before. The shock of the actual vote, if people had been adequately informed, should therefore have been well cushioned, and attention already directed to the next steps which would prove necessary. The fact that the shock was so great can therefore be laid at least to some extent upon the merchants of information who were apparently counting on some last moment, unforeseen, dramatic and exciting development which would ward off an event which was practically certain to take place.

This is the kind of thing I meant earlier when I talked about the historical flow of events out of the past into the present and on into the future. But if we continue to regard international affairs as a football game which can be transformed in the last minute of play by a spectacular forward pass miraculously caught by a hitherto unknown sensation, then we are not doing our jobs properly.

The other illustration touches on another current issue, but of a different kind—the very honest clash between the United States and British opinion on the question of the recognition of Red China and its entry or nonentry into the United Nations. I have my views on this subject, but they are supremely unimportant. What I am interested in, and what is important, is the existence of the clash. There are, believe it or not, powerful arguments on both sides, and my belief is that it is the paramount duty of our trade to explain to our audiences just what those differences are and why they exist. What is of the greatest importance to the free world is the maintenance and the strengthening of the present coalition. This is not achieved by calling each other names. I do not, for instance, think that the free world was strengthened when *Life* magazine undertook to settle the matter by calling old Winston Churchill an appeaser. That is not only abusive and untrue, it is simply too easy. What we are obviously up against is something much more complicated than a dirty word, and on both sides of the Atlantic not enough effort has been made to explain the other fellow's point of view.

The issue has been greatly complicated by our own basic sins—too great simplification, too much stress on conflict, too great haste in making up our minds, altogether too much readiness on both sides to cheer on their own side. A little calm, a little reflection, a great deal more information and background, and we might well arrive at some common understanding. As it is we have run and still run the risk of weakening essential friendships, not so much by lack of common principles as by lack of comprehension.

Now, having said all this in somewhat incoherent fashion, where do I come to some conclusion? I have given some reasons why the press and the other media of mass communication cannot do much more, or much less, than they are doing now to inform the public they serve accurately and fully. I believe that the press, until the level of public education has been raised far beyond what it is now, cannot do a much better job in its news columns than it is doing now. We are doing a pretty fair job, but only those who live close to it day by day can fully see the fundamental imperfections and difficulties that confront it. This is what made me say at the outset of these remarks that strict limits are set to the quality and competence of the job that we can do in our news columns and yet survive. We can perhaps do something more—but not much. It is really not reasonable to expect much more, considering the conditions of competition that exist, and the need of maintaining a mass audience, and the techniques that are inexorably imposed on us by science.

Yet, it seems to me, there is, certainly in a newspaper (and with greater difficulty in the other media which exist), an area in which the defects of the strictly news columns can be rectified; and I am talking now of the potentialities of the editorial page and its frequent adjunct, the opposite-editorial page. I am well aware that books and many articles are dedicated to a subject widely known as "The Decline of the Editorial Page," and the subject is usually illustrated by countless examples of the hard-hitting, ruthless editorials and editorial pages of the past. I am well aware also of the fact that polls have shown, and continue to show, that the readership of such pages is lamentably low. The bulk of newspaper readership does not read editorials. If we console ourselves by the fact that a large percentage of readers go for what we publish on opposite-editorial pages in the way of columns and the like, it remains true that a newspaper's entertainment features are much heavier drawing cards. This does not distress me, even though my own job in the trade has been for years the writing of editorials that few people read.

Let me digress for a moment. I am not, and never have been, a believer that newspapers are such a direct factor in the creation of public opinion as their owners, their publishers, and their editors believe they are. I am supported in this view by the results of the elections in the United States from 1936 to 1952, and by the result of the British general election of 1945. If we were as powerful as some of us have believed we were, the results of these national pollings would have been different.

I am a believer instead in what I call the livery-stable theory of public opinion. The phrase dates me, but there was a time in my own youth when cities were not as great as they are now, when more people lived in small towns, and when the New England town meeting, although no longer held, had been transferred to such community centers as the livery stable, the barbershop, the saloon, the streetcar, and the tea table. Change some of these locations to adapt them to the present, and the same theory will hold true.

In little groups the citizens of any democracy have discussed what they have learned by word of mouth, by ear, and from the public prints, and they have come to their own conclusions on the various facts presented to them. Take into account at the same time, the instinctive distrust of the average man in the disinterested motives of anything big. Not being big himself, he asserts himself by a rising suspicion in anything the size of a circus tent. If he lives in a one-newspaper town, he will tend to react against what that newspaper tells him. If he listens to radio or to television, he recognizes that what he sees and hears is part of some gigantic chain, and, again, his individualism asserts itself. He wants to feel his decisions are his own and are not being imposed on him by some big monopoly or, indeed, by anything big.

This is natural enough, yet there is always a small, reflective percentage of the population which is ready to listen to anything which sounds, to it, like a moderate, reflective, objective point of view. This relatively small group is important far beyond the extent of its numbers as reflected in any surveys of newspaper readership or of public opinion polls. Let me quote to you what is said on this score by Lord Bryce, the author of a classic analysis of American institutions, who remarked that two classes of persons have mainly to do with the making of public opinion:

> There are the men who seriously occupy themselves with public affairs, whether professionally, as members of legislatures or journalists or otherwise actively engaged in politics, or as private persons who care enough for their duty as citizens to give constant attention to what passes in the political world. These persons are, taken all together, an exceedingly small percentage of the voting citizens. It is they, however, who practically

make public opinion. They know the facts, they think out, and marshal and set forth, by word or pen, the arguments meant to influence the public.

The second class consists of those who, though comparatively passive, take an interest in politics. They listen and read, giving an amount of attention proportionate to the magnitude of any particular issue placed before them, or to the special interest it may have for them. They form a judgment upon the facts and arguments presented to them. Their judgment corrects and modifies the views of the first class, and thus they are, though not the originators, yet largely the moulders of opinion, giving to a doctrine or a proposition the shape it has to take if it is to succeed. Most of them belong to a party but are not so hotly partisan as to be unable to consider fairly both sides of a case. In countries accustomed to constitutional government, and when not swept off their feet by excitement, such men have the qualities of good jurymen and deliver a sensible verdict. What they think and feel is the opinion of the nation as a whole. It is public opinion.[4]

These two classes together, Lord Bryce believed, made up together a quite small percentage of the population, but it is that percentage which reads, or hears about, the opinions of editorials and of other media which express opinions.

In this modest context, the writing of editorials and the expression of opinion assumes a proportion far beyond the Gallup poll percentages, and I believe that this fact is widely recognized by the owners and publishers of the press and its competitive media. If it is not, the maintenance of the editorial page can be nothing but the expression of an exaggerated megalomania, and I just do not believe that a megalomaniac will spend as much money as an editorial page costs.

But, getting on to the other aspects of my thesis, the editorial page and the opposite-editorial page, to be effective and useful, must be something more. All I ask therefore is that the money spent daily on the production of opinion and of background news should be devoted to the objectives which I have suggested might be useful: the creation of a greater sense of continuity and of proportion, divorced from headlines and hot leads; the presentation of opposed points of view and the reasons for them; the determination to avoid the inevitable limitations and salesmanship of the news columns for the sake of the smaller, more reflective public which wants to have time to think.

I do not believe that this can be effectively done by the presentation, day by day, of the views of a dozen contrasting columnists. This is an abdication of a newspaper's fundamental responsibility. It is, to be sure, better than nothing at all. Especially in one-newspaper towns, it has its great usefulness. But it seems to me that a newspaper or a radio station with a consistent point of view, moderately expressed, can be a much more effective weapon of public opinion. If it presents opposed points of view, and simultaneously expresses an editorial point of view known to be its own, it vastly increases its effectiveness as an instrument of public opinion. Objectivity can degenerate into a colorless neutrality which deprives any organ of public opinion of any status beyond that of a public carrier as defined by the regulations of the Interstate Commerce Commission. A newspaper surely should be something more than a railroad or a trucking company.

Federal Centralization

and the Press

The problem to which I address myself and invite your attention is a very elementary one.* It has to do with the grave danger to our freedom and our security from the growth of federal centralization—a danger to be found, I think, not primarily in the realm of economics, but very largely in the realm of things of the mind and the spirit.

I want you to reflect this problem of federal centralization against a very large background of American experience and American history, against a background that might almost be called an achievement in avoidance. For in historical perspective, the most astonishing thing about the American experience is that we have managed in so extraordinary a fashion to achieve the things that Western nations and societies try to achieve without paying the price that history or Providence customarily extracted from them. We have achieved nationalism and national unity without chauvinism, without what the Germans call "Nationalismus." We have achieved colonialism on a very large scale—for everything west of the Appalachians was colony to the thirteen original states—and achieved it without colonialism, eliminating it so completely that not one out of a hundred Americans realizes that we have been the

---

* This lecture was delivered November 10, 1955.

greatest colonizing power in the nineteenth and twentieth centuries. We have achieved universal education without that vulgarization of learning which was so confidently predicted by the critics of the American experiment. We have separated church and state and embarked upon a policy of no ecclesiastical establishment without that moral depravity which again was predicted as its inevitable consequence. We have achieved majority rule without that despotism over the minority which was expected by de Tocqueville and by all those who have echoed de Tocqueville's famous chapters on the inevitable tyranny of the majority. We are in process of achieving world power without, so far, that imperialism which made world power more a curse than a blessing in the nineteenth century.

Have we achieved national unity, national centralization, national strength, without the impairment of local autonomy and without the impairment of the liberty of the individual which so frequently follows the establishment of a powerful central government? In a larger sense this issue of particularism and nationalism is part of a very ancient issue in politics, one of the oldest, one of the most persistent, and one of the most difficult of all political questions: The question of the reconciliation of liberty and order. It is a problem on which the old British Empire was wrecked—it is a problem which the Americans themselves proved unable to solve during the dark days of the Articles of Confederation. It was a crucial issue at the Constitutional convention—it was solved then at least in principle. But it was not solved in practice; witness the war of 1861 to 1865.

You can almost write our history in terms of the struggle over the broad and narrow construction, the struggle over nationalism and States' rights. This it was that appeared to divide Jefferson and Hamilton; this it was that created crisis after crisis during the dangerous years from the mid-forties to the Civil War and that split the nation asunder. This it was that appeared the crucial problem of the war itself. Need I remind you that the question of the nature and extent of national authority was by no means settled by victory at Appomattox? It persisted and persists to our own day. I suppose few questions have ruffled the surface and agitated the deeps of American politics in the last half-century as persistently as has this one. In one sense this problem of local autonomy and national authority has been a very real problem, and we cannot but stand amazed at the insights of a Jefferson or a Hamilton, both ardent patriots, both far-sighted statesmen, both devout nationalists—one putting his faith in the intelligence and virtue of the mass of the people, the other in the power and majesty of the state; one representing what was to be the American tradition, the other what has been the European tradition. It is a tribute to the understanding and the vision of these great founding fathers that we are still discussing the problems of state and nation very much in their terms.

Subsequent generations have added little to the analysis or to the clarification of the issues. Quite the contrary—it is not too sweeping an exaggeration to say that subsequent generations, and particularly, I think, the last generation, have done much to obfuscate the issues. They have invoked States' rights to rationalize economic interests; to obscure reality of national unity—the unity of soil and water and forest and resources, of wind and rain and drought, of economy and of society. Certainly it is hard to avoid the conclusion that most of the discussion of national centralization versus States' rights in recent years has been immaterial and irrelevant and designed to confuse the issue.

Perhaps the most urgent observation here is that the problem of governmental power, of the nature and extent and of the limits of that power, is not one that can yield to glib clichés, nor be disposed of by processes of incantation. We must look to realities, not to theories; we must look to functions, not abstractions. We must keep ever in mind that whenever government exercises authority in America, it is the American people who exercise that authority, although parenthetically I may say this is more nearly true of the national governments than of state governments, because of the far more equitable distribution of representation in the Congress and the highly inequitable distribution of representation in so many of the state legislatures. Above all this, we must keep in mind that the issue of state and nation is not a moral issue, although it can become one: It is a practical question. In itself, there is nothing either virtuous or wicked about state government and nothing either virtuous or wicked about national government. A highly centralized government like that of Britain is not necessarily a bad one, or even an inefficient one. A decentralized government like that of Germany is not necessarily a good one or even an efficient one. If we look realistically at the issue of the exercise of governmental authority, it will be clear, first, that the process of federal centralization has been steady and persistent from the beginning of our history, and particularly from the 1880's; second, that the process has been nonpolitical and nonpartisan, furthered by all parties when in power; third, that the process has generally adapted itself to the exigencies of the economy. Centralization, in the political arena, has almost invariably followed, not anticipated, centralization in the economic. Fourth, the process has been enormously stimulated by war and by military considerations generally. The implacable demands of military security make it highly improbable that there will be any diminution of federal centralization in the foreseeable future.

More to the point, in the light of this discussion, is the fact that historically federal centralization has not appeared to be the most serious threat to the liberties of the citizen. It would be asking a great deal to ask working men, for example, to subscribe to the notion that national government has been their enemy and state government their friend over the years. It would be asking a great deal to ask Negroes to subscribe to the principle that they must look to the states for their freedom, their rights, and their privileges and must regard the federal government with suspicion. Even in the realm of civil liberties, the states rather than the nation have been most derelict. Whatever the situation today, historically most of the threats, too, and the attacks upon liberties guaranteed in bills of rights have come from states rather than from nation.

Who can doubt that the situation today has changed and is changing? Who can doubt that federal centralization does now pose problems that profoundly affect the liberties of men and the security of the nation? Two things that are inextricably tied together, for we cannot have the one without the other. Why is this? It is because with recent years, old issues have taken on new form and new dimensions. We can see now that Jefferson's fears were in many ways valid and logical, for Jefferson was not afraid of a strong government—during his Presidency, the government did not lack for strength nor did the executive power lack for strength. The real issue as Jefferson saw it when he advised the addition of the Bill of Rights, when he wrote the memorable Kentucky resolutions against the alien and sedition laws, when he prepared his first great inaugural address—the real issue was not quantitative, it was qualitative. The real issue was not so much the distinction between state and nation but the distinction between those things that government may do and those things that government may not do. Even this distinction, needless to say, is not mathematically clear. Under our system government may not ordinarily restrict freedom of speech, but may do so in war time; it may not usually restrict freedom of press, but may do so in the face of obscenity; it may not demand excessive bail, but what is excessive varies from circumstance to circumstance; and so forth ad infinitum.

In short the whole matter is a matter of degree. The emphasis, therefore, should be more on the wisdom than on technical or even legal rights. Nevertheless, I think there is general agreement on those things that government may do and government may not do, should do and should not do. The thing a government should not do is to embrace above all, control of the communication of ideas: control of religion; control of political ideas; control of speech, of the press, and of association. This is one very large category and it is by far the most important single category. There are certain procedural powers government does not have—it may not violate due process but must act in accordance with rules of the Constitution and rules of law; it may not take life or property or liberty arbitrarily but only with due process and under the law.

Now the reason for this distinction between things government may do and may not do—the reason for setting all matters having to do with the communication of ideas in a special category exempt from governmental control—is as clear as is the reason for giving a preferred position to the first amendment. It is not a sentimental indulgence to favored or privileged groups as is sometimes supposed. Indeed, the element of privilege does not enter in at all. It is rather a hard-headed recognition that without access to information, without the right to communicate information, without discussion and criticism—in short, without freedom —we cannot make our kind of government work at all. Without freedom we will fall into error and that error may be irremediable. Freedom is not a luxury but a necessity. It is not an indulgence but a way of avoiding error and discovering truth. It is for that reason that it occupies, and must occupy, a preferred position in our constitutional system. What we have witnessed in the last decade, and especially in the last three or four years, is an ominous development, one that takes us back in a sense to the Jeffersonian struggle against the invasions of liberty by the leviathan state. It is the entry of government generally—not the national government alone, but all government—into areas heretofore thought immune from governmental invasion. It is not so much that government has taken on new and larger powers or activities in the economic realm— in social security or the development of hydroelectric energy or soil conservation. It is not even that it may enter into such controversial fields as education or slum clearance or public health. These developments we can take in our stride. If they are mistaken or misguided, they can be readily reversed. It is rather that government is now entering into fields of the communication of ideas, into precisely those areas that were thought immune from governmental operation; the areas of the press, religion, education, and association that were specifically exempted from governmental invasion by the Bill of Rights.

One of the most curious features of this development is that it appears at once so pervasive and in a technical sense so innocent. Nobody apparently wants it this way and nobody in government is prepared to admit that this is in fact what is happening. But almost every department, every branch, every agency of government contributes to the process in one way or another. Everybody talks about decentralization, and the weathering away of the TVA, and the return to the states of oil lands and grazing lands goes on apace. But in the realm that really counts—in the realm that will be decisive, in the realm that is far and away the most perilous—it is federal centralization that grows apace, not decentralization.

Let us look, then, at some manifestations of this process—at some of the areas where the growth of governmental authority threatens the integrity of our constitutional system and our ability to function as a democracy. What are the areas in which federal centralization appears to be spreading?

First, the area of education. A very important part of American nationalism has been the absence of statism, and one thing that has contributed to this fortunate and happy absence of statism is that education has not been the instrument of a powerful national government, but has been very largely a local affair, in this contrasting sharply with the position of education in many continental nations. Even those who today advocate federal aid to such things as school building or school lunch programs or scholarship aid would balk at suggesting control over the educational content of schools throughout the country. But in recent years we have witnessed a series of threats to private and local controls over education through the operation of security legislation and review, through Congressional investigations of one kind or another, and through a variety of other influences that affect the integrity of the educational system. Note that the Jenner committee, for example, recommended in 1953 a country-wide institution of loyalties programs for all colleges and universities [1]—and that Senator Joseph R. McCarthy, going Senator William E. Jenner one better, urged the withdrawal of tax immunity from any institutions that did not supervise teachers' loyalty to the satisfaction of his committee, or that harbored what he called "Fifth Amendment Communists" on their faculties.[2] Harvard college, you may recall, was a particular target of his criticism.

Other indirect invasions of the realm of education suggest themselves readily enough. In 1953, the Defense Department conditioned granting USAFI contracts to colleges on teachers' getting security clearance. As the Civil Liberties Union observed at the time, this would open the door to a similar action by all other government departments, and through the mere accident of their employment in an institution which desires to sign such a contract, the universities might themselves find themselves subject *in toto* to governmental clearance.

Similar pressures on education have come from voluntary organizations—that is, from nongovernmental organizations. I have in mind, for example, the demands of the American Legion, or the Veterans of Foreign Wars, or the Minute Women, or similar organizations, for censorship of textbooks and supervision of teaching. Most of the members of these organizations in their private capacities, it is safe to say, are dead against "big government" and in favor of private enterprise rather than governmental enterprise; but in the one place where enterprise really counts, namely in the mind and spirit of men, they throw their immense strength to the side of government—to the control over enterprise and, eventually, the smothering of enterprise. This inability of private organizations to see the inevitable consequences of their demands for censorship over security clearance or for intellectual controls is one of the sobering paradoxes of our time.

What we have here in the realm of education is not merely pressure from the outside, from government or pietistic societies, but from the inside as well. It is one of the tragedies of our day that all that George Orwell predicted and Arthur Koestler described seems to be becoming fact, even in the citadels of freedom—namely that in many cases the victim cooperates with the process of victimization. Thus Boston University discharged a teacher who refused to answer questions put to him by the egregious Jenner committee. Thus New Jersey has provided that all teachers at Rutgers must answer all questions coming up in legislative inquiries. Just how the constitutionality of some questions is going to be tested, unless someone refuses to answer, is not clear. The files of the American Association of University Professors and of the Civil Liberties Union bulge with complaints from teachers whose institutions have cravenly caved in before official demands and who undertake to police —the word itself is an affront—undertake to police their own faculties.

A second broad area into which government is moving increasingly, and with increasing energy, and which government may in time come to dominate, is the area of science. This has come about in a variety of ways. First there is the elementary fact that science is an essential ingredient of national security and the government itself must have a monopoly on production and control of atomic energy. The claim of the military to establish security safeguards in crucial fields of scientific research is a persuasive one. What was apparent only to far-sighted scientists when it was first advanced—namely that all realms of science are somehow related to security and that this principle would give government jurisdiction over the entire realm of science—has only gradually come home to the rest of us. What should have been apparent to anyone familiar with the psychology of the administrator—namely that he would invariably err on the side of caution and put his faith in mechanical regulations—is now becoming crystal clear.

A second factor making for the extension of central government control in the area of science is the power of the purse. It is natural that government should be sufficiently concerned with scientific research to finance it. In the process of farming out its projects to universities, like Minnesota or Harvard or Columbia or Massachusetts Institute of Technology or California Institute of Technology, government naturally indicates what it wants researched. Two things follow: Some degree of governmental dictation of the kind of research to be undertaken and some degree of governmental control over those who do the research and over the findings themselves.

What this means is that, more and more, universities are no longer free agents. They are committed to projects not of their own choosing, and this often to the neglect of that pure research without which even applied science will become mere engineering. They find themselves supinely permitting governmental supervision over their faculty, their research assistants, and even over the use to which their findings are put. This, needless to say, is the very negation of the function of the university. It is also an enormous accretion to federal authority precisely in those areas where the government is incompetent to operate effectively. I am not concerned here with the palpable incompetence of government, an incompetence whose monument will ever be the Gray commission report that denied us the services of Robert Oppenheimer.[3] I am concerned rather with the manner in which governmental security procedures create something like a federal veto power over scientists and scientific projects. The Gray committee cleared Professor Oppenheimer on loyalty grounds and then rejected him on grounds of discretion! Promptly the authorities at the University of Washington withdrew or cancelled an invitation to Professor Oppenheimer to lecture at that institution. Washington may not be ready for federal supervision over its water power projects, but it is clearly eager to anticipate federal suggestions over its intellectual activities. Well, may we ask, where is this process to end? Will universities eager for federal research money or eager merely to be thought above suspicion start submitting names of prospective professors to the proper security agencies in the federal bureaus?

A third pressure is in the realm of religion. If there is one thing that in the beginning more sharply distinguished the American experiment than any other, it was the separation of church and state. Ours was the first Western nation to try the experiment of getting along without a state church. Ours was the first major nation to manage without religious warfare or religious conflict. Everyone was agreed at the time that government had no business in the field of religion and everyone is, in principle, agreed on that now. Yet by indirection, through such things as the pressures of the Velde committee and through the operation of the security program, the federal government does indirectly impose itself upon religion. The spectacle of the Velde committee investigating Bishop G. Bromley Oxnam and the sallies of the Jenner committee into the field of religion are more than straws in the wind.[4] As Bishop Oxnam pointed out, the committee clearly invaded the field of religion. The book which was under attack (Jerome Davis' *Behind Soviet Power*) [5] had been sent to Methodist ministers by order of the administrative committee of the board of missions of the Methodist church. It was an official action of one of the official agencies of the largest Protestant denomination in America. So far as I know, this is the first time in American history that any committee had presumed to question the right of the church to send such literature to its ministers as it deemed wise.

The distinguished executive editor of the Washington *Post,* J. Russell Wiggins, the man who has probably done more to vindicate freedom of the press than any other journalist in the country, has said, "It was a dreadful day when the House of Representatives thundered its applause and shouted its cheers as an eminent member made the utterly baseless charge that the most respected bishop of the largest Protestant denomination served God on Sunday and the Communist front for the rest of the week."

A fourth area where the federal government is threatening the field of the control of thought is that of the foundation—that new institution which is one of the most remarkable inventions in social science in recent years, and very much an American invention. I refer not so much to the puerilities of the Reece committee as to the reaction to them.[6] The degree to which the champions of the foundations found it necessary to defend their institutions on grounds that Representative B. C. Reece chose was an ominous thing. Some of them seemed all too ready to concede that government did, in fact, have a right to pass on the intellectual activities of beneficiaries of foundation grants and too eager to prove that they had not in fact favored radicals or endowed subversives. No more specious argument than that tax exemption authorizes Congress to pass on the ideas and policies of the foundations was ever advanced. If this is true, it is equally true that tax exemption to churches authorizes governmental agencies to pass on the content of every sermon preached in every church or on all the doctrines taught in theological seminaries. If it is true, it is equally true that tax exemption authorizes state and local governments to investigate what is actually taught in the classrooms of Minnesota or Harvard or Chicago universities, a position which Senators Jenner and McCarthy are quite prepared to adopt. If it is true, it is equally true that tax exemption authorizes governmental authorities to inquire into the medical practices of doctors and tax exempt hospitals. Once establish the principle that tax exemption authorizes supervision, not merely of the finances of any organization but of its intellectual or moral activities, and you have an effective end to freedom for any intellectual and moral activities.

The fifth area where we have witnessed an extraordinary growth of federal centralization is perhaps the most ominous of all. It is in the realm of literature. Few of us, I fear, appear to realize what is involved in the impudent claims of governmental authority to investigate the principles, ideas, beliefs, the training, background, and character of all persons who write. I have in mind here not only the influence of the Attorney General's list and the list of the Un-American Activities Committee on publishers, librarians, school boards, and private organizations, but the consequences of the principle inherent in the government's position in the Lamont and O'Connor cases in the federal courts. Keep in mind that neither Lamont nor O'Connor served the United States government in any capacity whatsoever. They were presumably wholly outside the jurisdiction of governmental committees. On the specious argument that because overseas libraries have purchased some of their books, the McCarthy committee called these gentlemen to testify about their political beliefs and affiliations. Both Lamont and O'Connor denied the jurisdiction of the committee. The district court ruled in favor of Lamont and the case is now on appeal.[7] In the O'Connor case the decision went the other way!

The principle here is, I should think, crystal clear. If through one of its committees Congress can investigate the beliefs of any author whose books some branch of the government acquires, it can, of course, investigate the beliefs of all authors of books, magazines, and newspaper articles, or any other printed word by the simple device of acquiring a copy of the book, magazine, or newspaper for the Library of Congress or for any other governmental agency. The naked question here is whether the government can investigate any author or any book that it wishes to investigate. If it has this authority, it has the authority to control; that is, to censor all writers. If it has this authority, it can, in effect, supervise all literature.

It is not clear that this authority differs in any respect from the Russian or the Nazi censorship in its ultimate implications or in its potentialities. This indeed is precisely what the concurring opinion of Justice William O. Douglas said in the Supreme Court decision in the Edward A. Rumley case:

> Once the government can demand of a publisher the name of the purchasers of his publications, the free press as we know it disappears. Then the specter of a government agent will look over the shoulder of everyone who reads. The purchase of a book or a pamphlet today may result in a subpoena tomorrow. Fear of criticism goes with every person into the bookstore; the subtle imponderable pressures of the orthodox lay hold. Some will fear to read what is unpopular, what the powers that be dislike. When the light of publicity may reach any student, any teacher, inquiry will be discouraged. The books and pamphlets critical of administration or that preach an unpopular policy in domestic or foreign affairs, or that are in disrepute in the orthodox school of thought, will be suspect and subject to investigation. The press and its readers will pay a heavy price in harassment. That will be minor in comparison with the menace of the shadow which government will cast over literature that does not follow a dominant party line. Through the harassment of hearings and investigations, reports and subpoena, government will hold a club over speech and over the press. Congress could not do this by law; the power of investigation is also limited.[8]

And as the Supreme Court said in a decision in the Washington *Herald* case—a decision which Colonel Robert McCormick of the Chicago *Tribune* quoted with approval a few years ago—"a general offensive, inquisitorial, compulsory investigation conducted by commission without any allegation, upon no fixed principles, and governed by no rules of law or of evidence, and no restraints except its own will of caprice, is unknown to our constitution and laws. Let the power once be established, there is no knowing where the practice under it will end."

A sixth realm of the growth of governmental power is that of labor and of industry, chiefly through the extension of security requirements to all industries and businesses that deal with projects important to the national security, even at second or third hand. The possibilities here for the extension of federal authority over the whole realm of the economy beggar the imagination. That there may be a legitimate concern for the trustworthiness of those who work on super-secret projects is clear enough. It might be supposed that business itself, however, could take care of this problem as it always has in the past. As it is, security tests now extend to somewhere between ten and fifteen million workers—the exact number cannot in the nature of things be known—and distinguished heads of great corporations have to have clearance and so, too, do the janitors in their buildings. The result in one direction is a loss of men like Dr. Edward Condon, who threw in the sponge after going through four security clearances and being called up for a fifth on what is widely suspected to have been political grounds. The loss in another direction is in the time and energy and efficiency all down the line while the processes of security clearance grind on and on. But whatever the social or economic or intellectual cost, the political cost is clear and it is that with which we are concerned. Authority over who may and who may not work in certain key industries of the country has in effect been transferred from the private to the public domain, and chiefly to the national domain. And, *mirabile dictu,* the great industrialists and executives who bitterly and ceaselessly fought control of business during the New Deal years now appear to take for granted this far greater, and potentially far more dangerous, control over their business.

There are comparable pressures in the realm of labor. The Taft-Hartley Act required union officials to take the non-Communist oath in order for the unions to enjoy the services of the NLRB, and this requirement has been upheld by the courts. Whatever its constitutionality and whatever its wisdom, it is clearly another step toward federal centralization. Recently we have witnessed a great spate of bills looking to the tightening up and extension of federal control over labor through security techniques of one kind or another. The Butler bill, for example, which was happily defeated, authorized the subversive activities board to deprive unions of their rights to bargain collectively on mere complaint that a union was Communist dominated, whatever that phrase might mean. Senator Homer Ferguson and Representative C. William Reed have introduced measures which create a new category of Communist-infiltrated organizations as distinct from Communist-dominated organizations. These provide for the dissolution of any that are Communist-infiltrated without defining the term. The bill is not limited, note, to unions working in defense plants, but embraces all unions. In 1954, too, came a bill making it illegal for any member of the Communist party to hold office in any union and requiring Communist-infiltrated unions to purge themselves before they can enjoy bargaining rights. So far, none of these bills has been enacted into law; but they reveal the length to which men otherwise eloquently opposed to big government are prepared to go in extending governmental supervision in the realm of labor and of business.

A seventh area in which we are witnessing an extraordinary expansion of governmental power is that of the security program in general and the various lists in particular. What is striking here is not merely the nature and scope of the federal security program, but the extent to which it has been emulated and adopted by states, local governments, and even private industry. State after state has come up with its own little un-American activities committee, has taken over the lists put out by the Attorney General or the House committee, and has given to them spurious dignity and legality. Thus state, local, and private associations have identified themselves with the federal government and allowed the federal government to lay down controlling principles on matters of security —have made themselves, in effect, law enforcement agencies of the government, or at an even further remove, agencies to punish non-cooperation with a federal agency, no matter how dubious the authority of the agency or the claims of cooperation. Thus, for example, the New Jersey law providing for the dismissal of those who do not cooperate with federal investigation by answering questions. Thus, for example, the proposed Broyle's Act, which provides automatic fine and imprisonment of any persons who remain members of organizations on the Attorney General's list, and this even though the Supreme Court has said that the Attorney General's list has no legal standing.

Still another example is the pusillanimous retreat of the New York City authorities on the issue of employing the distinguished playwright, Arthur Miller, to write a script on the youth of the city. Miller was charged with the crime of having belonged to or sympathized with organizations on some governmental blacklist. There was no charge of illegal acts, no charge of disloyalty or subversion. There was no criticism, even, of what he had written, much less of what he proposed to write for the city. But the fact that he was a "controversial" figure was enough to persuade the New York City authorities to withdraw their invitation to him.

The moral is clear. All that is necessary to establish an effective blacklist is to create a "controversy."

Closely connected with, and indeed part of, this activity of government through the application of lists of allegedly subversive organizations is pressure in an eighth field—that of radio, television, the movies, and the theater. Wisely or unwisely, Americans decided to confide control of radio and television to private enterprise, not public. One reason for the decision not to adopt the model of the British Broadcasting Corporation was doubtless fear of the state, fear of censorship or of partisanship. Yet we have in considerable part forfeited the advantages and the benefits of the privately controlled system by instituting private censorship and controls, so that it is probably true to say that there is more freedom today on the BBC than on the American radio—more freedom and less censorship. Certainly the BBC knows nothing of political lists that in effect blackmail potential speakers. Nor does it seek to avoid employment of controversial characters or even to avoid controversial subjects. On the contrary it welcomes controversy on the radio. What purpose to deny governmental power to censure ideas if the most powerful media of communications themselves undertake censorship? Government can be challenged in the courts but it is almost impossible to challenge the policies of private corporations judicially. Government can be criticized in halls of Congress but we do not know how to go about effectively criticizing the internal policies of private corporations, privately adopted and privately pursued.

One aspect of this problem has received curiously little attention. That has to do with the rules which appear to guide, if they are indeed rules and if they do indeed guide, the decisions of the Federal Communications Commission. The FCC has authority to license radio stations. That authority is not, or at least should not be, an arbitrary one. The FCC should and does fix standards of public service. If it applies to standards of political or other orthodoxy, it is guilty not only of grave abuse of power but of seriously frustrating precisely the policy it was set up to defend—namely making sure that the American public would have a chance at competing views and that there would be no monopoly of the air by one party, one interest, one faith, or one philosophy. The spectacle of the FCC denying a license to a radio station on the ground that the owner was alleged to have belonged to or contributed to subversive organizations—allegations which later turned out to be false—is one to inspire gravest misgivings in the minds of all who cherish freedom of information. For if only those who contribute to the Republican party, or the Methodist Church, or the Red Cross, if only those who are careful enough or dull enough or ignorant enough never to join anything that anybody could possibly disapprove, if only these may be sure of getting government license to the air, then we have precisely that monopoly of the air we seek to avoid. The English, Scandinavians, and others who maintain state-owned and -controlled radio insist that their radio is in fact freer than ours. Both the radio and the FCC seem determined to prove them right.

The ninth example of federal invasion of the realm of ideas is in the operation of control over the whole field of foreign travel through passport and visa controls. Time was when passports were not needed at all.

Then they came to be used purely as statements of identification and formal requests for admission and for courtesy abroad. The use of the passport and the visa as a mark of approval or disapproval is one fraught with danger, one that must be resisted by all who fear the rise of the leviathan state. There is specious support in law or in administrative rulings to this use, but there is none in wisdom or sound policy. For if travel is to depend on the subjective judgment of anonymous persons in some bureau of the State Department on the imponderable issue of whether travel is or is not "in the best interests of the United States," then there is an end to genuine freedom for any who contemplate travel. What are the best interests of the United States and who is to determine them and on what grounds are they to be determined? How are these nameless persons to discover what is the interest of the United States and how it may or may not be served abroad? Is criticism of the United States in the interest of the United States? So it has been supposed, at least in the past. But pressure of federal centralization here is even more serious than appears on the surface. When the State Department assumes responsibility to decide that it is or is not in the interest of the United States for a particular person to go abroad, it follows implacably in logic that those who are permitted to travel do travel in the interests of the United States.

The principle here is precisely the same as that which President Abbott Lawrence Lowell of Harvard University submitted in response to a request for censorship of off-campus activities of Harvard professors. If, he said, we censor some and not others, it follows that those not censored speak with our approval and speak on our behalf.

So if we deny visas to some and not to others, it follows that those who do have visas are certified pure by the State Department and travel in the interests of the United States. This is a pretty tall order. It is a large responsibility for any department to assume. It is a heavy responsibility for any individual to carry. The day by day effect of this policy may be negligible: Here and there a scientist like Professor Linus Cole Pauling kept at home, here and there a political critic like Louis Boudin denied a passport, here and there an artist like Paul Robeson refused permission to go abroad. But the long-range consequences will be formidable. It is difficult to imagine a more effective instrument for silently inducing conformity of opinion on all critical public matters or of silencing public dissent than this. The ordinary traveler will not be affected, the average businessman, for example, or those who travel for pleasure. It is the scholar, the journalist, the scientist, the public figure—precisely those upon whom we depend for the criticism necessary for democracy to work—who will be affected. All of them will be tempted to conform or to be silent in order to be sure that when they do come to travel they will not have difficulty getting a passport from the State Department.

A tenth area which government is invading is that of voluntary association. Time does not permit a review of the significance of the private voluntary association in our history. I think it no great exaggeration to say that it has been the most important single institution in the whole of our history. Possibly one reason why the English triumphed over the French and the Spanish in America is that, where France and Spain colonized through the agency of the state, the English colonized through the agency of the joint stock company and the congregation; colonized, that is, through the agency of the private voluntary organization. Private voluntary organizations have played a decisive role in our history since the first landfalls in Virginia and Plymouth and Massachusetts Bay. Need I remind you that all our political parties, our labor unions, all our churches, all our professional organizations, all our reform organizations, all our fraternal organizations are private voluntary associations? These have furnished the grass roots experience of democracy, these are the organizations that carry on the day by day business of government in thousands of communities scattered over the land. These, too, have made an enormous contribution to the growth of a sound sense of nationalism by uniting those of common interest from state to state and region to region—uniting the lawyer in Vermont to the lawyer in Texas and the doctor in Virginia with the doctor in California, a stamp collector in New York with a stamp collector in Florida and a fisherman in North Carolina with a fisherman in Washington.

What we are witnessing today for the first time in our history is a concerted attack on the right of association and on the institution of private voluntary association through the compiling of lists—the Attorney General's list, the Un-American Activities Committee list, the scores of state lists like the Kenney committee list and the Canwell committee list and the Broyle's committee list. Even private persons— emulating Gilbert and Sullivan (for life is always imitating art)—are compiling little lists which take on a pseudo, quasi-authoritative character. De Tocqueville warned us over a century ago that the private voluntary organization was crucial to the working of the American system and he pointed out too that if once government started drawing up lists of approved organizations and disapproved organizations the practice of joining would dry up. For, once men were prevented from joining the organizations of their choice, it would be in vain, he said, that the government urge them to join organizations that had the stamp of approval. They would refrain altogether. As anyone familiar with universities and college campuses in this country knows, we are witnessing already that reluctance to join which may spell a drying up of the grass roots of democracy and a serious blow to effective nationalism throughout the country. It is no wonder that the young, familiar with the case of Milo J. Radulovich, familiar with the case of Midshipman Landy, familiar with the case of Russ Miller, familiar with a score of other cases of people who themselves joined, or whose mothers joined, or whose aunts or uncles or father-in-laws joined some organization that someone disapproved of, are steering clear of joining things. But once the habit of joining dries up, once people cease to join dangerous organizations, they will cease to join any organizations, including the Republican party and the Methodist church, for you never know.

Here, too, we witness the spread of federal instruments and federal standards. Nothing is more impressive than the readiness with which state, local, and private organizations adopt federal lists. Many communities are prepared to select the books in their libraries, the teachers in their schools, the speakers on their platforms, not on the basis of their own standards but on the basis of some anonymous federal standard, some name or some organization which somebody in Washington has seen fit to put on a list. Texans ready to die at a new Alamo for tidelands oil seem quite prepared to give up their sovereign right of selecting their own books or their own speakers. Medical and bar associations that fight fiercely against that fate worse than death—federal aid—are ready enough to call for federal loyalty oaths and to accept standards of thought, standards cooked up in Washington, for membership in their organizations. Here is one of the least dramatic but one of the most efficacious pressures for federal centralization.

Eleventh, there is pressure on the civil service through the loyalty-security program. Who that has read the hair-raising Adam Yarmolinsky report can doubt that the inescapable consequence of investigations and examinations of this kind is to create a civil service made up of conformers and accepters—what are popularly called "yes-men"? Many of us assume thoughtlessly that federal civil servants, because they work for the federal government, should inevitably be agents of or spokesmen for that government. But they work, of course, for the American people, and their ultimate responsibility and loyalty is to the people as a whole. May I say parenthetically one of the most ominous developments in recent years is the emergence of the notion of loyalty to the administration. We have long prided ourselves in America that we did not have a national bureaucracy any more than we had a special administrative law. We do not put our civil servants in uniform or give them special privileges or exempt them from the laws that affect other citizens. But there are more ways than one to create a bureaucracy or to create a bureaucratic type of mind, and one of the most effective ways is that which we are now using—namely to discourage any expression of individuality; to discourage outside interests, activities, and loyalties; to discourage criticism of government or policies adopted by political superiors; to induce a general mediocrity, a general acquiescence and a general apathy.

Finally, I come to pressure on the press itself—pressure which is perhaps the most dramatic. That is a growing tendency to internal censorship, the deliberate withholding of information about government from the American people. When Dwight Eisenhower was President of Columbia University, he popularized a principle of man's right to knowledge and the free use thereof. His Presidency of the United States may well be recalled in connection with the principle of the government's right to withhold knowledge and the free use thereof. Other administrations have withheld information; it has remained for this administration to elevate that policy into a principle. The principle we may designate the "Philip Young principle of the inherent nonavailability of information." This principle had, in fact, many inventors. The one who may perhaps finally be awarded a patent on it is Secretary of Defense Charles E. Wilson. On March 30, 1955, the Secretary cut down information forces of the armed services by one-half to one-third and sent a directive to govern the policy of giving out information. That policy was, quite simply, that information was to be a constructive contribution—I am quoting—"a constructive contribution to the primary mission of the Defense Department." What was constructive, what was a contribution, and for that matter what was the primary mission of the Defense Department was not made clear. After a few days, came, however, an "experimental balance sheet" for strategic information. According to this, officers were to strike a sensible balance on whether what they said might or might not be harmful to the United States. They were to consider the net effect of what they said on the military and the industrial power of the United States as compared with the power of other countries and whether what they said might help reveal weaknesses or might reveal strength within the United States. Apparently it is dangerous to reveal your weaknesses and equally dangerous to reveal your strength; that pretty well covered the whole ground. Just in case it left some gaps, the directive provided that officers were to invoke other considerations, e.g., "anything else you can think of."

This policy of the control of the flow of information has, as might be suspected, many ramifications. First, as with the security test, it extends from sensitive to nonsensitive and insensitive areas, and from classified areas to various degrees of nonclassification. I say various degrees, because the resourcefulness of the American people, or at least of the American administrator, has never been more fully dramatized than by the discovery of between thirty and forty new classifications that are not precisely secret and not precisely nonsecret, but something in between. In the second place it has spread from obvious agencies like the Atomic Energy Commission and perhaps some parts of the Defense Department to all departments. It is, after all, a sad confession of insignificance not to have anything important enough to conceal! So departments like Agriculture and Commerce and the Civil Service Commission now proudly have their own secrets and their own restrictions on what the public may know. Some of these restrictions are very sweeping indeed. Secretary Sinclair Weeks, in November of 1954, set up the Office of Strategic Information in the Department of Commerce. His purpose was to prevent unclassified data from being made available to foreign nations which might use it in a manner harmful to the United States. As the National Education Association pointed out: "If the policy of the Office of Strategic Information were carried out literally, it would bar the teaching of foreign students within the United States, the participation of foreign students and Fulbright scholars, exchange professors and fellows in university seminars, discussions and research programs, correspondence among university members and their opposite numbers abroad, and even fulfillment of contracts for technical assistance to foreign countries sponsored by the foreign operations administration." The policy has spread through the whole executive department and often into purely domestic matters; witness the withholding of important information about the negotiations of the Dixon-Yates contract.[9]

Third, it involves, not officially but unofficially, discrimination among reporters and newspapers and the intimidation and harassment of some correspondents who are persistently critical of governmental policies. Thus, for example, the Alsops, who have been strong enough to cry most loudly. If we take their story at face value, they have been made to suffer for their criticism of departmental policies a series of harassments and indignities. And the Raymond report of the Civil Liberties Union suggests that theirs is by no means an isolated instance.

The leviathan state will inevitably control the press, as it controls other media of thought. This invasion of freedom of the press through security regulations and inside censorship is nothing astonishing; it is predictable.

The press itself failed to foresee it or to guard against it. But that it is a logical part of a pattern of federal centralization cannot be denied—the pattern of the invasion by government of the realm of thought and communication. The press as a whole was remiss in not seeing the nature of this problem. It was remiss in failing to make clear the danger to the people—and to their servants, the government. The press is remiss even now in failing to relate the fight for its own freedom to the fight for freedom of the civil servant, of the applicant for a passport, of the teacher and the preacher—for failing to relate it to the whole pattern of attack upon the fabric of freedom. It has failed to make clear (has failed even to realize) that freedom is a seamless web.

Those who fear the leviathan state direct their fears and their defenses almost entirely to the political and the economic realm. They fight desperately against the invasion by government, especially by the federal government, of the realm of labor relations or tidelands or hydroelectric power, or public housing, or public health, or education. They are concerned with the impact of these political developments on private enterprise. But the invasions here are *relatively* unimportant, just as the whole concept of private enterprise as an economic concept is *relatively* unimportant. The only ultimately important area of private enterprise is the intellectual and the spiritual because it is antecedent to all others. Dry up private enterprise in the intellectual or spiritual realm and it will die of itself in the economic realm, a fact that every totalitarian government has known instinctively.

So too with the growth of the leviathan state and of centralization. Allow the state to invade the areas of thought, of education, of the press, of religion, of association, and we will have statism. It will be too late then to protest invasion of the economic realm. That will be a not very important detail. Those who fear statism, as all who are rooted in American history and tradition fear it, must resolutely oppose it where it is most dangerous, precisely in the realm of the mind and the spirit of men. For if once we get a government strong enough to control men's minds, we will have a government strong enough to control everything.

X · · · · · HERBERT L. BLOCK

An Independent Press

Each of us newspapermen has some responsibility in the field of journalism, although not as much as some of our friends and neighbors seem to think.* They frequently complain to me, as I am sure they do to each of you, that *"I don't see why you put that story on page one in your paper today,"* and *"You're certainly making the squares awfully small in the crossword puzzles in your paper lately,"* and *"That paper of yours—I had to crawl through the bushes this morning to find it."*

Each of us learns to bear these complaints with the fortitude of a man who is presumably responsible for the entire writing, editing, production, and delivery of a newspaper. And we do not really complain until we start getting blamed also for somebody *else's* paper.

We sometimes hear about The Press, as if it were a single publication. Statistics may seem to indicate that the trend is in that direction, but fortunately there are quite a few papers left and they are not all alike. I want you to know that I feel this as keenly as anyone and that when I refer to the press in its less happy moments I am not thinking of it as a single unit. I know that there are many fine newspapers and

---

* This lecture was delivered November 15, 1956. Delegates present at the annual meeting of the National Conference of Editorial Writers attended the lecture.

many more excellent individual performances—which could no more be recounted here than all the good news in the world could be included in a daily paper.

Leonard Lyons tells the story of Paul Gallico's being introduced to an audience as a man who was syndicated in 367 newspapers. When Gallico spoke, he said, "You hear a lot of figures about syndication, but when I say I'm in 367 papers, I don't mean 366 and I don't mean 368. I mean twelve!"

So if I talk critically about some parts of the press, please remember that I mean something less than all 1,765 papers.

In the past few years there have been many references to a "one-party press"—a press which is by no means unanimous but which by an overwhelming majority endorses or supports one political party. But I think the thing that should be of greatest concern to us is what Senator Paul Douglas recently referred to as a "double-standard press."

I think that some newspapers have tended to apply a double standard in judging the actions of parties or of government administrations. If a paper had closed its eyes to misdeeds in the last administration but cried out unceasingly about them in the present one, it might fairly be accused of maintaining a double standard. Perhaps there have been some like that, but I think that more often the shoe has been on the other foot—perhaps only because there are many more papers sympathetic to the present administration.

I think that newspapers which tolerated or encouraged the activities of a McCarthy when he was attacking members of one administration and found him an undesirable character only when he became injurious to the administration of another party were not entirely consistent in their standards.

Certainly many newspapers in the past four years seem to have altered their ideas about the responsibilities of a President as head of the government and leader of his party. Where the mistakes or misdeeds of even minor officials or politicians a few years ago were proclaimed to be typical of the "Truman Gang" and "Truman corruption" it was more likely to be said of recent officials whose conduct was questionable that "they have done a disservice to our President."

In some cases, papers which find it easy to forgive, forget, or ignore unfortunate statements by an Eisenhower or a Nixon, for example, seem to have memories like an elephant for those of a Truman or a Stevenson. And when I say "memory like an elephant" I am aware that this animal is sometimes used as a symbol for something besides persistence of memory.

Again, let me remind you that I am not talking about all the papers all the time. And the exposure of the security-risk "numbers game," which was accomplished by the Washington correspondents of many newspapers of various political views, was a fine example of the press performing its job of checking on government.

But Dixon-Yates, Al Sarena and conflicts-of-interest cases did not stir some papers to the same pitch of sustained indignation that they achieved over mink coats and deep freezes.

In 1952 a number of papers urged that a candidate or a party be supported to "preserve the two-party system." This alone did not seem to me to be a valid argument for voting for anyone, and still does not, even though the former "ins" are now out. But as a matter of consistency, papers which were worried about the two-party system then might well be concerned for the two-party system when the party they favor has the advantage of being in power and has also on its side most of the press and most of the money.

When newspapers hold one administration responsible for what they call the "loss of China" and hold another administration responsible for all the good news from abroad but decline to connect it with any bad news, I think this also suggests that a double standard is operating, and one that can be dangerous in assessing our situation in the world.

Wherever papers do not adhere to a single standard in judging government action I think it is harmful, not simply because it favors one party at the expense of another, but because it diminishes the independence of the press—because it is bad for journalism and bad for government.

It has been said by men who have spoken here in other years, but it can stand being said again, that the essential function of a free press is to provide a check on government—to act as a critic of government. This is why we *have* a free press. In a very real sense the press itself is a part of our system of checks and balances.

But even if there were an exact balance of papers supporting the two major parties, this in itself still would not be good enough. Theoretically, one might say that the two parties alone will check each other and expose each other's errors. But it does not necessarily work that way, even when there is a more or less even division of seats in Congress or in legislatures—or when the executive and legislative branches are in control of opposing parties. Expediency and even corruption and cowardice, in varying degrees, can be just as bipartisan as policies in the public interest. Infringements on civil liberties can be bipartisan or nonpartisan, and often are.

There are many members of Congress who feel that the Committee on Un-American Activities is an abomination, that it should never have been given the status of a standing committee of the House, that it operates under a charter so vague that it can hardly be held to account, and that it has been used—or misused—by members of both parties and charimen of both parties as an instrument for gaining personal publicity, for wreaking vengeance on individuals, for curbing the full exercise of civil liberties. But the congressmen who would vote to abolish it or to cut off its appropriations or who would decline to support it on contempt citations you can count on your hands, with a few fingers to spare.

In the closing days of more than one Congress, members of both houses have passed with a last-minute "whoop and holler" so-called internal security bills. Few would go into a campaign having voted against such bills, even though they might not know what was in them. And a President may sign such measures even though his administration might be known to consider them unwise.

There are also many political Pandora's boxes that neither party will open.

Early in 1956, at the time of the famous financial offer to Senator Francis H. Case,[1] there was much talk about an investigation of the oil lobby. What has happened since then? A committee headed by Senator John L. McClellan is supposedly investigating lobbying influences, or at least *was* when last heard from. But if Senator McClellan and his committee are filled with a passion to expose all the facts of the influence of such lobbies upon Congress, it is a passion they have kept remarkably well under control.

The feeling of most senators for the upper house as a gentleman's club is something that is also stronger than party lines. And the influence of oil flows across party lines.

Now, in citing such examples of bipartisanship it has not been my purpose to make out a case that all men in government are knaves or cowards. They are politicians, and while I think we should urge them to be more courageous, we should not be surprised that most politicians facing periodic elections *act* like politicians. But a newspaper, however outspoken it chooses to be in its political views, should not be a politician in that sense.

I do not think it is enough for a paper to consider itself independent simply because it reserves the right to endorse a candidate of a different party some time. Whatever its political preferences in elections, it has to be independent of government itself. In its day-to-day work it is obligated to keep an alert eye on *all* government and to say things that politicians do not say.

A newspaper also is not essentially a statesman or a diplomat. Among newspaper executives the temptation must often be strong to play a great role behind the scenes. I do not doubt that some of them, acting in this capacity, have done good on many occasions. But I think the desire to do this can easily be carried to a point where it separates such men from the readers and from the obligation to inform the readers. There is always the danger of getting so involved backstage that newspapers, or their executives, forget that their primary concern is to keep things in *front* of the scenes, where people can see them. I think there is such a thing as developing inside-dopiness—getting so deep inside the horse's mouth that you cannot see what is going on.

Many newspaper executives and many working newsmen have occasion to talk with public officials of both parties, and often these officials are flatteringly confidential. But I have noticed that government officials seldom make themselves or their policies look bad. Sometimes they even offer private assurances that they agree completely with whomever they are talking to at the time, and that what they are really trying to achieve is just the opposite of what they seem to be trying to do. There is often good reason why such statements are told in secret. Some of them could not be told to a room full of working correspondents without getting the government official laughed out of the room. I think newspaper people should take such confidences with a few grains of salt and remember to judge public officials on their public records. And I do not think a paper should abandon its independent judgment simply because an official says that something is good or bad—whether he says it privately or publicly.

In August of this year the State Department objected to a proposed trip to China by American newsmen, and throughout the country this decision was protested in editorials. The State Department then announced that President Eisenhower concurred in its policy, and press criticism of this decision dropped off sharply. Nothing new had been added by way of arguments or reasons. But for much of the press it was apparently enough that the President had spoken. I do not think newspapers should scrap their own opinions on the say-so of any man—even though the man may be the President, and one who is obviously not trying to be dictatorial. I do not think they should do so even if the man happens to be J. Edgar Hoover.

I think that newspapers surrender some independence of judgment whenever they try to fit their policies into a preconceived plan regardless of issues—whether they go along unquestioningly with a party or public official or whether they determine that come-what-may they will take a position exactly in the middle on public issues. A fixed position in the middle of the road can be more objectionable than objective. And sometimes papers which make a great show of being objectively in the middle are following the injunction of the minister who exhorted his congregation to "follow the straight and narrow path between right and wrong."

In any controversy, if there are a thousand wrongs on one side and one wrong on the other, it is possible to cite one wrong on each side and to point out that neither side is perfect. And I think it would be far better to say nothing at all.

It is said that the press of today is more responsible than it was in the days of vigorous and even violent personal journalism, and in some ways it is. But a single middle-of-the-road position cannot take the place of the clash of opinions. And papers which are reluctant to choose between right and wrong—or which neglect their prime duty to check abuses in government—are also being irresponsible, and in a way that is perhaps less obvious but in the long run more dangerous to the country.

The responsibility of the newspapers to exercise their critical faculties is today probably greater than it ever was. There are now few magazines of political commentary and they do not enjoy a large circulation —unless you include among political publications some of the so-called news magazines which mix political bias with their reporting. Such publications probably have wide political influence, but they can hardly be described as offering frank opinion as such.

We have in the United States no magazine of political satire and few which devote even small space to it. The movies, the radio, and television also comprise part of the press, but for the most part they have been happy to resign themselves to being what they call "entertainment industries." The movies, after first allowing themselves to be intimidated by Congressional committees, learned to lie down and roll over at the drop of a postcard from any vigilante group. And they have now become so adept at it that they are willing to be told not only what they should say but whom they should hire and fire.

I recently read of a proposed code which members of the West Coast television industry were thinking of adopting. This code proposed, among many other things, that "officers of the law are to be portrayed with respect and dignity. American principles of government, both state and federal, will be treated with respect and dignity in all their aspects, including the personnel thereof—both our houses of Congress, for instance, their procedures and their committees." Under such a code I do not know whether they would have considered it proper to put on the Army-McCarthy hearing. I do not know why members of any section of a free press should so choose to limit themselves, and I do not know of whom or what these TV people are afraid. But I do not think that the way to beat the other guy to the draw is to blow your own brains out first.

Today there is little sharp satire and not much pointed opinion expressed in a legitimate theater where more and more producers feel obliged to appeal to the largest possible audience. In this field the softening influence has not been intimidation, which the stage has resisted quite well, but current theater economics which require a show to be practically a smash if it is to be successful at all.

There may be Mark Twains and Bernard Shaws around, today, but—except in book publication—their outlets appear to be limited. And, while I never considered H. L. Mencken a great political philosopher and did not subscribe to many of his views, much of what he wrote still makes good reading, and his irreverent remarks about national heroes and established institutions were a healthy stimulant for the country.

There is less diversity of opinion and less criticism expressed today generally, and less of it in newspapers because there are fewer and fewer of them. Perhaps one remedy for this is for those newspapers with no competition in their areas—or at least no competition of viewpoint—to provide space for other opinions, through syndicated features, "battle pages," reprints of editorials giving "the other side," and so on, and some of them do. But I do not think they should try to please everybody in their own editorials or neglect their function to call for reforms or to provide needed criticism of government simply because these things may not be popular—or may not be popular with some particular interests.

Sometimes newspapers adorn their pages with fine mottoes about courage and independence, but the test is in what they do and when they do it. A celebrated minister, speaking of the success of many superficially spiritual books that have sold extremely well, said that there were a great many people who wanted to *feel* good without *being* good. Sometimes newspapers are that way too, when they want to champion the public interest but do not want to offend anyone; or when they want to put on armor and look bold but do not want to run the risk of meeting somebody else coming in the opposite direction.

Dictatorship is an inevitable subject for editorializing, and it would hardly have been possible for a newspaper to have avoided writing a great deal about it in this period of history. But heroic attacks on Communism, which the people of this country are against about as unanimously as they have ever been against anything, cannot take the place of editorial matter explaining and defending American civil liberties. And the public interest is hardly well served by whipping up fears about the internal dangers of Communism to a point where people think that Communists are about to take over the country and that in the face of this danger we had better suspend the Bill of Rights.

Many papers were extremely vigorous in their denunciations of Perón and in their defenses of *La Prensa,* when that Argentine newspaper was under attack—and rightly so. But I have the impression that considerably fewer rose to the defense of the New York *Post* when it was attacked by the McCarthy committee or to the defense of the New York *Times* when it came under attack by the Eastland committee—despite the fact that their own freedom of the press was involved in these obvious attempts at intimidation by government. There are many notable exceptions, but in too many cases it seems that the vigor of the crusade is in direct ratio to the distance from danger.

Denials of democratic rights abroad anywhere are a good subject for comment. But as one of the hundreds of thousands of people who have no vote of any kind by virtue of being resident in the District of Columbia, I respectfully suggest that papers around the country might promote our concepts of government in a more immediate way if they would apply pressure on their congressmen to bring democracy to the capital of the United States.

I think our papers have a duty to keep their readers informed of developments abroad and of the importance of those developments to us. But most of us have little circulation abroad. And when we go crusading we are generally most effective in our own country and our own communities. Sometimes crusades get off to a fine start toward a worthy objective but seem to drift off somewhere down the road. As I mentioned a while ago, there was great indignation over the contribution that a lobbyist tried to press on Senator Case. There were demands for thorough investigation and for revision of the laws regarding political contributions. But the indignation subsided, and congressmen and senators who had been worried for a while relaxed, took a deep breath, and went home without doing anything.

As for the oil lobby itself, only a few papers have made a serious effort to break the vicious circle in which the government, through special tax concessions, in effect subsidizes an industry to increase its pressure on government. A few newspapers and a few individuals like Tom Stokes have long been prodding the public conscience about such influences. But many newspapers seem to show little more interest than do the politicians themselves.

It may be that politics is the art of compromise and that the successful political leader is one who is not too far behind the people he is leading. But that is not a good formula for independent journalism. If a local vigilante group seeks to decide what is proper and patriotic for people to see and hear and read—particularly if such a group operates under the sponsorship of an organization like the American Legion—it is more difficult to stand up to it than it is to Nasser and Khrushchev, to Eden and Mollet, and all the powerful governments across the oceans. Politicians may shun the task. But the press should not.

An independent press can not only apply pressure on politicians to do better, but it can also create a climate in which they can follow the dictates of their consciences without feeling that they may be committing political suicide. But it cannot do so if it acts like a politician itself. To do this requires some courage, but I suspect it is not really as dangerous as some would suppose. It is a common complaint among editorial people that their work apparently does not sell papers as do the comic strips and other features. And yet editors sometimes quiver over a flurry of letters complaining of some editorial policy. I think we should face—and not without some satisfaction and pleasure—the fact that newspapers are not bought solely for the editorials or by people who are in agreement with their policies. This should remove the needless fear that a paper takes its life in its hands when it speaks up with conviction in those columns.

Editors who cannot put finger to typewriter key without first holding the finger aloft to test the weather would do well to think about a couple of the most famous and successful papers in the country—the St. Louis *Post-Dispatch* and the Chicago *Tribune*. One is regarded as a "liberal" paper, the other as "conservative" or even "reactionary." There is no reason to think that the climate of St. Louis is particularly conducive to liberalism or that the climate of Chicago promotes the particular brand of conservatism espoused by the *Tribune*. The only differences are in the climates created by the papers themselves. Their policies are poles apart, but both have had strong policies which they have not been afraid to express even when they might be unpopular. Both of these Middle West papers have not only managed to survive but to do extremely well. And far from endangering the success of the papers, their vigorous and outspoken policies have, if anything, contributed to their strength.

When Colonel McCormick voiced the opinion that his paper was liked because it had, as he put it, hair on its chest, he may have been under-estimating the many nonpolitical features which prompted people to buy the *Tribune*. But in any case he did not seem to be suffering in the cash register for having the courage of his convictions, however mistaken some of those convictions may have been and however much they may have been out of line with prevailing opinion.

It can always be said, whenever it is felt that a stand ought to be taken against odds, that there is no use wasting the effort in a "lost cause." Or the argument is often given that a paper will be "more effective" if it waits for the issues on which it is most likely to win. But the paper which does that is really saving itself for the time when it will be least effective, when its voice is least needed. And it is likely to make of itself a mere chanticleer boasting of having brought up a sun already risen.

Editorially, it is not the business of an independent paper to guess what is going to happen. Its business is to say what it believes to be right and in the public interest. And the time to say it is when it is most needed. The time to speak up most vigorously against mob violence is not when everything is quiet. The time to speak up against abuses of government is not when the threat has passed, but when committees are hauling before them representatives of the schools, the clergy, and the press. The time to speak up for the Fifth Amendment or for individual conscience is when the rights of witnesses are most heavily under attack. The time to speak up about the mistakes of administration—state, local, or national—is often when they may seem to be most popular and when the fewest voices are raised to point out their errors. As for "lost causes," no good cause is ever lost.

The New York *World*—which, incidentally, folded for reasons having nothing to do with its editorial policies and which I understand need not have gone under at all—is recalled as a newspaper which had a splendid editorial page. In what may have been its best years it seemed constantly to be fighting losing battles. It was against prohibition when it was thought that repeal was all but impossible. It was for international-ism when the mood of the country seemed to be isolationist. In the happy 1920's it criticized and lampooned the policies of such unques-tionably popular men, at that time, as Calvin Coolidge and Herbert Hoover. It was for social welfare measures in a time of normalcy. It was for civil liberties in a period of postwar hysteria.

Yet who would say that this was not a great and effective editorial page, that it did not raise the standards of the profession, that it did not and does not still influence others by the force of its example? Or who would say that the causes it championed were really lost?

I do not want to close without a word about a man who was, in himself, an example of conscientious journalism—the late Carroll Binder of the Minneapolis *Tribune*.

I recall a magazine article that he wrote a few years ago which may not have been among his more important works, but which was nonetheless characteristic of him in its way. It was an article bluntly critical of some journalism awards—specifically the manner in which he felt certain committees arrived at their decisions. I am sure that his views on this subject were shared by many others at the time, although not expressed publicly. But Binder felt that this article had to be written and he wrote it. It was hardly the kind of piece calculated to add to his own awards. But in his lifetime of work, I think he won the finest prize of all —the knowledge that he had done, as far as he was able, what he thought ought to be done.

This came back to me when I was thinking of the things I have been trying to say about our profession. I think the fourth estate is at its best, and proves itself the equal of any, when it is not trying to be some other estate, but when it is being faithful to itself and its essential function in a free country.

I think it is at its greatest and proudest whenever a newspaperman can feel of what he has done: This may not be shrewd diplomacy; it may not be weighty jurisprudence; it may not be good business or clever public relations or smart politics; but *it says the thing that needs to be said*— and that is the job of the independent press.

An Art to be Practiced

All of life is of course an art to be practiced.* But as I am only an amateur philosopher and indeed often find it difficult these days to be philosophical at all, I shall speak here of that particular area where I have claims to competence. It is politics.

My own happy breed of men and women are political reporters and the special flavor of their work arises from the fact that their identity with their subject becomes with the passage of time absolutely total. It is fortunately possible for reporters to cover crime without acquiring the criminal mentality. They are able to make the trial of a spicy suit for divorce or a spectacular case of larceny live in deathless prose and at the same time lead blameless lives, at ease alike with their bankers and with Dorothy Dix. Not so the political reporter.

If his political coverage is to have any depth—and no other kind is worth writing or publishing—he must become saturated with his subject and intimately acquainted with the true nature of the politicians he deals with.

He must know them and the political imperatives they are bound to obey. These political imperatives take many forms, and they are dif-

---

* This lecture was delivered October 24, 1957.

144

ferent for each politician. They include geographical considerations, social and economic forces, and the interests of his party, both local and national. Such knowledge is vital because the political reporter on occasion comes very close to being judge, jury, and lord high executioner of the politician. To undertake this assignment without proper information is worse than unfair, it is base.

Eventually reporter and politician grow into that relationship which is such a cross to every President and the bureaucrats around him; that is, they have no secrets from one another. Possessing as they do, a complete mutual understanding of political situations and the forces creating and operating upon them, how could it be otherwise?

I consider this relationship one of the great bulwarks of the republic quite apart from my personal stake in it. My one real complaint about it is that reporters—and their publishers—tend to become too kind to their favorite politicians and Presidents. Too often they find it difficult to maintain that detachment which combines in correct proportions understanding with critical analysis. The pampering by the press of politicians, no matter how exalted their status, is a crime so heinous it should be forbidden by law.

When I was younger and more sanguine, I used to make certain suggestions for remedying any such bent on the part of my colleagues. I proposed, for example, that Washington correspondents should be returned to their home offices at stated intervals and made to cover police and the department of sanitation, both excellent experience for political coverage. I argued that this would reacquaint them with reality, shake them loose from connections which had grown too comfortable, and generally restore their perspective. I was fond also of quoting Parnell to the effect that the greatest enemy of Irish freedom was the English dinner napkin.

I soon learned that I was not destined to win any popularity contests at the National Press Club. I have settled long since for a column of my own, where my efforts to practice what I preach have earned me a few figs—with thistles.

I am indebted to that notable phrase-maker, Adlai Stevenson, for the title I have attached to my remarks. Stevenson's favorite definition of the difference between the two major parties of the United States is this: "For Republicans, politics is a status to be maintained; for Democrats, it is an art to be practiced." Stevenson of course gave his own party the best of it since it is always more interesting to watch a man trying to walk the length of a tightrope than to see him immobilized in the center of it. Reporters generally will agree that the arts of politics seem to come more naturally to Democrats than to Republicans. The reasons suggested are many.

One is that throughout its long history—and it is the oldest political party in the Western world—the Democratic party has tended to identify itself with causes affecting people. People arouse a greater and more bewildering variety of emotions than property and they do not stand still. People's causes attract reformers who are often wrong but rarely unpicturesque.

Again, Democrats make good stories because they tend to be rather more romantic about the party of their choice. Harry S. Truman actually believes that it is better to be a Democrat than a Republican; he is willing to give a Republican his civil rights, but in his view the party that will make your teeth white, your eyes shine, and your hair curl is Miss Democracy. Former Secretary of the Treasury George M. Humphrey would probably agree with him on that last point but for different reasons.

When the late Vice-President, Alben Barkley, described the golden thread which ran through his party from Thomas Jefferson to Andrew Jackson to Grover Cleveland, et cetera, he almost talked poetry—for the first hour, that is. I could never seem to interest Dear Alben in my constitutional amendment forbidding speeches longer than twenty minutes.

For some curious reason Democrats also are more impervious than Republicans to the patina imparted by worldly success. I have had this put to me in various ways. My favorite comes from a disgruntled Republican who pointed to some indubitably rich Democrats, including a shirt-sleeved Averell Harriman, and said disgustedly: "Look at 'em! No matter how rich a Democrat gets he still sweats."

Will Rogers expressed the fun of watching Democrats many times. He explained that he was not a member of any organized party, he was a Democrat. A Democrat, he said, will shoot at Republicans only when he cannot find another Democrat around to work on with his knife.

Republicans rather wistfully complain that their array of sterling qualities does not command the same memorable descriptions. They quite genuinely deplore the Democratic party and with some justification regard it as the Auntie Mame of politics. What seems to baffle them is that she can be a best seller. They are quite touchingly sensitive, too, about their presumed devotion to private property, and can tell you in some detail how much of it remains in Democratic hands.

Certainly no one can take it away from Republicans that they too have had their moments—as with the Bull Moose and the sons of the wild jackass. But unquestionably theirs is a superior talent for hiding the family skeletons in the closet. It is no accident that "the team" emerged in January, 1953, as a hallmark of the new management at the White House.

In all seriousness and leaving the partisans to their fun and games, the objective observer descries in Stevenson's definition the dividing line between successful politicians and those whom history delights to forget. The difference is not a party matter. Men who have come alive for the voters, including Republicans and Democrats—Teddy Roosevelt and Franklin D. Roosevelt, Al Smith and Fiorello LaGuardia—have all treated their trade as a creative art. They practiced it untiringly and they got results largely commensurate with their efforts.

Every corner of the governmental machine and the programs which these politicians directed and controlled felt what Walter Lippmann has so well described as "the brooding presence of impatient men." They were impatient because they recognized the scope of their responsibilities and knew how much depended upon them personally. Such men communicate a sense of urgency and excitement to politics. Their creative energies release in turn the creative energies of those around them and of the nation. Suddenly people cease to feel that to muddle through is the best that can be hoped for. It not only seems important to act, but it appears possible that good will flow from it.

The command to practice politics as one of the highest arts and noblest sciences has been laid down by writers, philosophers, and rulers since recorded time. They have pronounced it necessary to the happiness of mankind and they have admitted to no limitations on its importance.

The *Oxford English Dictionary* defines politics as the science and art dealing with the form, organization, and administration of a state and with the regulation of its relations with other states. Note the inclusion of "the regulation of its relations with other states." Disraeli called it the art of governing mankind. Noah Webster typically brought it down to earth. Politics, he wrote, is the theory and practice of managing or directing the affairs of public policy. The key words are "managing or directing."

To Gouverneur Morris politics was "the sublime science which embraces for its object the happiness of mankind." Morris had a right to speak, being associated with that immortal band—politicians all—who wrote the American Constitution and founded this republic.

De Tocqueville speaks of "the agitation of mind" common at that period. It is past time for a fresh outbreak of that valuable disease.

People who denigrate politics are perverting its meaning and failing to understand its purpose. For it is through politics that man by the exercise of his will can dominate his public fate. Politics uses all the knowledge that can be assembled for man's most important function, which is to get along with other men—both within his own nation and outside its borders. It is a function noble and almost divine in its suggestion of loving fraternity.

We can elect to choose our national destiny by way of the art of politics or we can sit down and let fate overwhelm us. If we merely cling to status we shall only put ourselves at the mercy of the leaders of other states who are resolutely managing and directing their public affairs for the benefit of themselves or their nations. The most formidable of such leaders are acting from motives we hate and for purposes we abhor. They have cynically created the problems we now are facing. We can expect them to go on creating more problems within the limits of their ability to confuse, to harass, and eventually to destroy us.

But these men are not ten feet tall. The Russians, the Red Chinese, the Syrians, are not bigger, brighter, fiercer, or smarter than we are. They are merely men in a world of men. Contrary to a popular misconception, their police state governments are not more efficient than our democracies. What is in truth really frightening about their operations is that they are so inefficient; it is possible that the stupidities of a few men, or even of one man, may bring total destruction on us all. *The Last Days of Hitler,* by Trevor-Roper,[1] is recommended to anyone who doubts this— and there are companion volumes to drive the lesson home.

What is lacking here is the determined will to manage and direct the overwhelming forces at our disposal. Somewhere along the line we have been overtaken by a perverted definition of politics. We have ceased to expect the best from our politicians; we have sometimes seemed to demand the worst. We are tolerant when they abdicate their true functions and when they cater to our national faults. We have driven our best minds from politics because of the low esteem in which we hold it. We have ridiculed the intellectuals who sought to guide us by the light of reason and we have allowed them to be accused freely of treasonable purpose. Happily the swinish climate of anti-intellectualism has moderated, but we are by no means rid of its legacies of conformity, inertia, and timidity.

In our commitment to a materialism which puts comfort ahead of all other considerations, we have allowed our young people to forget the rewards of public service. It is an attitude which infects American life at all levels. At the same time the multiplicity of our society has led to the proliferation of the experts. Two kinds in particular now hold high place: the professional manager and the scientist. Yet both of these, because of their enforced specialization, have in large part removed themselves from the ordinary hopes and fears of mankind and are no longer qualified for the ultimate leadership. The worlds of science and technology are making great contributions to our well-being, but they rarely yield men capable of managing and directing mankind's affairs.

What are our principal problems today? In human terms our greatest is race relations. Inflation is a growing cancer in our economic life. The rapid growth of the population of the United States and its flight to the cities are drastically changing the whole face of the nation. These changes have brought in their wake a whole train of enormous difficulties of which a crisis in education and the proper use of land, water, and resources are outstanding.

The avoidance of war in the face of a determined, implacable, and evangelistic enemy is and must remain the heart of our foreign policy. The task grows more difficult by the day. It bristles with such thorns as the maintenance of friendly relations among our allies and the search for an approach to colonialism in new nations which by a sad irony of fate demand freedom from outside influences while committed to feudal or authoritarian social systems.

One has only to state the problems to show that they lie in the realm of politics. The alternative to our slow destruction is to recognize this and put the national will to work.

I have not heard it suggested anywhere that this country could not have put a satellite into outer space as soon as or before the Russians did. The failure to do so was a political failure, it was the lack of vision to see what it would mean to our world leadership to be surpassed in so striking an endeavor. The Russians used their dictatorial power over their subjects to win that triumph. Our victories must be voluntary. They always have been and they will be again when the American people are made acquainted with the facts.

The cruel embarrassment of Little Rock was well within the capabilities of wise men to foresee and to avoid. Politicians practicing their art could have mobilized forces within and without the South. The real troublemakers have never at any time represented more than one per cent of the people—but that one per cent had leaders.

The iron truth of today's dynamic world is that nobody can maintain status by standing still. This is a hard lesson not always learned in high places. There will be decisions in the world—political decisions— and they will determine our fate. Whether those decisions are made by us or by the Russians depends upon our ability to make our politics achieve the ends we seek.

I wish I had some magic formula to suggest. There is none. There are no wonder men or wonder women. There are only you and I and others who believe in freedom. There is only what we are able to get out of ourselves for our children, our country, and our God.

XII   GERALD W. JOHNSON

Personality in Journalism

The fame of the men, in whose honor these lectures are given, is beyond our power either to add or to detract.* The most we can do is to recognize it, and that cannot be done better than by applying the words of a great orator, for us the living to resolve "that from these honored dead we take increased devotion to that cause for which they gave the last full measure of devotion." That cause, I beg leave to remind you, was and is something more than patriotism; that cause was and is to make men know the truth that the truth may make them free.

This is, however, a statement of the ideal and it is usually the case that the ideal, to be of practical utility, must be restated in terms of our everyday life. My present effort in that direction is confined to one small segment of the whole subject and it is of necessity no more than the reflection of one man's experience and observation in relation to that segment. A man is a fool if he approaches a subject of this size posing as Sir Oracle whose dicta take rank as universal law. The best I can offer is a guess—an informed guess, I hope, but still a guess, to be accepted or rejected in the light of the hearer's own experience. To emphasize that, I have chosen a subject that itself will raise a question, not to

* This lecture was delivered October 30, 1958.

151

say a protest, in the mind of every newspaperman. That subject is "Personality in Journalism," chosen at a time when it is generally agreed that the day of what we have known as personal journalism is long past.

I hope, however, that you will bear with me while I define my terms. I submit that the occupation of collecting and disseminating news, like all Gaul, is divided into three parts; these three I denominate as, first and lowest, job-holding; second, newspaper work; and third, journalism. These three activities are carried by three classes of animate objects, to wit: first, trained seals; second, reporters; and third, stars.

The difficulty with this classification is that it is extremely fluid. A reporter may flash into stardom on one big story and subside again the next day. I have known more than one star who under the erosion of time and circumstance eventually degenerated into a trained seal. Of course, every trained seal poses as a journalist, and with such success among the ill-informed that they have rendered the term "journalist" almost an epithet within the craft. Nevertheless the distinctions, while highly variable, do exist and represent the more or less permanent status of most persons engaged in handling the news.

My concern on this occasion is with one of the two classes that merge into each other rather vaguely. There is no sharp line of distinction between a reporter and a star, but between either and the mere job-holder, the trained seal, the line is very clear. Find a man who says of his connection with any of the media of publicity, "It's a living," and you have a mere job-holder; but find one who says, "It's life," and you certainly have a reporter, perhaps a star.

Naturally, this must not be taken too literally. Catch a very good reporter just after his pet story has been murdered by the copy-desk, or catch even a great star who has spent a week covering a national political convention and is suffering the great-grandfather of all hangovers, and you have a man who takes a dim view of newspaper work or any other phase of human activity. A man is not himself at such times and his comment then should be off the record.

Most of the men who regard the craft of handling news as merely a living need not give us much concern, for they are transients. They soon pass on to some type of work to which they are better fitted. But a few are highly successful and they become the real trained seals, performing not for the joy of craftsmanship, but solely in the hope that somebody will toss them a fish. Some of them write brilliantly, but not for the purpose of conveying information, only in the hope of pleasing the front office, or for some even more disreputable reason. Some become nationally notorious and think they are nationally famous; but none is

really part of the craft except in the sense that an infection is part of
the victim, and all have the capacity to give honest newspapermen
bad moments when they regret that they did not in youth take up
plumbing or bricklaying in a serious way.

Let that be enough for mere job-holding. I now invite your attention
to the very elusive activity that I have named journalism, but which I
cannot define in terms that satisfy me, to say nothing of Noah Webster.
It is a sort of emanation from reporting but it is not reporting, for it
conforms to no stylebook. It is literature, but a very special form of
literature, one that baffles the most astute professors of English. And it
is an activity so intensely personal that I set above it in that respect only
Solomon's great mystery of life, the way of a man with a maid.

The classical model of this form, in so far as it has a model, is Julius
Caesar's commentaries on his conquest of Gaul. A modern example of a
very high order of excellence is John Hersey's *Hiroshima*.[1] But the odd-
est with which I am acquainted dates from 1822 and is a report of a
prize fight written by William Hazlitt. I choose it to illustrate my point because this story, viewed strictly as reporting, is almost fabulously bad.
Hazlitt violates every rule known to a self-respecting copy-desk. He
has no lead. He ambles. He dashes off after every fugitive idea that
crosses his path, now to this side, now to that. He is sublimely indifferent
to personal names, place names, and dates. He actually lost count of
the number of rounds, and it is from other sources that we learn that
the bout went seventeen. I cannot recall a piece of writing that, judged
by the accepted standards of news reporting, would better justify firing
the cub reporter who turned it in.

Yet after a hundred and thirty-six years people still read it with de-
light and many account it the greatest description of a prize fight that
exists in the English language. For when you have read it you know what
happened, how it happened and, to a very large extent, why it happened. Hazlitt spotted the blow that really beat Hickman in the third
round, and thereafter the reader is in no doubt that it is merely a matter
of how much longer he can stand up. But the story does more than
that. It presents the event as a whole—the fighters, the crowd, the tension, even the weather. All those extraneous circumstances that at first
seemed inexcusable padding contribute to the total effect and not one
could be omitted without some loss. But if you ask me how he did it,
the only answer I can make is, "He did it because he was Hazlitt." Which
carries us no further toward an explanation.

Is that, however, a valid objection? For my part, I am inclined to regard as a weakness of the modern world our reluctance to recognize any-

thing that we cannot explain. I am aware that the Great Man theory of history has been largely discredited for good reasons, but I doubt that those reasons do much toward solving the problem of personality.

Sometimes I am inclined to think that they were wiser in the days of the medieval guilds, whose members had a stock phrase to describe their peculiar body of knowledge. They referred to "the art and mystery" of carpentry, or weaving, or brewing, or bricklaying. The phrase was forgotten until H. L. Mencken dredged it up to use in a satirical sense with reference to things about which there is neither art nor mystery.

Nevertheless the words are not meaningless. Every trade, craft, art, and profession has certain techniques that must be mastered before the theorist can practice. These may be taught, and a student of even mediocre intelligence can attain some degree of proficiency in their use. These may be described as the art appertaining to the occupation. But certain students exhibit an aptitude somehow to learn what has not been taught. Let us go back a hundred years and consider two boys, both handy with tools, both interested in wood-working, both serving a long apprenticeship under a master craftsman. When their term is over we have two cabinet-makers. That is the art of the trade. But one of the two is Duncan Phyfe and the other is not; and that is its mystery.

It is of this mystery that I propose to speak, not to teach it, for John Dewey, Mark Hopkins, and Socrates rolled into one could not teach it, but to describe it and to urge recognition, not merely of its existence but also of its high value to the craft of the news-handlers and to the craftsmen themselves. Not every man is given the ability to penetrate the mystery of his own craft, but every man who knows that it exists may cherish the hope of penetrating it, and this hope marks the difference between those who make a living by their labor and those who live by it.

Mencken once made a remark to me that I heard rather carelessly, but remembered; and as I thought it over, its implications became darker and darker until today I consider it a bit of pessimism that is enough to make Schopenhauer look like a humorist. He said, "Johnson, you and I are very fortunate people in that we can make a living by doing what we would do anyhow; not many can say that."

It is true as far as I am concerned, and I fear it is true as regards most men. If I had millions I know that I would still be fevered by desire to write the perfect news story. I know well enough that I shall never do it, nor even come within many miles of it, not if I outlive Methuselah; but I am addicted to the hopeless effort as firmly as a drunkard to his bottle, and through that addiction I have gained the means of sustaining life. How many men, given a fortune today, would return tomorrow to the treadmill on which they had spent their most productive years? A considerable number, certainly—probably all scholars, artists, and scientists, and positively all born newspapermen, but a majority of workers? That I cannot believe, and the fact gives a dreary plausibility to Thoreau's remark that most men live lives of quiet desperation.

I do not claim that this signifies any particular merit in either the craft or the craftsmen. Sometimes, indeed, I am inclined to think there may be a touch of the puerile about the whole business and that the greatest of journalists is essentially childish. For the perfect news story would be simply one that transfers from the reporter's mind to another mind an experience, exact to a hairsbreadth; complete in its inclusion of every significant factor, emotional or intellectual; and rigid in its exclusion of everything insignificant or irrelevant. It is an ideal, of course, a feat far beyond human accomplishment, but that is not the point. What is the basis of every journalist's intense desire to accomplish it? Perhaps it is nothing more than the emotion of the excited kid who bursts into the house exclaiming, "I know something that you don't know!" and who it is impossible to deter from telling his story instantly. Be that as it may, the emotion is certainly one form of rapture.

Furthermore, I submit that there is nothing more intensely personal in the whole realm of human experience. To talk of the elimination of personal journalism then is to talk arrant nonsense. We do it because we fall into semantic error. What we mean by "personal journalism" never was journalism at all but propaganda in the sense in which Rome uses the word in the title *Congregatio de propaganda fide,* that is, "propagation of the faith." Henry Watterson, for example, usually accounted the last of the great personal journalists, devoted much of his effort, not to the communication of truth, but to imposing the opinions of Watterson upon his readers—not necessarily an ignoble effort, but not journalism.

To the extent that the opinions of Watterson—or of Greeley, Dana, Bennett, Bowles and the other giants of old—coincided with truth, they were not merely important; they were more important than the most scrupulously accurate narration of events unaccompanied by any explanation of the relation of the events in question to conditions resulting from past events. It is possible, indeed it is common for a man to be in possession of the facts without having an inkling of the truth, and the function of journalism is to communicate the truth. The messenger who brought King Louis XVI word of the fall of the Bastille was a reporter up to the moment when the King exclaimed, "But this is a revolt!" and the man replied, "No, Sire, it is a revolution." With that, he became a journalist.

Every news editor knows this and acknowledges it by his assiduity in seeking to supply "background material" for his current news stories, but we are perversely reluctant to admit it in our discussions of the theory of the business. The trouble is that we have here a factor not amenable to analysis and control, which comes into collision with the necessity for order and discipline in the management of any enterprise as large as even a small-city newspaper. We have accordingly adopted the staff system at the policy-making level, especially on the editorial page. In view of the great and increasing complexity of the operation, this is doubtless the only practical expedient available to the modern newspaper, but it ignores the disconcerting lesson of experience that, when it comes to getting at and dragging out the truth behind the facts, one head is sometimes better than two, and usually better than half a dozen.

This is contrary to accepted professional doctrine, and I have nothing to offer in its support except the observed fact that influence upon public opinion seems to have shifted from the anonymous editorial to the signed column or, in the case of radio and television, to the identified commentator. This I believe to be the measure of the impact of personality. I cannot accept the explanation that the signed column is powerful because it is syndicated to an enormous clientele. It was years after I had joined the Baltimore *Sun* that Frank Kent and H. L. Mencken first began to appear in any other newspaper, but either of them could shake Baltimore more profoundly than the heaviest thunder of the editorial page.

Superficially, this would seem to indicate that the public reposes more confidence in the columnist than in the newspaper but that, I think, is an oversimplification. It is nearer the truth to say that most of us have more confidence in our own judgment of a man than in our judgment of an organization. There are columnists—some of them widely syndicated—in whose integrity or intelligence I have no confidence whatever, but that they influence my opinions is undeniable. When such a writer adopts an attitude toward a subject to which I have paid no attention I am immediately more than half-persuaded that the opposite attitude is the right one. Since on those subjects with which I am familiar the fellow has been wrong three-fourths of the time, I judge that it is three to one that he is wrong this time. But I have found the composite opinion reflected by the editorial page neither as consistently right as a good columnist, nor as consistently wrong as a bad one; so it is a less reliable guide than either.

I feel that I can understand a man, especially if I know his past record, because he is constituted pretty much as I am; but an institution is different and I am suspicious of my own ability to judge it correctly.

But there is another consideration. I think that most of us feel that the highest social value attainable by an institution is intelligence; the higher value, wisdom, is attainable only by a person. This is because intelligent conduct is the result of following well-known rules, but how a man arrives at wisdom nobody knows, and that applies to the wise man himself. Wisdom implies knowledge, of course, but its essence is the form of a man's response to his learning, and that is a mystery of personality. But while its nature eludes us, we know that it is invariably associated with three other personal qualities—experience, diligence, and integrity. I have never yet seen a really wise man who was not intellectually and emotionally mature, a hard worker, and rigidly honest; he may or may not be brilliant, versatile, witty and so on, but he must be seasoned, industrious, and upright.

My conclusion then is that personality in journalism, far from being an inadmissible intrusion, is essential to the highest excellence. But please note well that I have carefully distinguished between journalism and routine reporting. The injection of personality in writing a weather forecast would be a monstrosity, and the bulk of a reporter's daily labor, however much it may differ in form, is basically as purely routine as the weather report.

The fact that all this argument leads up to is that the great journalist is an individualist, but establishing the fact is a waste of effort since nobody denies it. However, there is a truth behind the fact that seems to be unknown to newspaper management in some cases and in many more cases is consistently ignored. This is the truth that the journalist is one of the few individualists remaining in a world that has less and less room for anybody but the organization man.

In a world driven to more and more minute specialization, I can cite only three classes of men who are in the nature of things generalists, as opposed to specialists. They are the judge, the clergyman, and the journalist. As regards these three, everybody's business is legitimately their business. In these days lawyers customarily specialize, but the man on the bench may not. I suppose professors of theology may specialize, but the pastor of a flock may not. Even newspapers employ financial writers and sports writers and dramatic, music, literary, and art critics, some of whom have gathered well-earned fame; but for all that they are side shows. Under the big top are the intellectual acrobats who can land on their feet no matter where they are dropped, and the business of communication is dependent upon them to an extent not approached by any other widespread human activity, the church alone excepted.

And it is not only the press that urgently needs this highly personal trait, this ability to uncover the truth behind the facts. The world at large needs it more urgently than the press. In the current *Harper's Magazine* is an article by one of the most eminent and I may add one of the most highly specialized specialists of our time, Dr. Robert Oppenheimer, the physicist who directed the construction of the first atomic bomb. Oppenheimer notes with alarm the great and rapidly widening gap between scientific knowledge and the experience of the average layman. He makes the startling assertion that "nearly everything that is now known was not in any book when most of us went to school; we cannot know it unless we have picked it up since. This in itself presents a problem of communication that is nightmarishly formidable." [2]

Who is to solve this problem? Not the specialists, for Oppenheimer points out that they have great difficulty in communicating with each other. They cannot do so at all except by resorting to the common language of mathematical symbols, as medieval scholars resorted to Latin. But the typical American understands mathematical symbolism no better than he understands Latin or Greek; a translation is imperatively required.

Nor can a successful translation be expected of a mere reporter, no matter how highly trained he may be in the matter of factual accuracy. He may get the facts straight enough, but he will not communicate the truth behind the facts unless to the skill he has acquired by training he adds wisdom acquired God knows how, but certainly not by following the rules in any stylebook.

Oppenheimer spoke conservatively when he described as "nightmarish" the responsibility that rests upon newspapermen and other servants of the media of communication at this juncture in the world's history. It is all of that, but that is not the aspect of it that a first-rate man considers most intently. If the job is nightmarish, the reward on the other hand for its successful accomplishment will be fabulous. When I say "reward" I do not have in mind money or fame; I mean the consciousness of having done something in the world, realization that one has exercised power, the assurance that because one has lived and labored the world is not, and never will be again, exactly what it was before.

This is the reward that every giant figure in history has sought, but that very few have attained. It is all very well to assert that great men do not make but are made by history, yet few of us can persuade ourselves that the world would have been exactly the same had Alexander, or Caesar, or Napoleon never lived. Perhaps if they had not existed the work would have been done by someone else, but that is like saying that

Hamlet was not written by William Shakespeare but by another man of the same name. The work was done, and whoever did it stamped his image and superscription on the face of the world, which is the greatest accomplishment within the reach of man.

As Oppenheimer points out, a vast new body of hitherto unknown truth has been discovered in recent years, the greater part of which is completely outside the experience, therefore beyond the comprehension of the majority of Americans. This is a situation that cannot be allowed to continue, for it is knowledge of the truth that makes men free and without it civilization will not only cease to advance, but will drift back in the direction of barbarism and slavery.

Much of the labor of making this truth available must fall upon the press. But it is not hack work. None of it is within the capacity of the trained seals, and not much of it can be done by reporters, even good ones. For it is not mere reporting. It calls for a very accurate weighing of the significance of the facts, on the one hand, and on the other, a rare understanding of the average layman's habits of thought.

That kind of knowledge you do not get out of books. It is an element of personality. But the man who has it, and who applies it diligently, exactly, and honestly during the next ten years will hold a plastic world in his hands and will shape and mould it to an extent never approached by any of the tin-pot emperors and strutting dictators who have occupied so much of the front page in recent years. The reward of the great journalist will be to stamp his image and superscription upon the future.

If that is a bit too dramatic for your taste, let us tone it down a bit by substituting a metaphor from the Second World War. Let us say, rather, that the first-rate journalist, the journalist with personality as well as technical skill, the journalist whose knowledge is transmuted into wisdom, will make his mark as did that shadowy figure known, but never seen, by our armies in Europe. So when the triumphant battalions of liberty sweep forward driving ignorance and superstition before them, however fast they advance they will always find before them the cryptic inscription, "Kilroy was here."

The Third Reader

W hen I was small, I would hear old-fashioned peo-
ple say the newspaper was the common man's school, and from this
I formed a mental picture of the press as something like McGuffey's
Third Reader.*

This image from childhood flits back in my mind and serves as a re-
minder that the end target of all the elaborate operations of the modern
press is still the reader.

But we can no longer think of a product for him as akin to the old
Third Reader. His grandchildren have gone to college and their world
is full of things that the old scholar of the Third Reader never thought
of or needed to.

Have we in the newspaper kept up with the modern reader and his
modern world?

Walter Lippmann, in his magnificent birthday address to the National
Press Club, reminds us:

> We are only the first generation of newspapermen who have been as-
> signed the job of informing a mass audience about a world that is in a pe-
> riod of such great, of such deep, of such rapid and of such unprecedented

---

* This lecture was delivered October 22, 1959.

160

change. We have all had to be explorers of a world that was unknown to us and of mighty events that were unforeseen. . . . The Washington correspondent [that was his audience] has had to teach himself to be not only a recorder of facts and a chronicler of events, but also to be a writer of notes and essays in contemporary history. . . . We do what every sovereign citizen is supposed to do, but has not the time or interest to do for himself. This is our job. It is no mean calling and we have a right to be proud of it.

Lippmann holds with the old-fashioned notion that the primary function of the press is to inform; that it has a responsibility to its readers; that this function is essential to a self-governing society; that the press is a strategically vital institution, parallel to the public school system. That it is and must ever be more than just a business. Indeed, on no other basis could we justify the historic immunities to the press, written into our Constitution. On no other basis could we justify the erection of schools of journalism in practically all our publicly supported universities.

The implication is that the press is necessary to a democratic society —that such a society requires a source of information, independent of government, that is dependable, competent, and responsible to its high obligation. Anything that weakens the press, that corrupts the press, that diverts the press from this central function, is a peril to the kind of society that the fathers of the Constitution and the creators of our land grant colleges had in mind, that indeed has been the basic principle of the American system. This is so axiomatic that you may ask why I take your time to say it. I might answer that we need constantly to remind ourselves.

But a more urgent reason is that the pressure of our times, in all the complexities that Lippmann suggests, crowds hard upon us. Any of us concerned with the education of journalists must feel this urgency, this exacting demand for adequate men.

It is by no means only the man in the ivory tower who feels it. The very day I was reading Lippmann's address the chief of a Washington bureau telephoned me to ask help in finding a man to take charge of the bureau's library. A rather routine technical job, you might think. But he did not see it that way. "I want a man with a real feeling for history," he said, "a man who'll see the whole story and all its possible background and initiate the research we'll need on it, even if we aren't always conscious of the need." This is a new man—librarian, newspaperman, researcher, historian. I do not have him in stock, in standard sizes and salaries, to meet such a demand. Do you?

The importance of the press in its function grows greater as its task

grows more difficult. Our society becomes more complex. The world
crowds in upon us its complicated problems even as our own multiply
and deepen. The citizen is hard put to it to understand the central issues
of his government, even when they are fully reported to him.

No other time ever had to try to puzzle out the riddles of an adequate
defense as posed against the dangers of annihilating destruction in war
and possible radioactive poisoning without war. Nor the other defense
problem of a sufficient shield that does not bankrupt the nation or inflate
its economy to ruin.

Our leading economists tell us that our cities are in decay, our schools
starved for support, our hospitals insufficient and medical costs more
than most of our population can support; this calls for rethinking of the
support of the public sector of our economy, which can be sustained
only by our taxes.

We are faced with problems in labor-management relations which have
rent the country and blockaded its production, and the measures that
are used do not meet the problems. An administration that has thrown
its weight to curbing the power of labor faces a dilemma in acting as impartial arbiter of a fundamental strike.

Drew Middleton, London correspondent of the New York *Times,* can
report candidly on a parallel issue in England. He writes, Sunday, October 11, 1959: "Although theoretically the government is neutral in
conflicts between capital and labor, capital and government are so closely
allied in any Conservative regime that its bias inevitably is on the side of
capital."

How often do we get such candid reporting on our own government?

The Khrushchev visit was a landmark in many ways. We talked a
lot about the importance of Khrushchev getting an impression of America. But the American impression of Khrushchev was a revelation too.
The President gave us his own impression of an extraordinary man. How
much of this need have been new to us had our reporting from Moscow
gone further than it had from merely echoing a government doctrine that
you cannot do business with the Russians? The tone of the reporting
and the picture we got of Khrushchev changed with the length of his
stay here. Part of this came from a reversal of attitude by our officials
handling the tour. But the interaction of the official attitude and the press
performance was such that an old wire service man remarked to me:
"We can turn it on and off too, about as well as the Soviets." This is
worth thinking about.

A week ago Sunday I heard Governor Pat Brown of California,
on a television panel, answer two questions that pricked up my ears. I

looked in the Boston and New York papers that I read next morning and found no trace of it.

One question was whether Lyndon Johnson would be an acceptable candidate in California. Politely but definitely, the governor of California said, "No." California consumers were paying through the nose for the price privileges conferred on Texas oil and natural gas interests.

The other question was what issue the Democrats could have in 1960 against an administration claiming peace and prosperity. Governor Brown immediately brought up the issue of high interest. In his state necessary growth was blocked by high interest, and he thought it a most inflationary factor.

I cannot think of two newsier items, both wrapped up in the perennial American game of guessing the next Presidential election. I would think many a listener to Governor Brown would be suspicious of such a gap in the newspapers next morning. I would expect some to connect it with that phrase of the sociologists that I am hearing now very often from newspapermen—"the local power setup." The implication is that the newspaper plays along with the elements of power in the community—the people who run the town. This is what makes cynics of young reporters.

As mergers increase and more and more cities are reduced to a single newspaper ownership, the danger that the newspaper will become chiefly a voice of the local power setup increases. As this concentration proceeds, what form of countervailing power is available to the elements in the community which do not feel their interests affiliated with the elements of local power? In short what chance for the opposition for those who do not feel represented by the board of trade?

To be sure, the mere fact of the newspaper having to convince its advertisers of a mass market, that it covers the potential readership, is a safety brake. It must retain a degree of confidence that will keep people buying the paper. But they may buy it for the comics, or for the advertisements, or for the television program, or for the birth and death notices. Or the baseball scores. Or the stock quotations. These indeed are all services, properly merchantable. But they do not guarantee a citizenry informed on its public affairs. Nor will any amount of reading weekly news magazines enable them to keep an eye on city hall or their local utility rates. And it is only the exceptional reader, whose sophistication comes from some experience of publicity of his own, who can sense what is left out of his newspaper. He may detect a news slant or an inadequate report. But it is impossible to ferret out facts that are not printed at all. This is not a fancy. In one New England state this past winter the largest newspaper in the state was keeping from its readers the case for the budget of their state university, which it was opposing.

Here in Minneapolis you are fortunately located on the journalistic map. You have the diggingest reporter in Washington in Clark Mollenhoff, and one of the most seasoned and wisest of labor reporters in Sam Romer, to handle two of the most strategic areas of news, and you have a newspaper management that is alive to the issues of the modern world.

My acquaintance with the St. Paul papers is limited to their managing editor, Bob Eddy, one of the finest newspapermen I know, and their Washington correspondent, Robert E. Lee, who looks and acts more like Richard Harding Davis than anyone else in the business.

Some other places have good luck in their newspapers. But one has to call it luck, for great newspapers are no more equitably distributed among our cities than championship baseball teams. We have to take our luck with both.

We have some magnificently independent newspapers. But we do not have anything like enough of them. Too few of those we have are appreciated and admired by the very public they seek to serve. This is basically a failure of education in a land which has had more of it than any other, and longer. For independent journalism goes to the very core of the American tradition. History ascribes heroic stature to such editors as Matthew Lyon, Horace Greeley, Samuel Bowles, Josephus Daniels, William Allen White.

They had to be tough.

When William Allen White was conducting a one-paper resistance to the no-strike law of his friend Governor Henry J. Allen, White said: "Only in time of stress is freedom of utterance in danger. Only when free utterance is suppressed is it needed; and when it is needed it is vital to justice." When White wrote that editorial, his own state justice department was preparing to prosecute him. They had to drop the charge.

The rigorous independence of Joseph Pulitzer was written on the wall of the city room of the old New York *World:* "The World has no friends."

It takes toughness.

The Arkansas *Gazette* has withstood a boycott for demanding decency and responsibility and legality in its city and state government.

Ralph McGill persists in puncturing irresponsible demagoguery in a state that is drenched in it.

The Louisville *Courier-Journal* has stood out against a demagogic machine that has taken over control of its own party in Kentucky.

The Toledo *Blade* under Paul Block's chemical analysis of his community's needs, pursues its own course regardless of what the power elements think of it.

Any of us can add to such a list. A number of small newspapers would stand out on it. Some have turned in heroic performances, such as Buford Boone's Tuscaloosa *News* standing up to the dominant White Citizens Council in his home town.

This is a hard course to take and it is more than can be asked of an enterprise which must survive by the willing support, both of the commercial interests and the general readers. All we can ask is detachment in informing the community and independence of the elements of privilege which have axes to grind at the expense of the community.

Even a newspaper so established in dissent as England's *Guardian* (Manchester) lost heavily by its opposition to Anthony Eden's Suez adventure. The publisher, in the doughty tradition of his father, C. P. Scott, told his editor to stick to his course. But the drop of 25 per cent in local readership was not recovered in its own local area. The *Guardian* dropped its place name to focus on the role of a national newspaper that in reality it had long enjoyed. That course is not open to a local newspaper in our continental area. A dissenting daily cannot draw to itself the minority of the whole land or any large part of it. In my own youth the old Springfield *Republican* waxed vigorous as an independent newspaper, stout in its mugwump opinions, just so long as the Berkshires provided a constituency of independent farmers. When that was gone, the *Republican* lost out to the complacent commercialism of its rival's sound business principles.

The problem of maintaining an independent press—newspapers guided by the objective detachment of professional journalism, unswayed and undominated by the power elements of their communities—will inevitably increase as economic pressures bring more mergers to more concentrated control.

The peril is roughly parallel to that of the public school system that seeks to present any realities of modern life, that are not already understood and accepted by the Chamber of Commerce and the American Legion. An independent and informed press should be the chief support of a free school system against the pressures of ignorance and bigotry and special privilege. The schools and all other vital institutions of an open society must look to an untrammeled press for support.

But where is a valiant and beleaguered editor to look for support? Or where is a complacent or weak or irresponsible publisher to find effective criticism? We come back to a question Walter Lippmann asked a dozen years ago about the press. Who is to criticize the critic? Who is to police the policeman? He asked it when the Hutchins Commission,[1] reporting on the state of the press in 1947, urged an increase in mutual criticism among newspapers of each other's lapses and proposed establishment of some body of citizens to appraise the performance of the press and inform the public of its judgments. Lippmann thought both proposals unrealistic. Time has supported him.

Where then may we look? The schools of journalism in our free tax-supported universities are the only place I can think of that could become adequate to the role. To be professional critic, appraiser, examiner of the newspapers. This would require that they accept or develop the full status of professional schools.

They have a precedent in our law schools, whose law reviews provide highly respected and highly influential critiques of our judicial process. More of this is needed, and will be increasingly, in respect to a privately owned press with a public responsibility, than to the law whose officials in authority are subject to voter control, even if indirectly.

It seems to me that the responsibility upon our schools of journalism to set standards and keep score on performance is apparent and will become a conspicuous lapse if it is not soon accepted.

A chance was lost when Sigma Delta Chi, itself an outgrowth of our journalism schools, permitted itself to be dissuaded from the post-mortem examination of the press performance in the 1952 Presidential campaign, when the charge of one-party press was raised and left unresolved.

The research burden was not so great but that a young copy-desk editor in Boston, using his own nickels to buy newspapers, turned in a revealing performance all by himself. Ted Rowse in his book, *Slanted News*,[2] examined the thirty-five largest circulation papers on their treatment of two strategic issues of the campaign, the Nixon fund and the Stevenson fund. He did not have any research staff to add up column inches and evaluate stories. He picked a shibboleth that was a valid test of the tone, the attitude, the direction of policy by the biggest papers in the campaign. Thirty-five was only a sample, but it was the top sample. It was what one man could bite off to do for himself. It showed the problem is not insuperable.

Indeed, I know that there have been instances of journalism schools making surveys of press performance in their local areas. One notable instance was a cooperative enterprise of the school and the newspaper guild in that area. It can be done. Such a function can stem only from independence and detachment. This I think we have a right to expect of any part of a university.

I have one other suggestion. But before I make it, let me say that I am convinced we must find the answer ourselves, within our own institutions. As editor of *Nieman Reports,* I receive many suggestive articles about the way problems of the press are handled in other countries. These are often suggested as a cure for invasion of privacy, or trial by newspaper, or the curbing of irresponsible publication. But I do not believe we can look abroad for any direct answer to our own journalistic problems.

Our system is unique and it needs to be. We are serving an open society whose members bear direct responsibility for the issues of their public affairs. It is like no other society. It is not enough that a few be informed. No other country that shares our traditions has even the physical dimensions of our country. London and Paris circulate their papers across the land. The American syndicated columnist is unique. London and Paris want no syndicated competition in the provinces they dominate.

I spent my summer vacation in Britain and came away depressed with their journalistic situation and the chance of learning anything there except a plight to avoid. But I did discover in Francis Williams' wise and penetrating book on British journalism, *Dangerous Estate,*[3] a clear statement of their situation which my own experience as an avid newspaper reader for a month supported. Williams' evaluation of the British press situation is in part suggestive for us.

Francis Williams I would describe as approximately an Elmer Davis to British journalism. He resigned the editorship of the *Daily Herald,* once a vital voice of Labor, when its ownership turned it to the business of selling sensation. Williams finds that only 2.8 per cent of the British people read the serious, or as the English say, "quality" newspapers.

Now London dominates the British press. More than half the circulation in the country comes from London and it puts the few serious provincial papers under increasing squeeze. For simplification, look just at London then. Daily the brilliant, informed *Guardian* (Manchester) sells 185,000 papers all over Britain. The majestically independent *Times* sells about 225,000. Williams tolerantly brackets with them the very readable but quite unobjective *Telegraph* to add another million readers on the serious side. But in contrast the *Mirror,* which may lead the paper with a stunt dreamed up in the office, sells nearly five million, and the intensely partisan *Express,* which Lord Beaverbrook himself says he prints only for propaganda, sells more than four million. Almost equally sensational and uninforming I found the *Mail, News-Chronicle* and *Herald,* which add up to five million or so more.

On Sunday the *Observer* and the *Sunday Times* are among the most readable and informed newspapers in the world. But the *Observer,* which I found the most interesting paper I have ever read, sells only 600,000, the *Sunday Times* a little more, while the *News of the World,* with no real news of the real world, sells more than seven million, and a flock of its competitors in sex and sensation pass five million each. These are more to be classed with our comic books than our newspapers of any level.

In short a small circle make up the informed public opinion of Britain. To the great mass of readers, the newspaper is what T. S. Matthews has called a sugar pill and is bought about like chewing gum, with as much nutriment. Those who get information must get it from the B.B.C.

Williams says better than I can, of the mass circulation Sunday papers of Britain, that "they are, as regards a large proportion of their contents, not newspapers at all, but entertainment sheets." With nothing against entertainment, Williams insists that "they must accept some of the obligations of the journalist in the field of public affairs."

Williams' appraisal of the British newspaper situation is:

> The great journals of information and opinion are secure in their position. They exert an influence on thought and decision not easily to be calculated. . . . The great mass circulation papers command their millions. . . . Only the middle group of serious popular papers is in serious difficulty, and that not so much because of any journalistic defect, as because trading conditions impose on them with increasing severity. . . . Their decline is as much a public tragedy as a journalistic one, for such newspapers perform a service no others can provide. [He means something between the heavy London *Times* and the saucy *Mirror.* Almost all the American press would fall between these extremes.]

The present danger to journalism, as Williams sees it, "is of its becoming simply a business . . . that it be pressed into a pattern that denies it all purpose other than the purely commercial one of attracting the largest number of paying customers by whatever means comes most readily to hand." In such case, he goes on, "the responsibility of journalists becomes very great. The defense of journalism, as more than a trade and greater than an entertainment technique, is properly the journalists' and no one else's. They have both a professional and a public duty to look after their inheritance."

What can we say to Williams' challenge that the defense of journalism as more than a trade is the duty of the journalists? Is there any organization of American journalists we can expect to meet this challenge? Can we expect it of the guild, which is not a professional organization but a trade union? Or would there be a natural suspicion that the guild had an ax to grind against the employing publishers, as a labor union? Is an evolution of the guild's role in journalism too much to look for, now that it has more security than in the days when it had to fight for recognition and found frequent enough necessity to be aggressive?

For the function I am seeking, it is of course a limitation of the guild that it began as it did, as a trade union, instead of an independent association of newspapermen dedicated to the professional standards of their calling.

This means no criticism of labor unions. Nor do I see any sign that union membership has made reporters less dedicated to the journalistic grail of objectivity. At the time the guild was organized, in the depth of the great depression, and in a craft enmeshed in an institution whose other crafts are highly unionized, the rise of a reporters' union was perhaps inevitable, if only to protect its members, who presented about the only group whose salaries could be cut when business fell off.

The guild, I am sure, has brought more pay to the newsroom. Unhappily this has had a leveling effect which has brought the star reporter's pay closer to the office boy's, and has left less margin to recognize exceptional talent, and consequently has let it leak away at a debilitating rate. It has increased the difficulty of weeding out those who proved to be misfits and has maintained staffs with too many members unqualified for newspaper work. To be sure, this happens in other institutions, notably the public school, and in all civil service. But it has no less deadening an effect on those institutions.

It was further unfortunate that the guild, created in the days of vertical union development, grouped reporters and copy editors with a miscellany of workers whose only relation to the profession of journalism is that they worked in the same building.

It has had the effect of making reporters liable for cooperation with the people who tie the bundles and drive the trucks, and we have had such fantastic phenomena as that in New York last winter when a nondescript union of curious leadership could deny the millions of a vast metropolitan area their prime source of information for a month, besides wiping out the profits of the papers for a year.[4] Such a strike, on such a base, surely cries out for some form of a Taft-Hartley act that will protect the public from having their most vital information denied them at the arbitrary whim of people who never saw a journalism school and never gave a thought to the responsibilities of journalism.

The simple fact is that we do not have American journalists joined in a common bond of professional association, independent alike of management and union. The potential of such association, it seems to me, is very great, and its absence a serious vacuum. I know, for example, that the association of university professors has been a powerful influence in maintaining the freedom to teach.

Perhaps I am taking my case to the wrong institutions: the journalism school and the guild. These happen to be the institutions that invited me to speak my mind on this occasion. If the only immediate effect is to irritate my hosts, nevertheless, out of the irritation may sooner or later come a thought that will strike them as more workable than mine.

It is perhaps rash and tactless to lay this problem so directly in your laps. But I am quite sure that it is not unrealistic to say to you that this is a problem we must all face and that it will press upon us more inescapably as newspaper control becomes more concentrated and more papers come into the hands of those who run them only by their balance sheet, sometimes at long distance from their local issues.

I cannot do better than to close with Williams' words, as he ends his provocative last chapter:

> Those who serve journalism serve one of the great professions. The allegiance it properly commands is absolute. Those who give it that allegiance need stand in no man's shadow.
>
> For a newspaper is more than a piece of property; it is a living personality with a character and tradition deriving not only from those who own or edit it, but from its readers, from the interests it has historically served, and from the community of which it is a part. . . .

Reporting Politics

M y present view about newspaper reporters is that
it is their job to be read, if possible, but they had better not be either
seen or heard.* I am therefore always very hesitant to speak to people
about my general views. However, I hope you will forgive me if, as I
have been asked to, I meander for a while about some opinions, reflections, and conclusions that have been suggested to me by what is now
almost exactly a quarter of a century as a political reporter.

I think I ought to begin by defining what I mean by political reporting.
I mean something very broad and comprehensive—not just election reporting but reporting of everything that bears in a major way on the pos-
ture and affairs of the United States as a country. This would include
everything that seems likely to influence our historical development and
current situation. This is an awfully big area in which to be reporting,
I am afraid.

As to the equipment needed, I think it is also well to be clear what
the desiderata are. The first requirement is a good pair of feet. The feet
are just about as important as the head, particularly for a political reporter. This is functionally unavoidable. A sports reporter has the event
which he is due to report neatly and often quite comfortably served up

---

* This lecture was delivered October 17, 1960.

for him. A political reporter has got to find the event; if possible he has got to foresee the event and this can only be done by what, now that I have reached the age of fifty, seems to me an inordinate investment of shoeleather. You can easily see why that is so. Your chance of discovering something significant is ten times as great if you talk to ten politicians and experts than if you talk to only one. Indeed, I would say that it would be one hundred times as great, because each conversation gives you a kind of cross-bearing on the next conversation. At the end of seven or eight of them you begin to have an idea, if there is a body buried somewhere, where to dig for the body. So you have got to have a darn good shoemaker and darn good feet to put in the shoes if you want to be any kind of serious political reporter.

The second requirement is a head of some sort, preferably, in my opinion, a head with some historical equipment. I do not see how it is possible to be a political reporter on a major scale without being able to situate events in history. To look even at the political tendencies in Sunrise Township in Chisago County, Minnesota, requires one to look at these tendencies in some kind of historically relevant framework. Without that, particularly if you are dealing with national affairs, nothing really has much meaning at all. Without a historical setting, events become a whole series of quite unrelated anecdotes and episodes without much importance or meaning; therefore you need some historical grounding in the head.

You also have to be able to write grammatical English, which is an increasingly peculiar habit nowadays. But it is necessary if you are going to be a political reporter and not a sociologist.

The fourth requirement is a strong sense of what I call loyalty to the facts. Here we encounter a very interesting moral problem—a genuinely moral problem. The political reporter is rather sure to have his own side and his own sympathies. No one is absolutely neutral; certainly no political reporter known to me in my lifetime has ever been absolutely neutral. You inevitably develop, in every election that you cover, either an intense sense of repulsion or some mild attachment for one candidate or another. This cannot be avoided. It is only human to do so and there is no use telling political reporters that they ought not to do this, that they ought to be eunuchs. Nobody really wants to be a eunuch and they are very unlikely to follow your advice. The question is if political reporters have these feelings and attachments, how do they deal with them? The answer to this question, it seems to me, is quite simple. And it is an answer dictated to, or imposed on, any political reporter who has much care for his own reputation by the practical nature of his situation. The answer is that whatever his preference in an election or in any given political situation may be, he must, above all, be loyal to the facts. He must report the facts according to their importance and significance. He must not shove under the rug facts that may be displeasing to the candidate he likes or facts that may be helpful to the candidate he finds repellent. For if he indulges in these practices, he will, in the long run, lose his reputation as a serious and reliable political reporter.

There are some people in my business who have done very well out of lost reputations. They are known to be so reliably and passionately partisan that people on their side will always be able to hear from them *exactly* what they want to hear and *only* what they want to hear. This seems to me to be a rather boring, although sometimes profitable branch of the trade. It certainly is not a branch of the trade which is held in great respect in the trade itself. The principal check on partisanship in a political reporter, then, is a practical one. If he becomes disloyal to the facts persistently and in a conspicuous manner, he will lose his reputation.

It is morally permissible, in my opinion, for a reporter to say to himself, "Okay, I prefer Mr. A. to Mr. B. either because I think Mr. A. has a certain quality as a candidate or because I think Mr. B. is an unholy phony, provided that what's favorable to the unholy phony and what's unfavorable to the attractive candidate gets honestly and factually reported without undue emphasis either way."

To anyone who may think of entering this peculiar trade, I have a final, rather difficult piece of advice to offer, and that is: do not be too humble. Frank Kent, who was a great political reporter in his day and a great wit, told me when I first went to Washington, "Joe, there's only one thing that a Washington correspondent must always bear in mind. That is that there's only one way for an honest newspaperman to look at 98½ per cent of public men and that is down." I think that is perhaps a little exaggerated, but I do not think it is possible to be both a serious, self-respecting newspaperman and a spaniel. And I have seen many newspapermen get fairly far as spaniels but I have never seen one last the course as a spaniel. I think this warning—this piece of by-the-way comment—is increasingly important nowadays because public men more and more expect spaniel-like behavior from men in the newspaper business.

When I first went to Washington it was unthinkable for a serious Washington correspondent to have a serious conversation with any public relations man, particularly any government public relations man, including the President's press secretary. To public relations men you talked about railroad schedules and such subjects, or about more private subjects if they were nice guys. If you wanted to talk about public subjects, you would talk to the official himself. Now, partly because government has grown a great deal bigger, partly because I think too many newspapermen have forgotten the advice I have just been offering, we are told we must be briefed by public relations men. I will not do it. I am too old fashioned. When I am received by a public official with his public relations man present, it is my disagreeable habit to say that I assume that the presence of a third party implies either that the public man does not trust me, in which case I do not want to talk to him, or does not trust himself, in which case he is not worth talking to. And if you think about it, this is quite accurate.

A newspaperman should never waste a public man's time. He should never be resentful if the public man refuses to see him. He should never, by the same token, be grateful to the public man because he is seen. A newspaperman has a job to do that is tinged with the public interest. His task is to act as a kind of transmission belt—or sewer pipe, if you prefer—by which the vital facts having a bearing on the public situation are disseminated to the public. He has no reason, therefore, to be grateful to a public man when he is received by him. The newspaperman is doing his job, just as the public man is doing his job, when they join in the vital work of informing the public. The essence of the relationship is that an informed public is the only means by which our kind of society can be made to work. Therefore, the newspaperman on his level and the public man on his level have a community of interest to see that the public is informed.

In this last rather odd piece of advice I have been giving I have already sketched one of the enormous changes that have come over political reporting in the twenty-five years since Ogden Reid sent for me after the Hauptmann trial [1] and told me that I was to be rewarded for my performance as a trial reporter by being turned into a political reporter. It is very hard for me to sum up for you the marvelously cozy and agreeable atmosphere of the Senate press gallery twenty-five years ago. I have been there so long now that, as I counted the other day, I discovered I am a very senior inhabitant of the Senate chamber. I am senior to everyone in the Senate except Senator Carl Hayden, Senator Harry Byrd, and Senator Richard B. Russell. It makes me feel rather venerable. There are five or six newspapermen who are senior to me. But you have been around an awfully long time when you have been around twenty-five years.

In preparation for this evening, I was thinking about the changes that have occurred in political reporting since then. The first change is in the content of the news. When I went to the Senate, it was at the very end of the classical period of American political reporting—a period when, except in very unusual circumstances, even American national politics did not desperately matter. It was a time when our national politics were very entertaining and it was not very much out of place to make jokes all the time about it. It was a period when old Senator George Moses of New Hampshire used to appear every morning on the Senate floor and say, "Gentlemen, what outrage shall we perpetrate to-day?" And it was a period when politicians' personal relationships had great importance, when ordinary old-fashioned pork and patronage had enormous importance, when you really did not need to know in order to understand political events, how many jobs Senator J. Will Robinson was getting out of Roosevelt, or in an earlier period how Senator Reed Smoot had succeeded in loading onto the federal payroll so many people from Utah that when he was defeated in 1932 they had to hire two special trains to take them all back to the Rockies. These were matters of real significance and they generated a number of entertaining legends which also had significance.

If you do not mind, I will now proceed ruthlessly to tell what I have always thought was the funniest of these legends. It was about a man who was a great friend of mine, Pat Harrison of Mississippi, who in 1936 was the second man on the Democratic side in the Senate. At that time, or a little earlier than 1936, he was terribly afraid that Theodore Bilbo —"The Man" Bilbo—was going to run against him for the Senate. And he wanted to get Bilbo onto the federal payroll in order to buy him off. He went around to see George Peek who was Agricultural Adjustment Administrator, and said, "I want a job for this glorious patriot, Bilbo, and it's got to pay $6,000 a year." That was a lot in those days. Pat explained at great length how patriotic and what a glorious fellow Bilbo was. Finally, knowing perfectly well what he was getting into, Peek said, "Okay, Pat, I'll give your man Bilbo a job." Pat thanked him profusely and got as far as the door on his way out when he turned around and said, "Now George, don't get me wrong, this man Bilbo is a very fine citizen. I think he'll do a good job for you. But he was brought up in the piney woods country back home. Education there is kind of peculiar and I don't believe I'd let him make any public speeches for you because he might say some things that would embarrass you later." George Peek said thank you, Pat, and good-by. This time Harrison got halfway out of the door before he came back and said, "Now George, don't get me wrong, this man Bilbo is a very fine citizen and he'll do a splendid job for you but he was brought up in our piney woods country, and they don't have much money there. They don't get to handle very much folding money and I don't believe I'd let him handle any funds for me because there might be a little mistake." Peek said, "Senator, I'm very grateful to you for your little tip; I'll bear that in mind and everything will be all right." The third time Pat got all the way out of the door and shut it behind him. Then he opened it and said to Peek again, "Now George, don't get me wrong, this man Bilbo is a very fine citizen and he'll do a splendid job for you. You're not making a mistake in hiring him. But he was brought up in our piney woods country, and people are pretty rough and crude there in those back woods. I just don't believe I'd put any very pretty girls on Bilbo's office staff." And George looked at him, and he said, "Well, Senator, I see exactly what you mean. All we have to do is gag him, bind him, and geld him and he'll make a perfect public servant."

When I came to Washington, there he was, the perfect public servant, drawing $6,000 a year cutting out newspaper clippings in a kind of cubbyhole in the AAA with a lady secretary whose face really would have stopped a train and did stop Bilbo.

That was not unimportant, mind you. It was important because it established a kind of relationship between Peek and Harrison. It told you what Harrison would do about Peek's legislation; it told you who Peek would go to if he wanted help in the Senate, all that sort of thing.

But even when I first went to Washington, all that was vanishing. When I joined up with Bob Kintner as a columnist, I was still a Senate reporter, but I was immediately educated in a very much larger world. I think it is fair to say that Kintner was one of the very first Washington reporters to see that everything had really changed in government. He saw the importance of making friends with the New Dealers, of studying the theory as well as the practice of the New Deal legislation, of familiarizing himself with this brand new world that had nothing to do with the old political world which the senior political reporters in Washington were at that time accustomed to and were largely writing about.

I was very lucky to be educated in this larger world by my new partner. I have tried to keep up with *ideas* in government as well as with the *practice* of government ever since. Even so, if you think about it, Bob Kintner and I never wrote a single line about foreign policy or defense policy from 1937 until well after Munich. There really was no news of that kind written in the United States then. No American newspaperman except two or three State Department specialists *ever* wrote about these subjects. They were untouched, except by foreign correspondents, until the great awakening and the great surge of apprehension that was felt after the Munich agreement. Then I, like all the other people in my business, had to learn yet another vast new area—foreign and defense affairs. There were some people who had managed to become knowledgeable about politics and about New Deal ideas who did not want to go on into this new area. They, too, fell by the wayside in the end. And now in the period since World War II, you have foreign policy, you have defense policy, you have internal politics, you have social and economic ideas in government, and you have the constantly increasing pressure of events abroad on events at home. All these topics must somehow be studied and related to one another. Hence the task of a political reporter who makes any serious attempt to cover the political waterfront has been vastly extended, complicated, and rendered vastly more onerous. Political reporting has been transformed from a job that was cozy to do to a job which, now that I have passed the half-century mark, I find myself breathing louder and louder to try to catch up with. And I never quite succeed in catching up, really. I must say, moreover, that in our business as a whole not everyone has tried hard enough to catch up.

I will give you two quite simple examples of this. One was Secretary George C. Marshall's Harvard commencement speech in which he announced the Marshall Plan. The identity of those who were to get special degrees at the Harvard commencement was kept a deep secret. There was no special announcement, therefore, that Marshall was going to Harvard to receive a degree and to make a key speech. For this reason the commencement was covered entirely by the political reporters on the spot, as it often is. But the political reporters on the spot knew very little about the European situation. Consequently, Marshall's announcement of his Marshall Plan, which, if anything has changed history in the postwar period, did change history, very nearly went completely unnoticed. Officials had to call up and point out that the speech was of outstanding importance, before it received adequate attention in the national press. The Washington correspondents began to get into the act from that point onward.

I think you have seen similar examples in a rather different way in much of the reporting of the recent United Nations session.[2] There has been a great deal of emphasis on nose-counting. The fact that Khrushchev did not get a majority vote has been constantly pointed out. It has been made to seem as though this episode did not go too badly for us. In point of fact, it went very badly indeed. Mr. Khrushchev's aim was to inspire terror. He did inspire terror. His further aim was to soften up situations by frightening people. I think one can detect that he did soften up situations by frightening people. The majorities that we got were a great deal less than the majorities of the past. If you study, for example, the UN vote on the admission of Red China and if you make a very modest extrapolation for the probable way the new African countries will vote next year, you have to conclude that the recent vote probably presages defeat for the American position at the next session of the United Nations. Now I do not think that the reporting from the UN has been biased. I do not think it has been factually inaccurate, but I do think that because the events of the UN were not put in any kind of general context, either historical or foreign, the reporting was quite misleading. I am afraid that we shall see the proof of that in the next twelve months. We are already seeing some proof of it.

I sometimes wonder what has happened in this country to lessen our alertness to key developments. Let me offer the example of Laos. Laos is a very small place but it is a geographically crucial place. It is the key to Southeast Asia. It is almost impossible to believe that southern Indo-China will not fall into the grip of the Communists if Laos ever falls. At this moment you will find Laos falling, but the accounts are carried on the third page of newspapers in our country, if they are carried at all. It seems to me that this is an event of sufficient significance—an event that may well compromise the whole future of Southeast Asia—to receive more attention. I do not think we show due sense of proportion when an event of this importance can take place, so to say, obscurely and without being very much noticed.

Here I have telegraphed part of the next point I want to cover, which is whether in our trade as political reporters we are doing our job adequately. I do not honestly think that we are, partly because of failures like the failure with respect to Laos. This, mind you, is partly a mechanical failure. In the first Laos crisis, when Laos was physically invaded by Communist troops from northern Indo-China, a very large congregation of newspapermen gathered in that country, myself included. We sent out a great deal of copy. Since there was so much copy coming in, the newspapers of this country gave the situation considerable prominence and people got interested in the crisis. The present crisis is not primarily of a military nature. It has the interminable character and general mistiness of outline which are common in all Southeast Asian political crises. There is no nice, neat precise drama that you can report easily. Now, there is no large congregation of newsmen in Laos and there is no large outpouring of copy. So I do not criticize the editors in our country because Laos is on page three. I criticize, in a way, the reporters—the

Washington reporters particularly, myself included—who ought to be making a great deal more of a row about what is happening in Laos. Some of us, perhaps, ought to be going there, although it is difficult to do so in an election year.

I think I would criticize both the people in my branch of the trade and in the editorial branch with respect to defense reporting. Here is an aspect of our national situation of the most desperate significance. It is a vast subject in itself, of such hideous complexity that it always makes your head ache when you try to get on top of any part of it. The tendency, therefore, is to take government handouts. This is always a bad thing to do, and worse in the area of defense than in any other. For in this area government handouts are always and persistently mendacious. All government handouts lie; some lie more than others. Defense and defense reporting has such enormous bearing on our national situation that I think political reporters and the newspapers in the country ought to interest themselves in it intensively. Then they should interest public opinion in it in a way that has never yet been done. I mean by that in a continuing and persistent way; not by just reporting a Sputnik or a Nautilus launching, but by trying to make people think enough about it, so that it becomes a normal thing for intelligent people to understand the basic theory of deterrence. It is not a very difficult theory, but I know hardly one intelligent person in a thousand in the United States who has ever tried to get on top of it.

I will not bother you with it now, but the fact that this theory of deterrence on which our whole national defense rests and for the realization of which we are spending some forty billion dollars annually (and that is not enough)—the fact that this theory is not generally understood does seem to me a rather alarming fact. This situation shows that those of us in my business are not quite doing our job. We are not doing our job as I believe it ought to be done mainly because of all the increasing complexities and difficulties, plus the growing scope of the task which I have been emphasizing.

I must add that I think in these past seven and a half years the American newspapers and the American political reporters have failed in their jobs for what are essentially partisan reasons. I do not mean by that, for one instant, that I endorse Truman's view about a one-party press. I do not mean by that, either, that any large number of my colleagues in Washington receive orders from their editors or publishers to slant the news. The number of newspapers and magazines in which I consider the news to be consciously and continuously slanted is very small indeed. Some of these newspapers and magazines may be quite important. I would note *Time,* until recently; for there has been a very substantial change in *Time* in this election campaign. But conscious and continuous slanting is an isolated and unusual phenomenon. It is not a question, I think, of slanting the news so much as it is a change of approach that one sees when there is an administration in Washington to which most of the newspapers in the country are friendly.

I think it is a splendid thing for the country to have its newspapers *unfriendly* toward the government because then newsmen dig more, they will not stand for as much nonsense and they will not accept twaddle at face value. I would like to see every administration gone after by the newspapermen as Truman's administration was, for example. I think it is undeniable that Eisenhower's administration has not been gone after in this manner. Had it been, a tremendous feeling would have been generated by now on, for example, the matter of defense. The surge of apprehension we felt with the first Sputnik would have caused a vast discussion of this subject. Deficiencies which undoubtedly exist would have been pointed out and emphasized, and people in government would not be getting away with what they *now* are getting away with.

There is also this matter of American prestige which has entered into the present campaign. No practical foreign correspondent known to me, whether he is a Republican or a Democrat, has even a momentary doubt that our prestige and influence in the world have vastly declined in the last seven and a half years. One can prove it statistically. There is no strategically significant region on the face of the globe where we have not suffered serious setbacks or where the Soviets have not made important progress. They have established important political claims in the Middle East. They are doing very well in Africa. They have turned up in South America. I have already touched on Southeast Asia. They are at work in Japan through the Communist party without upsetting very many Japanese. They are able to prevent the President of the United States from paying a state visit to our chief Pacific ally.[3] Even in England, the Labor party—and after all, the Labor party is the official opposition party—carried a majority vote the other day in favor of unilateral disarmament and open anti-Americanism. Now if these things do not mean to you that our prestige and influence have declined in the world, well then I suggest that you look at the Berlin situation.

You cannot suppose that Berlin would have been threatened six or seven years ago. There was not the slightest danger then to Berlin. If Khrushchev had indulged, six or seven years ago, in the kinds of threats he has used in the past year and a half, the result would have been grave for him. For that reason he would not have indulged in them and he did not indulge in them. It seems to me that we should not have to wait for a presidential candidate like Kennedy to come along to talk about our prestige and influence. It seems to me that we ought to have been doing it ourselves and to have been doing it a great deal earlier. I find all this a disturbing and disheartening phenomenon.

Here in the Twin Cities you are very lucky in your newspapers. They are comprehensive; I have followed them all from time to time. They are comprehensive, they are fair, and they are serious. If you do not think you are lucky, just try living in some other cities I can think of where there are quite different kinds of newspapers which are not comprehensive, fair, and serious. You would see what I mean. Most American cities have good papers and are well served by their papers. The difficulty is that something happens to reporting in the climate of Washington. I think we as reporters have a good deal more responsibility for our own reaction to this Washington climate than the overtly Republican publishers and editors. As I already have pointed out, I cannot think of more than four of five nationally or even locally significant publications that ask their reporters to eliminate this or emphasize that or to forget about the negative and emphasize the positive. This is not a common practice, thank God! It is just that somehow or other in the present climate in Washington a great deal that seems to me and to others on the scene to be desperately significant somehow has not been brought home during these years. I am afraid it will be brought home eventually by events. That is always a most unpleasant way to learn unpleasant truths and it disturbs me greatly that this omission by the nation's newspapers has, in this manner, occurred.

I have now given you the reflections that have been suggested to me by looking backward over twenty-five years in my peculiar trade. They have been passionately interesting and very enjoyable years. They have taken me everywhere from the Senate gallery to the beach at Inchon and from Laos to Sunrise Township in Chisago County, Minnesota. I am very proud of my trade and I think it has a very high public function. If I have criticized my trade's deficiencies, it is because I judge its performance entirely by my opinion of its very high function. It has its high function because our society can operate only if it is informed. I think the vast majority of the people in my trade—the reporters, editors, publishers and everyone else—are good, patriotic, and intelligent men whose aim and purpose in life is to inform the public that they serve. But I also feel that the fearful changes in the world and the new challenges which confront our country rather insistently demand some changes of approach and viewpoint in this trade of mine. Otherwise, the full flow of vital information will not continue, and this flow is what we live by in America.

XV

PIERRE SALINGER
JAMES HAGERTY

The Press and

Presidential Leadership

I am glad to have the opportunity to discuss the subject of the press and the President.* As I understand the assignment that has been given us, it involves three topics: first of all, the role of the White House Press Secretary; second, the relationship between the press and the President; and third, our philosophy of public information. James Hagerty and I represent two-thirds of the most exclusive fraternity known to man, the Society of White House Press Secretaries. There is only one of us missing, Roger Tubby, who served President Truman for two months. It is a rather chilling statistic to us from time to time to recall the fact that there are fewer living former White House Press Secretaries than there are living former Presidents.

The role of the White House Press Secretary can safely be said to have magnified through the years and really achieved its current standing during the administration of my predecessor, James C. Hagerty. As the role of the White House Press Secretary has increased in importance, so too, I believe, has the output of information. Each succeeding administration has stepped up efforts to get out information to the various

---

* This lecture was delivered November 9, 1961. Mr. Salinger spoke first. Mr. Hagerty's lecture begins on page 190.

mass media so that there has been an ever-widening view of the Presidency. This is a very, very good thing.

Hagerty did one thing that was revolutionary—at least it was considered revolutionary at the time that he was in office. For the first time he permitted cameramen to come to a press conference and to film the conference. This year, we have gone one step further and permitted live television at presidential press conferences. Both of these steps have great significance to the American people in that they give the people an opportunity to have a much closer look at their President; there is nothing more important today than for the people to know what the President is saying and thinking about a whole variety of very important subjects.

It is a lamentable fact that there are only eight daily newspapers in the United States which carry a full text of the President's press conference. Citizens who live in areas other than these eight cities must have some other way to find out precisely what the President has said in addition to what is reported in a condensed account available in their paper. The use of video tape to record some presidential press conferences which are not set up for "live" coverage permits television stations throughout the country to rebroadcast the press conference in its entirety, if they wish, so that the people can see the President answering the full array of questions. Of course, on the occasions when we have live press conferences, the people have the opportunity to see the President in action. It is very interesting to note that a poll was taken recently which showed that of the first three press conferences which were televised, 90 per cent of the people who were polled had seen one or more of them. And even more interesting was the fact that 85 per cent of these people had turned on the press conference on purpose. In other words, they had not reached it through dial-flipping; they intended and wanted to see the President.

Now, of course, televising the press conference has created problems. There are people who say the conference is too big—has become monstrous—and there are people who hearken back to the good old days and say, "Why, wouldn't it be nice if we could do it the way they did it in Franklin Roosevelt's time, when the press used to gather in the President's office twice a week and have a much more informal chat-relationship with him?"

There are several problems. One of them is the great growth of the information media since Roosevelt's time. Today there are 1,200 accredited White House correspondents, and even though a great many of those do not attend a particular White House press conference, it is still a fact that the average attendance at President Kennedy's press conference has been 400. This does remove, I agree, some of the informality that occurred in Roosevelt's time, and yet I do not really see any solution to that problem. I did propose a solution about two months ago: "If you really think it's too big, perhaps the solution of the problem would be for the President once a week to see Scotty Reston and Walter Lippmann in his office." We mulled that idea over for a while and then we had to discard it, because we could not decide which one would say, "Thank you, Mr. President."

But, seriously, the growth of communication which has brought the press conference to its present size is one of the inevitable consequences of the growth of the entire communication industry. We, in putting the television camera into the press conference room, have tried to do it in such a way as to have the least loss of the "classical feeling" of the press conference.

You hear a lot about reporters being able to ask more questions under the old system, or that the questions are not as good nowadays. I was recently reading the *Columbia Journalism Review,* which I recommend highly to anyone who wants to keep abreast of what is going on in journalism. I found a very interesting little article there about presidential press conferences. They discovered, by going back to some of President Roosevelt's press conferences, that in two early Kennedy conferences, one on February 13, 1961, and the other on March 23, 1961, reporters asked forty-two questions; whereas transcripts of two Roosevelt conferences showed that there were only thirty-eight questions asked. But this is the important thing: in the two Kennedy conferences the average questions were fifty words in length, and in the early Roosevelt press conferences the average questions were fourteen words long. You can conclude from this that it is taking reporters a lot longer to ask questions these days. Perhaps that is why we get letters from time to time castigating the reporters for the way in which they ask the questions. But in defense of reporters (and I am in a position now where I defend reporters at all times) I have gone back to the press conferences in the Truman era and the Roosevelt era—I even looked at a couple Herbert Hoover had—and the questions were not any better then. You either get very good ones or very bad ones. I do not think there has really been any deterioration of the questions under the new pattern.

Now, I was talking principally about the press conferences, but the opening up of communications has been more than that. Of course, one of the reasons for the gradually evolving communication with the people by the President has been the addition of new media. Certainly television and radio do bring people a different view of the Presidency than they can get from the written word. I will give you a couple of examples:

early this year we allowed a team of cameramen from ABC—and this is not a side deal I made with Hagerty before he left the White House—to spend a day at the White House, and they actually spent several hours in the President's office. They filmed everything that went on, including conferences with, as I recall, Dr. Walter Heller, chief of the President's Council of Economic Advisers, who used to teach at the University of Minnesota. They also filmed conferences President Kennedy had with John McCloy, the President's disarmament adviser, and others. Out of this shooting total they produced a one-hour program called "Adventures on the New Frontier." It probably was the most revealing view of the workings of the Presidency and the workings of the White House that has ever been seen by the American people, and it is another attempt to take the mystery away and to show how the Presidency operates and what the President is doing.

Now, the relationship between the press secretary and the President varies from President to President. People talk about the different styles of press secretaries. I would rather talk about the different styles of Presidents, because it is the style of the President that determines the style of his press secretary. I will speak only about President Kennedy, because I have never wanted to get into a debate about some other President's practices with the press, or some other press secretary's practice.

President Kennedy, probably more than any other public official that I have had anything to do with, has a keen sense and understanding of the whole field of communications. I have said on occasion, and I have not meant it facetiously, that in fact he does not really need a press secretary. There are certain things which I can do to relieve him of some burdens, but as far as the thinking is concerned, he has the keenest mind on communications that I have ever seen. This makes my job relatively simple.

The only way that a press secretary can be truly effective is to have a close working relationship with the President. If the President will not take him into his confidence, if the press secretary is not aware of what is going on at the White House, he is totally ineffectual. He cannot help the press, and he might as well not be there, because one of the great problems that a press secretary has is not only to get out the news and to see that what the President is thinking and saying is disseminated, but also to help reporters escape the trap of going down a blind alley or writing a story which is erroneous, or which could cause serious problems. Unless he knows the inner doings of the administration and what is going on, the press secretary cannot successfully do this.

I see the President every morning when he first gets to work. Usually

I have a list of things ready that I would like to discuss with him, things which I feel are going to come up during my own two press conferences a day, and things for which I want guides from him, especially on matters of policy—in other words, guides on how he wants me to answer these questions. I see him again in the evening before he goes home, and during the day I may see him as many as three or four times, depending on problems which may arise and may require me to see him at that moment. Access is highly necessary as is, I say, the confidence.

The procedure at the White House has not basically changed for many years so far as the relationship between the press secretary and the press. There have been two-a-day press conferences between the press and the press secretary for a number of years. I tried at one time to reduce them and I did so. I felt maybe we could survive with one a day for a while, at least until Congress came back. But in the five days that I tried it I still had two on four of the days, so I decided I might well go back to two. Most of the White House information business is transacted at these two-a-day briefings. Announcements are made; briefings are presented. These sessions are wide open, and reporters can ask questions on any subject. There are no restrictions on what they ask. And so the day-to-day information work of the White House is basically conducted in these briefings; they serve as the continuing bridge between the White House and the public and the press during those times between presidential press conferences.

We have attempted some other innovations which we think are of great importance in communication. One of the most important has been in the field of our relationship with foreign correspondents. It has always been my feeling that a great deal of our problem overseas, when we read unfavorable stories in foreign newspapers or had unfavorable broadcasts, was the failure of our communication with foreign correspondents in our country. There are a great many such correspondents—there must be over a thousand in this country.

Interestingly enough, the majority of them are not in Washington but in New York. They are there because they have to cover the UN. They are usually from papers which can afford to send only one man to the United States, so the correspondent makes an effort to cover Washington from New York. Of course they do not really get a very accurate picture of Washington that way.

About a month ago, after a considerable amount of work, we opened a foreign correspondent center in New York which will be devoted to helping the New York–based correspondents find out what is going on in Washington. We are running a special wire, concentrating on important news from Washington, to them in New York. We tape the briefings held at the State Department each day by that department's press officer, Lincoln White. The minute he is finished in Washington the tapes are played in New York. Parts of my own briefings which deal with foreign policy are taped and played in New York in the same way. These new efforts bring what is going on in Washington to New York and give many correspondents contact with the capital that they have not had in the past. An even more important function of this news center will be to assist these foreign correspondents in getting out of New York to other parts of the country to find out more about America than they are likely to find by staying in one place all the time. A number of these correspondents have said in the past, for example, that if they wanted to write a story on agriculture, they did not know of any way to contact somebody who could really give them an inside picture of American agriculture. Working through the foreign correspondent center, arrangements could be made through government agencies, through private industry, and through farm organizations, which would bring this reporter to a place where he could get a factual story on agriculture to send back to his paper in his country. We very much hope that this experiment will be successful. It has just started, and I do not want to claim any success for it at this moment, but it is an interesting approach, and it is one that is highly necessary at this time.

Now, I would like to speak briefly on the whole subject of presidential communication. There has been a great deal said about it lately. When the President was campaigning last year, one of the things which he said repeatedly in his speeches as he went across the country was that the reason he wanted to be President was that the seat of power is in Washington in the Presidency. In the Presidency he could make things move. He felt that from this position he could provide impetus to the government. If that is true of any function of government, it is true of communication, because the political communications of the country center with the President. He has the power to provide impetus to the whole effort of government communications.

The President communicates with the people in our country, and with people abroad, whether they are our allies or our enemies. He communicates with them in a variety of ways, but sometimes we think that the only way the President communicates with people is through a press conference, through some public appearance, or through some national telecast, and when he is not doing that he is not communicating. The fact of the matter is that he communicates in a whole variety of ways which do not appear as communications basically, but which are, in fact, highly important communications. If he writes a letter to a leader of a foreign country and that letter is published, that is a method of communication. If he invites a group of people to his office and discusses their problems with them, whether it is a group of farmers, a group of veterans, or so on, he communicates his interest in that particular subject. The people come out of the office and rediscuss the subject with better awareness of the President's views. If the people are connected with any particular organization, they usually go back to their organization and report what the President has told them. All this fans out throughout our whole society.

If the President arranges a concert at the White House, it is more than just a concert at the President's home. It is an indication to the American people that the President is interested in music and culture, and it is a communication of this idea to the people.

Now, of late there has been in Washington a group which is preaching the doctrine that the President is not communicating. I do not know whether this doctrine has reached Minneapolis yet. Maybe one of the reasons it has not got out to Minneapolis is that I find the farther I get away from Washington in the United States, the better I find the President is communicating. One of the reasons for this is—I do not know whether Mr. Hagerty will agree with me on this or not—but I find that Washington is a terribly isolated city, insulated against opinions from the outside. Those of us who work in the capital are responsible for that a great deal. We talk to each other in Washington. Some noted columnist may write an article saying the President is not communicating. Soon five other columnists will write an article saying the President is not communicating. Now maybe he is not communicating with them, but if they could just spend twenty-four hours out of Washington—in Kansas City where I have been, or in other parts of the country—they would find that there is a great deal more communication than they think.

The problem is, it seems to me, that the people of Washington are frequently out of touch with the country. For example, one of the things people in Washington say is that the President should take his case to the people more forcefully. Well, you ask, "What do you want him to do?" The reply is, "Well, he should go on television and talk to the people more." Now, if there is one thing that is true about presidential communications, it is the fact that the President has a great power to rally the American people to a great cause, or to some great need. But it is also a fact that he should do so only when it is urgent and necessary. In other words, the complete impact of presidential discussion, unless it is timed right, unless it is used, I believe, sparingly, tends to dissipate presidential influence. There is frequent reference to President Roosevelt's fireside chats; they are looked upon as a model in this field. The fact of the matter is that after 1933 and 1934, when the economic situation began to improve some in the country, the crises began to fade a little, and for a number of years thereafter Franklin Roosevelt had only three fireside chats a year.

President Roosevelt understood the impact of presidential communication and he understood the need for timing. This is one of the most important things any President has to remember. President Kennedy knows it as well as anyone. You have to use these powers with a maximum of effectiveness and at the right time. The President has held from the start that his administration should provide the freest possible access to information; we have in every way possible implemented that directive. There still are areas, I agree, in Washington where news media do not have access to information they should have. But the number of changes that we have made and the changes that have been wrought in recent years are gradually breaking down the remaining barriers of unnecessary secrecy in Washington and making it possible for people to get the information they need. And with the power of the President behind such a directive and the continuing power of the White House implementing it, we will be successful in this endeavor.

The topics assigned to us are rather flexible in scope and Pierre Salinger has outlined them for you, but before I start to answer specifically the topics so assigned I would like to outline my past duties, perhaps giving you something of the feel of the office of press secretary. Maybe now that I am out of office and can speak more freely than Mr. Salinger, I can give you by indirection a little idea of the tremendous responsibility that he has in these days.

I want to make three or four things clear to set a tone in discussing the office of the press secretary as it relates to these assigned topics.

In the first place, the press secretary to the President is the personal choice of the President. He is a member of the President's personal staff, and he works for no one except the President of the United States. He does not work for the press; he does not work for anyone except the President. He is appointed by the President and he is removable only by the President. He has responsibility, therefore, only to the President of the United States. He speaks for the President when the President does not want to speak himself publicly.

Pierre has alluded to the fact that each President and each press secretary have a different way of handling their jobs, and I would most certainly agree. You must have a personal relationship. Mine, with President Eisenhower, was—well—like father and son, next to my own father, he is the greatest man I have known. This is as it has to be.

I have been asked this question many times: if the Vice-President had been elected President in 1960, would you have been his press secretary? The answer is no. I think Pierre would agree with me that you can only work for one President in your lifetime. The associations that you have with that President are so close that I am sure I could not work for anyone else in that job.

Turning to the questions: the first topic is the relationship to the President in matters of news policy.

Here again I would like to set the record straight in the question of news policy. In any policy, whether it is news of foreign affairs or domestic affairs—anything—the President of the United States sets that policy and no one else. He is the boss, any President is. Certainly, he has his staff, he has his Cabinet, on the military side he has the Secretary

190

of Defense and the Joint Chiefs, but they do not set the policy on anything. It is the President and only the President. They act as advisers, consultants if you want; they present ideas to be talked over, but it is the President who finally determines everything. Then his staff, his advisers, and the Cabinet follow through.

Now, of course, as far as news policy is concerned, President Eisenhower (and I can speak only for my own job and my own experience—I would not presume to speak for President Kennedy or Mr. Salinger) asked my advice in this field. That is what he had me there for. He trusted the press secretary and he would ask for advice on matters dealing with news policy. You are there as press secretary to serve as an adviser, your are a friend, you are sometimes even the President's alter ego. You are certainly a buffer, and if needed you are the fall guy. It is as simple as that. We all make mistakes in this job, and again, if mistakes are made, it is your responsibility, not the President's.

I have alluded to the fact that you cannot work for a President in this position unless you have complete devotion to the man you are working with. You are on call all the time and you have a great many matters, complex matters, which you have to deal with in relation to the President and his formation of news policies. The timing, for instance, of the various announcements from the White House normally is left at least to your advice and discussion with the President.

Domestic problems, domestic stories, are rather easy to handle, but the overseas announcements take a great deal of the press secretary's time. Let me give you a little example of what I had to do and what I know Mr. Salinger has to do. Suppose you have a joint announcement involving the government of India and the government of the United States concerning a visit, as at the present time, of Prime Minister Pandit J. Nehru to this country. You would think that it is a simple thing to issue a statement from the White House on behalf of the President and the Prime Minister. But the press secretary, working with his opposite number from the government of India, has to discuss with the government of India the time of their publications in India. Prime radio time must be given important consideration as well as the time their papers go to press. You then have to try, with the time differential against you most of the time, to work out a suitable release time which will be fair to the news media of both of the countries. This is fairly simple when you are dealing with only two countries, but many times you have three or four governments that must be consulted. You have three or four nations operating on differing times, and the apparently simple problem of working out a time for an announcement from Washington that coincides with times acceptable to the news media in those other countries becomes more of a struggle than it should.

The press secretary also (at least this was true for me and I have more than a passing hunch this is true for Pierre) is asked for judgments in his field by members of the entire apparatus of government—not just the executive branch. At times, in working out arrangements or announcements abroad, he is asked to make important judgments by representatives of the foreign governments.

News policies for the eight years that I was operating under the directions of President Eisenhower were very simple. If a development did not deal with the security of the United States or with intelligence endeavors of the United States, it should be released. Now that sounds very easy to say, but I found that many times it is your own people within your own government in your own administration that put you in a difficult spot. Unfortunately, in a government the size of ours, there are many departments that are what I call stamp-happy. They mark everything "Top Secret." It does not make any difference what it is, the fellow down the line puts a "Top Secret" on it, and it comes all the way up. I have even received from a department a release that I was going to put out the minute I got it, stamped "Top Secret." This does get the press secretary in trouble at times.

So, again summing up the relation of the press secretary and the President's news policy, he acts as the President's spokesman. He acts only under the direction of the President. The worst thing he can do is to volunteer information to the news media unless he is sure he knows what he is talking about, and unless it reflects the attitude of the President. I do not know what Pierre has now, but I had a little card that I used to hand out to members of the White House staff and other members of the administration that I thought was a pretty good one. It was a saying by Calvin Coolidge: "I never remember getting in trouble for something I never said." This a fine thing for a press secretary always to remember. Unless he knows the answer, he can just say, "I don't know the answer, but I will find out." Then he checks with his boss; the President tells him the answer, and he in turn gives it to the news media.

The second topic deals with the contacts between the President and the news media.

The press secretary is about every sort of a man that you can think of as far as the news media are concerned. By the nature of his job, he is the principal source of White House information. He is the enemy and the friend of every working newsman in Washington—and they remind him of that at least five or six times a day. He is on call all the time—

even when he is not in his office and is enjoying an evening out with friends, it is quite possible that out of the woodwork will come some working newsman to ask questions that deal with the administration. It is also possible that on any given night between the hours of eleven o'clock at night and seven o'clock in the morning you will get many phone calls. I kept fairly good track of them in the eight years I was there, and I averaged six telephone calls a night for eight years, Saturday and Sunday included.

Why is the press secretary subjected to these demands? This is part of his job. With the rapid movement of communications and with the wire services—both our American AP and UPI, Reuters, Agence France-Presse, and even with Tass—if anything happens any place in the world, or in your own country, the first word the government might get is a telephone call from a wire service man late at night. So you have to encourage this. But nevertheless, this is part of the job of a press secretary, to be on call at all times.

On the trips of the President here in this country and overseas, you are a schedule-maker. You have the general feeling that you are moving a Barnum and Bailey circus every time the President moves. Remember, the President just does not move alone! In addition to the newsmen, and they can range from one hundred to two hundred or three hundred, you move with Secret Service men and with your Signal Corps detachment of the White House, because the President of the United States, regardless of where is is, can never be out of touch with his home base. I should say a moderate trip with President Eisenhower had an average of two hundred and fifty people altogether. And the press secretary is the poor guy who has to make the arrangements for moving them. He has to be a mother hen.

I have a great deal of admiration and respect for my colleagues in the news business, but they can be the most frustrating and annoying people on these trips. They are all prima donnas. They all want single rooms when only double rooms exist. They may not like the color of their room-mate's hair; they want somebody else in there. On planes they always want a window seat, usually alone. The television industry always insists that the press secretary is responsible for the shipment of tape or film, and if it disappears in their home offices, they say, "It isn't our fault; that press secretary gave us the wrong information. We put it on the wrong plane and it's his fault." If any mishaps occur, it is the press secretary's fault. I was in Europe when President Kennedy was there, and the press plane was leaving Vienna on a nice new runway of which the Viennese were very proud. The engines started up, the plane moved about three feet, and then one of the wheels went through the pavement and we were stuck there. It was the press secretary's fault. Absolutely, it was Pierre's fault. These newsmen were not kidding—he was responsible.

On a more serious note, the press secretary, because of his association with the President, who is at the end of the run of all the far-flung worldwide operations of our government, each day also gets an education in the affairs of the world. And it is not too long before he looks at the world like a President of the United States has to look at it. He does not take the more narrow or parochial view of the world, or even of our country. He is consequently amazed at the narrowness, sometimes, of the questions that are presented to him, or at questions that deal with fragments of the problems around the world. He tries his best, in answering the questions, to pass his education on these problems along to the newsmen, and most of the time he succeeds.

Salinger brought up the question of press conferences, and I would like to say two or three things about them. I have very strong feelings about a presidential press conference. I had them before I went into the government, and I have them now that I have been out of government. First, the press conferences by the President of the United States are the press conferences of the President of the United States, and no one else. There are times, particularly in times of tension and even danger, when the President of the United States cannot have a press conference because of very delicate negotiations that are going on overseas, and it would be harmful to the United States if he did have a press conference. Even if he said "No" or "No Comment" to the questions, the very fact that the questions were being asked of the President would in itself make a world story. But the press conferences themselves are more than just hearing the President of the United States. I have always felt that they serve as a two-way street between the President and the newsmen asking the questions, because the President, by the very nature of the questions that he gets from newsmen around our country and around the world, gets an idea of the general questions that are worrying them and their papers. And the newspapers reflect the worries and concerns of their readers in various sections of our country or throughout the world.

Each medium has advantages over the others. They all contribute to the general fund of information that makes news. Because news personnel in this country are the best trained in the world, they make us the best informed nation in the world. In addition to that, the President has dinners at which he has people from all over the country. He has bull sessions with reporters, usually when he is outside of Washington with a smaller press contingent, rather than having to pick and choose from the 1,200 men accredited to the White House. The danger, however, and it always does exist, is that the President in these private sessions may be quoted incorrectly by accident, or sometimes deliberately, and a wrong impression is given of the conversation that he had. These, then, are some of the problems that the press secretary has with the news media in Washington.

The last question with which I am concerned is the administration's philosophy on public information as a factor of presidential leadership.

I certainly want to discuss this, maybe from a little different angle than Salinger did. I do not know what is meant by "leadership." It is used very, very loosely. It makes good headlines. But what do we mean by leadership? Does leadership mean tearing your hair out and beating your breast, as some would have the President do? Is this leadership? Or is the leadership by a President a more quiet sort of leadership? Is it the constant pressure that the President, and only the President, can keep on any problem, either domestic or foreign? I personally think it is the latter.

As Pierre says, questions now are raised in Washington implying that the President is not communicating enough, is not giving enough leadership. I heard this nonsense for eight years. The words and music do not change at all. A President of the United States is the judge of this. He is the recipient of more information than any other person in our country and I think you have to leave the judgment to the President of the United States and not to the columnists or anyone else.

Now, of course, public information is a factor in informing our people, getting the people of our country to advance their collective thinking along certain lines. I do not think there is any trouble with this in domestic affairs, despite partisans of either the right or the left. I think the nation as a whole usually arrives at the intelligent solutions of any problems in the long run.

But it is the foreign side that again raises the question. President Eisenhower, I would say, spent at least 75 per cent of each day, not on domestic problems, but on foreign problems and their ramifications. Napoleon once said, when asked to what he owed his successes, "It was simple, I was fighting allies." Just think that over. We deal with allies. The United States is in military alliance with certain nations; it is in diplomatic alliance with others. You have the whole question of the free world, the neutral world, and the Communist world. And the President has to make his decisions, not on snap judgments, but on what is best for the United States and what the reaction will be in the free world, the Communist world, and the neutral world.

This is what takes time—to get a public position. And on something I know nothing about, so I can talk about it freely—the Berlin situation at the present time—I am sure that to get a united allied position on this situation is taking President Kennedy hours and hours and days and days, so that when we act with our allies we can act as a unit and not permit the Communist world to split us asunder on any public differences we might have.

There is need for public understanding, more public understanding, and each day the news media of the United States present more information than is obtainable by any other peoples in any country of the world. But the tragedy is that more than half of it goes begging each day, because the American people are disinclined to learn about it. Now these may be strong statements. But I do not think it is any secret that every newspaper survey that I have ever known about contends that the comic, the sport, and the society pages have more reader interest than the front page. And I have certainly seen in my new business that any time we put on news or documentaries we run a bad second or third to cops and robbers, private eyes, and all the rest. My question is why? I think it has something to do with the individuals in our country.

Two things more on public information as a factor of presidential leadership. Let me tell you a political story of mine. I had a friend a long long time ago whose name was Paul. He was talked into running for assemblyman in Brooklyn in New York City. This was rather too bad for Paul because, first he was a Republican, and secondly, the district was overwhelmingly Democratic and the incumbent had been re-elected for five times. But nevertheless Paul went into the fray with a gallant heart, and he went up and down the district. He spoke at street corners, at Bar Mitzvahs, at Irish wakes, at Protestant picnics—any place—any place he could talk to more than one person at a time. And he assailed his opponent, let's call him Joe. He assailed his record, he assailed his motives —everything. He thought he was doing pretty well, and I must admit, at the time so did I. The Sunday before election he met an old friend who was an experienced and wise district leader from another borough. The district leader said, "Paul, how're you doing?" and Paul said, "I'm doing fine. I'm going up and down the district, I'm raising the devil with Joe; I'm attacking him all the time." The district leader sort of smiled sadly and shook his head, and then he floored Paul with this $64 question. He said, "Paul, you say you're talking about Joe. I'm sure Joe is talking about Joe. Who's talking about Paul?" Well, his stunned silence to that question was equalled only by his stunned shock two days later when Joe clobbered him by about four to one in the voting.

Let us bring this story up to date and let us put in the United States and the free world in place of Paul, and the Soviet Union and the Communist world in place of Joe and let us ask the question. The United States and the free world are talking about the Soviet Union and the Communist world; and the Soviet Union and the Communist world are talking about the Soviet Union and the Communist world; but who is talking about the United States and the free world? I do not think enough of us are, and that includes all of the news media, my own to boot. There is too much feeling in this country among too many people that the United States is wrong until proven right. It is about time we started to say the United States is right until proven wrong.

We also are dramatizing and talking too much about the minus side of the whole world-wide picture, and we are not giving enough to the credit side. We have a lot of credits on our side. I think the Presidents of the United States—any one that I have known, certainly President Eisenhower, and I am sure President Kennedy—would agree with what I am going to say. Altogether too often in this country we pay too much attention to crises, to threats, to bluffs manufactured in Moscow and Peiping instead of the problems they are having on the other side—instead of the credits on our side. If we would all get together and talk and think about that more, under the leadership of the President, we would be much better off.

Magazine and

Newspaper Journalism:

A Comparison

Since I assume that many of you are either writers or editors or are in the process of becoming one or the other, this will be, I hope, less a formal talk than a family conversation.*

Like almost everyone I know in the magazine business, I came to it by way of a newspaper office. I made the move for pretty standard reasons—two of them.

The first was strictly cash. Shortly after I was married I was working for the Associated Press in Washington in one of the better jobs in that bureau. I was in charge of the AP staff covering the Senate, and I was relatively well paid as newspaper salaries went in those days. But my wife and I soon discovered that if we hoped to raise a family we would have to produce children that were not in the habit of eating. I had been trying for some time to supplement a newspaper salary by occasional magazine writing. After time out for World War II, I embarked on the rather precarious, constantly exciting career of free-lance writer and finally ended up as a full-time staff member of a magazine.

The other reason for the change, I think, is quite common, and I believe relevant to my subject. I left newspaper work because I was increasingly dissatisfied with the kind of reporting I was doing. I found

---

* This lecture was delivered October 11, 1962.

198

I had to work too fast under certain limitations which made it impossible for me to do the best kind of reporting. I was preparing about five thousand words of copy a day, and I filed most of it by telephone. If I got to think about a story at all, it was in the few steps running from a Senate hearing room to the phone booth. It was much more important then (and I assume it is today) for an Associated Press reporter to get his copy on the wire ahead of the United Press than it was for him to file a thoroughly reflective piece.

I also felt myself increasingly hampered by the conventions of objectivity that were standard then—and still are to a large extent—with all newspaper organizations, especially with the press associations. I was constantly reporting what somebody said, even if I knew that it was untrue, misleading or self-serving. There was no way within the canons of press association work that I could indicate that a senator or witness before a Senate committee was telling a damn lie.

I felt, too, that I was not learning as much as I wanted. I worked under one of the best wire service bureau chiefs that I know of, Byron Price, who later became director of the office of censorship. He was a great teacher, among his other talents; but the circumstances of my work made it increasingly difficult for me to dig into the complex issues in Washington that interested me intensely. I seldom had time to get much below the press release or the official statement.

I began to find that I was writing the same story year after year, or a story very similar to it: the opening of Congress, the introduction of a given bill, some one or another of the political ceremonials which become pretty repetitious after a few years. I began to look around for newspaper jobs that I thought would be more satisfactory—would give me time to write more careful, more interpretive copy. I found that most of the openings then available were not much better than the Associated Press, either in money or in scope for writing.

In retrospect, it was very fortunate that a number of coincidences made it possible for me to go to work for *Harper's Magazine*. While I was free-lancing, and indeed years before while I was still in college, I had done some writing for *Harper's* because it was the kind of magazine that interested me most. It was concerned with public affairs and with the kind of interpretive writing that I wanted to do. But it was sheer luck that *Harper's* needed a Washington man at about the time that I decided to leave press association work.

I have found in the magazine business many of the things that I had hoped I would find: more time, more space, more freedom to evaluate the events I was looking at—and a little more pay, although not a great deal. I would not want to lead anyone to think that the magazine world is enormously more lucrative than the newspaper world.

I also found some things that I had not expected. First, that the magazine field is much more competitive than the newspaper field, except in the narrow competitive sense of Associated Press versus United Press. In most large American cities now there is a one-newspaper–ownership pattern. Every magazine, on the other hand, is competing not only with two thousand other magazines but with newspapers, radio, and television and with all other kinds of demands upon a reader's time. Magazine writers have to think much more about the competitive aspects of their work than an average newspaper reporter does.

I have found that it is much more difficult to get out a reasonably satisfactory issue of a magazine than it is a reasonably satisfactory issue of a newspaper. The formula works pretty much the same, day after day, in putting out a newspaper. You know what sources to use and what places to go look for news; you send one man to the city hall, and another one to the courthouse, and another to the legislature, and another to check the hospitals. You expect to have the same kinds of news available on a regular repetitive basis. For any magazine except the news magazines, and even to some extent for them, any such repetitive formula would be fatal. One thing that is most dangerous to any magazine is to permit a feeling to grow up among its readers that "I know pretty well what's going to be in next week's issue; it will be the same mixture as before. I can skip it this week and turn on the television set or buy some other magazine." Providing an element of *surprise* is essential for anyone who is working in this field as either editor or writer.

On most of the papers that I have worked on we had a certain sense of satisfaction when the final edition of the day came out and we could have a last cup of coffee and look over the result of the day's work. Usually we thought it was pretty good. I have never seen a single issue of *Harper's* for which I felt the same satisfaction. Every one has been in a sense disappointing, falling far below what we had hoped for it and bringing a sort of feeling of frustration—plus a hope that next month somehow could be a little better. This was one aspect of the work that I had not anticipated.

Among the reasons for these differences, which I had not fully detected until I entered magazine work full time, is that the nature of magazine journalism is quite different from that of newspaper journalism. Magazine journalism is only in part reporting the news. In part it also is recording and analyzing history as it is being made. I think this is true of all magazines, not only the news magazines such as *Time* and *News-*

week but the specialized magazines such as *Scientific American.* Even *Vogue* or *Mademoiselle* is in a sense both recording the news and recording the history of an aspect of American life; such magazines will be useful historic sources seventy-five years from now to someone who wants to know how American women lived in the 1960's. I hope that *Harper's* will be of use to a historian looking back and trying to understand what was happening in broader aspects of American life at this particular period.

Magazine journalism also is different because no magazine can attempt to give complete coverage in the sense that the better newspapers attempt to give complete coverage of a geographic or subject-matter area. The magazine has to be much more selective; its editors have to make many more decisions about what subjects are really significant, and which ones will have some lasting significance in the years ahead. And the magazine man has to try to bring to these selected events or situations more reflection, more expert advice, and, hopefully, more mature judgment than the newspaper reporter normally does in covering a story.

There is another function that some magazines try to assume: to cover the kind of things that newspapers miss. Most newspapers are very good at covering events that happen at 3:00 Thursday afternoon. But something that happens slowly and imperceptibly over a period of weeks or years is likely not to be reported at all, or, if it is reported, to come out in dribbles in such a piecemeal fashion that the reader really does not grasp the whole of it.

A case in point is a story that broke recently in Nashville, Tennessee. I was first aware of it when I saw a two-paragraph story on page 17 of the New York *Times,* saying that John L. Lewis and Cyrus Eaton had just been convicted in the federal district court in Nashville of conspiracy to violate the antitrust laws. I was at first sure there must be a misprint here, and I read the story over again wondering what on earth Cyrus Eaton and John L. Lewis could be conspiring about—the archlabor leader and the archcapitalist, the archfoe of Communism in the unions and the close friend of Khrushchev. I did not quite understand what they had in common, and the *Times* did not tell me. And there was nothing in the *Times* the next day. So finally I wrote the editor of the Nashville *Tennesseean* to ask for some clippings from his paper on the story and to ask who the reporters were who were covering it.

I found that two men named Nathan G. Caldwell and Gene S. Graham had been digging for more than two years on this story. It had been reported in driblets over this two-year period, but even in the *Tennesseean* there was no one wrapped-up piece that could tell you what had happened—why John L. Lewis had conspired with Cyrus Eaton to put a large part of the membership of his own union out of work and to put the treasury of the union into the ownership of coal mines. This seemed to us a significant story, ramifying through economics, politics, sociology, and the world of labor, so we asked Caldwell and Graham to do a piece for us. They had never written a magazine piece and it took quite some time to get one that was satisfactory, but we were pleased with the eventual result. I am glad to say that eventually the two authors won a Pulitzer prize (1962)—not for the piece they did for us, but for the body of the work they did on this story.

I am still mystified why this was not reported in the national press or in any of the news magazines until after it was reported in *Harper's*. It is an instance of the kind of thing that magazines ought to do from time to time simply because there are certain categories of news that newspapers miss.

The kind of function I have been describing obviously demands, or should demand, a good deal higher quality of writing than you are likely to find in the average newspaper story, simply because the magazine writer *is* free to devote more time and thought and judgment to his task and to seek more advice.

Here, however, is where we come across our greatest frustration of all. It is astonishingly hard to find good writers, and getting harder all the time. For one thing, the newspapers are not producing good writers in the numbers that they used to. For many years, particularly up until the 1920's, the newspapers in the country were the natural incubators for novelists, poets, playwrights, magazine writers, men of letters of all sorts: all the way from Mark Twain and Lafcadio Hearn up to George Ade and Heywood Broun and hundreds of others one could name. One reason for this was that most newspapers in those days were dominated by editors —the editor usually owned the newspaper. The editorial side ran both business and editorial operation. People like Henry Watterson, for example, or the Bowles family in Connecticut, were first of all editors and writers and only secondarily businessmen.

This is still true in some places; I think Minneapolis and Des Moines are very fortunate in having newspapers run by a family which thinks of itself primarily as an editorial family. But in the great majority of cities, newspapers are now run by businessmen who think first of all of the return they are going to get from this investment, who would not know good writing if they saw it, and who could not care less whether good writing appears in their papers. Consequently there is no pressure on reporters or editors to produce the best writing that they are capable of.

There is no reward for a well-turned sentence, no punishment for a pedestrian story. It is very likely that no executive on those papers will ever notice either.

I worked at one time, just after I got out of college, on a daily paper in Oklahoma under an editor who had been trained by the great Oliver K. Bovard of the St. Louis *Post-Dispatch*—one of the great editors of the last century. My editor marked up every story that appeared in the paper with a red pencil and called it to the attention of the copy editors and the reporter, and sometimes put it on the bulletin board to call it to everybody's attention. If you did something particularly bad or particularly good you heard about it immediately. You knew that his eye was on every line you wrote and that good writing was appreciated, bad writing punished. I do not know of any such editor operating in that state today; it certainly is not true on that same paper since Walter Harrison, the man I speak of, is gone.

Another factor is that our school systems no longer teach people to write. In my father's day, anybody who got out of grade school was presumed to know how to read and write and even to spell, and often he could write quite well. By my time there already had been a considerable slippage in standards. Now, I do not think I need to tell you, it is quite possible to get through high school without being able to write a line of coherent English. Indeed, it is quite possible to get through *college* without being able to write coherent English. The Columbia University Law School recently started a course in basic English because it found that people who had gone through four years of college could not draft an intelligible page of legal prose. It no longer is a prerequisite, apparently, for a B.A. degree or a graduate degree that people should be able to write with reasonable competence.

There are good reasons for this, the predominant one being that we are not willing to pay for it. People can learn to write in school only by considerable practice, which means doing papers two or three times a week and having them not only graded but marked up and criticized, one by one, by a persistent and demanding teacher. With the masses of children going through school today, no school system that I know of can afford English teachers who will do that sort of thing. Many teachers handle 115 to 120 students, whereas in my grandfather's or even my father's day, a one-room school house maybe had a dozen children. The teacher was a poor teacher, by today's standards; but she did teach children to read and write and did have time to give individual attention to each one.

Since we no longer are able to recruit as many writers from the newspaper field as we used to, we turn more and more to other fields, particularly to the colleges. In theory you should find in a good university experts in almost any field of human knowledge and, since these are learned men, they ought to be able to write as well. Alas, this is rarely true. Most college instructors, we find, write a form of "pedagese" or—as Dwight MacDonald has called it—academic Mandarin, either because they are not able to write any better or because they are afraid to.

One of the best science writers I know of is a man named Loren Eiseley who is now head of the Anthropology Department at the University of Pennsylvania. He told me that he wrote in secret, almost as a vice, for nearly fifteen years before he became head of the department. In commenting on the reason for this he said, "If I had let any of my colleagues know that I wrote for a general audience, or what they called a popular audience, it would have ruined me academically, and I would never have gotten ahead in my chosen profession." He went on to say that there is a common assumption that any man who makes himself intelligible to laymen cannot be a scholar; that if he writes a best-seller he must by definition be doing shoddy work or has sold out to the "interests" in one way or another. He will, in effect, have his academic buttons cut off and be drummed out of the ranks. But once Eiseley got to be head of his department and no longer feared this kind of sanction, he burst into print in a great many directions at once, to the glory, I think, of American letters and scholarship.

As a consequence of this, magazines are engaged in a constant effort to recruit and train their own writers, gathering them from any source they can. It is often a tedious, painful, and expensive process. If you find any normally intelligent human being who is really enthusiastic and eager to learn, he can usually learn to write with fair competence—just as he could learn plumbing or cabinetmaking or electronic engineering. I do feel a little aggrieved sometimes that we have to start this process at such a late stage in life. I wish that they would learn writing in school just as they learn the cabinetmaking and plumbing and electronic engineering. But I know this is utopian.

One of our great efforts is to dispel the myth that it is impossible to get an editor to read your manuscript unless you know his aunt or the banker who holds a mortgage on the printing press. We spend our lives begging people to let us read their manuscripts. I was long puzzled because we are seldom able to convince authors, particularly novelists, that a rejected novel actually has been read by a responsible editor in the publishing house. Writers are always sure that it has been glanced at by the office boy—or perhaps even returned unopened. Three or four times a year we get manuscripts in which pages are stuck together so that the author can see whether we really looked at those pages.

I have finally decided that this is a necessary syndrome and that it is an unkindness to try to convince people that their work is, in fact, read. A writer puts in, say, two years of his life producing a book manuscript —the loneliest, hardest kind of effort. If he cannot then find a publisher, he has to believe either one of two things: first, that the manuscript has never been looked at, or, second, that it is no good and that he has wasted two years of his life—that his brilliant idea is really not so brilliant after all. To many people this latter conclusion is simply intolerable; and I think it is probably a wicked thing to try to destroy their illusions.

On the other hand, there is a great deal of compensation in this search for new writers. In a sense, it makes life a perpetual treasure hunt, to be constantly sifting through manuscripts, talking to acquaintances, people that you meet on trains and planes, in hope that tomorrow maybe you will hit upon the germinal mind of an intellectual pioneer on the growing edge of American society—a person who is producing or about to produce the ideas which will in some degree change the course of history or the development of American culture. It is an exciting business. This more than makes up for the frustrations and drawbacks and rather modest financial recompense. For me, it has made magazine work the most consistently exciting and absorbing work I have ever done.

Notes

INTRODUCTION

1 "Social Control in the Newsroom: A Functional Analysis," *Social Forces*, XXXIII, No. 4 (May, 1955), 327.

2 "The Status of the Newspaper Press," lecture delivered at the Ohio University, Athens, Ohio, 1949.

3 "The Mass Media in a Free Society," Department of Journalism, New York University, 18 pages. The lecture was given at Montana State University, April 26, 1956, under auspices of the Don R. Mellet Memorial Fund. Dr. Siebert is director of the Division of Mass Communications, Michigan State University.

4 For an authoritative recent discussion of the social responsibility of the press, see the excellent treatise on the subject by Dean Theodore Peterson, College of Journalism and Communications, University of Illinois, entitled, *Four Theories of the Press* (Urbana, Ill., 1956), 77–103. See also Wilbur Schramm, *Responsibility in Mass Communication* (New York, 1957).

5 "Organized Self-Control of the Press; The American View of Codes," *Problems of Journalism* (Proceedings of the American Society of Newspaper Editors [Washington, D.C., 1958]), 73–79.

6 Kenneth MacDonald as quoted in *Problems of Journalism* (Proceedings of the American Society of Newspaper Editors [Washington, D.C., 1956]), 209.

MARQUIS CHILDS

1 Brooks Adams, *America's Economic Supremacy* (New York, 1900).
2 Robinson Jeffers, "Shine Perishing Republic," *The Selected Poems of Robinson Jeffers* (New York, 1927), 168.
3 Temporary National Economic Committee, *Monographs* (43 vols.; Washington, D.C., 1940–41).
4 On March 12, 1947, before a joint session of Congress, President Harry Truman requested $400,000,000 be sent to Greece and Turkey for the period ending on June 30, 1948. This aid, he stated, was necessary to maintain and strengthen democracy and to cope with the Russian threat in these areas, as well as to preserve order in the Middle East. The bill resulting from the President's request was passed by Congress and signed by the President on May 22, 1947.

THOMAS L. STOKES, JR.

1 The committee in 1947 investigated alleged Communist infiltration of the Hollywood movie industry; they accused stars and writers of membership in Communist organizations. The writers challenged the committee's questioning as an invasion of civil rights and as a result were cited for contempt. The public was concerned over the abuse of civil liberties and the invasion of freedom of speech.
2 The committee headed by Representative J. Parnell Thomas investigated Dr. Condon in March, 1948. He was accused of being one of the "weakest links" in atomic security and of appointing himself head of the atomic-physics section of the Bureau of Standards. The committee disregarded favorable testimony from the FBI reports in their investigation. Dr. Condon played a leading role in the development of the atom bomb and was cleared at that time for top-secret work.
3 David Lilienthal was appointed chairman of the Atomic Energy Commission by President Truman. His appointment was approved by the Senate (50–31) in April, 1947, after a Senate battle opposing him led by Senator Kenneth McKellar of Tennessee whose deprivation of patronage in TVA had made him Lilienthal's foe. Lilienthal was former head of TVA.
4 The Mundt-Nixon bill to curb Communist party activities was one of the most controversial bills to come before Congress. It was assailed as to its constitutionality and effectiveness. Overwhelmingly approved in the House, it was left locked in a Senate committee.
5 The executive order of March 21, 1947, provided for a Federal Employees Loyalty Program designed to prevent employment by the federal government of persons not loyal to the United States. It also established a Loyalty Review Board within the Civil Service Commission to provide regulations and general procedural instruction for the program as a whole, to furnish advisory recommendations in loyalty cases, to act on appeals, and to provide coordination and standards to assure compliance with the order.

6 This bill called for investigation by the FBI of appointees of the Atomic Energy Commission. The bill was vetoed by President Truman and the veto was sustained by Congress.
7 This bill was vetoed by President Truman, but the veto was overridden by Congress.
8 Senator Ball's increased minimum-wage law failed to pass Congress.
9 The Congress enacted a much weaker bill than that initiated by Taft, Ellender, and Wagner. They failed to enact the provision for low-cost housing in volume.
10 See Chapter I, note 4.

JAMES B. RESTON

1 See Chapter I, note 4.
2 Climaxing a long disagreement between the U.S.S.R. and the Western powers, the Soviets imposed a blockade on Berlin beginning on June 24, 1948. Two days later on June 26, the United States and Great Britain began airlifting supplies into the Western-held sector of the city. The airlift continued until September 30, 1949, even though the blockade officially was removed at midnight May 11, 1949.
3 This was announced in an address delivered at Harvard University on June 5, 1947.
4 The President and Senator Taft were in a continual conflict over domestic affairs, Senator Taft being the Republican leader in matters of domestic affairs. Hungary was a victim of the "cold war" battle. Moscow forced out of office there the anti-Soviet and pro-American politicians in reaction against the Truman Doctrine (see note 5 below). On June 5, 1947, Truman declared that the Communist seizure of power in Hungary was a "terrible outrage" and the United States would not stand for it.
5 On March 12, 1947, President Truman addressed a joint session of Congress to present a new foreign policy aimed at curtailing the spread of Communism and providing economic aid for nations striving to maintain freedom. The Greek-Turkish aid program was the first expression of the policy; see Chapter I, note 4.

REINHOLD NIEBUHR

1 Senator Gerald P. Nye was chairman of the Senate Munitions Investigation Committee. This committee investigated the munitions industry, wartime profits, and neutrality in 1934–36 and was most concerned with those individuals who profited from war, especially the munitions makers who constituted a great threat to peace in the interwar period.

ELMER DAVIS

1 Robert Waitham, *The Day Before Tomorrow* (New York, 1951).

ALAN BARTH

1 Robert V. Brown, "Ike Press Support 67 Per Cent; Stevenson Backed by 14 Per Cent," *Editor and Publisher,* LXXXVII (Nov. 1, 1952), 9–10.

ERIC SEVAREID

1 The reference is to Charles E. Wilson.
2 The reference is to John Foster Dulles and his predecessor Dean Acheson.
3 The reference is to Herbert Brownell.
4 The reference is to the papers published by Colonel Robert R. McCormick, notably the *Chicago Tribune.*
5 McCarthy attempted to block Bohlen's confirmation as Ambassador to Russia. McCarthy's primary purpose was to establish a beachhead for a broader attack on the administration's foreign policy.
6 Whittaker Chambers, an editor for *Time,* accused Alger Hiss of having been a dues-paying Communist and a valuable source of information for the Communist party during his employ in the State Department. Hiss sued Chambers for libel, and in the pre-trial examination Chambers drew forth documents allegedly stolen from the State Department. He later led agents of the investigating commission to his Maryland farm and there from a scooped-out pumpkin produced rolls of microfilm of state papers he had had for ten years. He accused Hiss of procurement of the papers for transmission to the Soviet Union.
7 The United States withdrew the American military mission to China in January, 1949. This was an indication of the doubt expressed by the United States government in the ability of the Nationalist government to master the situation on the China mainland. It was the official opinion that there was too much reliance on the United States by the Chinese Nationalists to win their war against the Communists. The complete story of America's official change in support was presented in the White Papers which were released August 5, 1949, and entitled *United States Relations with China; with Special Reference to the Period 1944–49*. This discussed in detail the Department of State's reports on the United States' relations with China, specifically mentioning that the Nationalist government had failed to use our aid efficiently.
8 Ray Bradbury, *Fahrenheit 451* (New York, 1953).
9 Bradbury, *Fahrenheit 451,* pp. 49–53.

GEORGE V. FERGUSON

1 Senator Joseph R. McCarthy in March, 1950, contended publicly that the State Department employed or had employed Communists or Communist sympathizers who had official status in the Department. One of those attacked was Owen Lattimore, Professor at Johns Hopkins University, who was consulted on Far East policy. Professor Lattimore was investigated by the Senate Foreign Relations Committee on the basis of these charges. On July 17, 1950, the committee, by majority vote, found these charges to be false.
2 General Charles Gates Dawes was chairman of an international group of experts primarily concerned with the means of balancing the German budget and stabilizing the currency. They were to ascertain Germany's ability to pay its war debts. The committee's investigations and delibera-

tions began on January 14, 1924, and lasted for three months. On April 9, 1924, their official report was presented to the Reparations Commission; this report was popularly referred to as the Dawes plan.

3   A. Mitchell Palmer was Attorney General in President Wilson's Cabinet. In 1919–20 he led a vigorous campaign against the Communists and other groups for which he was severely criticized. A Congressional investigation of Palmer ensued with his being vindicated by a majority vote of the investigating committee.

4   James Bryce, Viscount, *The American Commonwealth* (2 vols.; New York, 1893–95).

HENRY S. COMMAGER

1   The Senate judiciary sub-committee on internal security headed by Senator William E. Jenner secured directly or indirectly as a result of this recommendation the dismissal of many professors and teachers who refused to answer to loyalty oaths stating whether they were or had been Communists or members of Communist front organizations.

2   Senator J. R. McCarthy was chairman of the Senate permanent committee on investigations. His label "Fifth Amendment Communists" resulted from the refusal, on the basis of the immunity guarantee of the Fifth Amendment, of some witnesses to testify before his committee.

3   Dr. Robert J. Oppenheimer was suspended as a consultant for the Atomic Energy Commission on December 22, 1953, for his personal associations with Communists. The AEC Personnel Security Board headed by Gordon Gray in a report dated May 24, 1954, cleared him of disloyalty but decided against reinstating him. On April 5, 1962, Dr. Oppenheimer was named as the winner of the AEC's $50,000 Enrico Fermi Award for his contributions to nuclear energy.

4   The House Committee on Un-American Activities headed by Representative Harold Velde charged, through testimony of witnesses, Bishop G. Bromley Oxnam of the Methodist Church with being a Communist. Bishop Oxnam testified before the committee for ten hours on July 21, 1954, at his own insistence. The Jenner Committee (see note 1) also heard testimony allegedly implicating clergymen as Communists.

5   Jerome Davis, *Behind Soviet Power* (West Haven, Conn., 1949).

6   The Reece Committee appointed in September, 1953, to investigate tax-exempt foundations, particularly scholarly foundations and societies, held its public hearings in May and June of 1954. These hearings were characterized by a carefully structured case and hand-picked witnesses who testified against the foundations. The one witness for the foundations was interrupted in the midst of his testimony and not allowed to finish; no others were permitted to testify in support of the foundations. The mass of innuendos, insinuations, allegations, misstatements, materials out of context, and guilt by association characterized the committee's hearings. For discussion of these hearings see Bernard DeVoto, "The Easy Chair," *Harper's Magazine*, CCX (April, 1955), 14–21.

7   *U.S.* vs. *Lamont,* 236 F.2d 312 (1956), affirmed the favorable ruling of the district court.

8   *U.S.* vs. *Rumley,* 345 U.S. 41, 73 S.Ct. 543 (1953).
9   Because Congress had refused to grant the TVA necessary funds to build
    a steam power plant to replace the power it was supplying a Tennes-
    see Atomic Energy Commission plant, President Eisenhower on June 16,
    1955, directed the AEC to negotiate a 25-year contract with two private
    utility groups—Middle South Utilities, Inc., headed by E. H. Dixon and
    Southern Company, headed by E. A. Yates—to replace the power being
    delivered by TVA. The contract was signed on November 11, 1955. The
    administration was sharply criticized for involving private companies in
    government-owned business.

HERBERT L. BLOCK

1   During a 1956 debate on a natural gas bill, Senator Francis H. Case
    made a speech implying that gas producers had attempted to buy his
    votes. This led President Eisenhower to veto the bill and the Senate to
    investigate "campaign contributions from gas lobbyists."

DORIS FLEESON

1   Hugh Redwald Trevor-Roper, *The Last Days of Hitler* (New York,
    1947).

GERALD W. JOHNSON

1   John Hersey, *Hiroshima* (New York, 1946).
2   "Tree of Knowledge," *Harper's Magazine,* CCXVII (Oct., 1958), 56.

LOUIS M. LYONS

1   This was the Commission on Freedom of the Press; the chairman was
    Robert M. Hutchins, chancellor of the University of Chicago. The com-
    mittee of thirteen was composed of educators, philosophers, lawyers,
    a poet and a banker. They spent three years investigating what should
    be done to improve the nation's press. The published report was en-
    titled *A Free and Responsible Press* (Chicago, 1947).
2   Arthur Edward Rouse, *Slanted News* (Boston, 1957).
3   Francis Williams, *Dangerous Estate* (New York, 1958).
4   Beginning on December 19, 1958, nine of New York's major daily news-
    papers were closed nineteen days by a strike of the Newspaper and Mail
    Deliverers Union (independent). This strike cost the industry approxi-
    mately fifty million dollars.

JOSEPH W. ALSOP, JR.

1   Bruno Richard Hauptmann was tried for the murder of the Lindbergh
    child. The trial opened in Flemington, New Jersey on January 2 and
    ended on February 13 with a verdict of guilty. The trial was marked by
    spectacular features—throngs of reporters and photographers. Haupt-

mann's appeals to the New Jersey Court of Errors and Appeals and to the Federal Supreme Court failed; he was executed on April 3, 1936.

2   The Fifteenth Session of the General Assembly opened on September 20. On September 23, and again on October 3, Premier Nikita Khrushchev demanded abolition of the post of Secretary-General and its replacement with a three-man executive. Dag Hammarskjöld refused to resign. This Soviet attack was precipitated by its disapproval of UN action in the Congo.

3   President Eisenhower's proposed trip of June 19–22 was cancelled at the request of the Japanese cabinet on June 16, because of their concern for his safety. This concern was a result of left-wing demonstrations which by the end of May opposed the government, the United States–Japanese Treaty of Mutual Co-operation and Security signed on January 19, and demanded cancellation of the Presidential visit. The active demonstrations by the group against Press Secretary James Hagerty on June 10 strongly influenced the cabinet's decision of June 16.

Lecturers

JOSEPH W. ALSOP, JR., has been an author and newspaperman since 1932. Besides writing a syndicated column in the New York *Herald Tribune*, he is a frequent contributor to *Saturday Evening Post, The Atlantic Monthly,* and *The New Yorker*. His most recent book is *The Reporter's Trade*.

ALAN BARTH has won wide recognition for his editorials in the Washington *Post,* including the American Newspaper Guild Award for distinguished editorial writing. His book, *The Loyalty of Free Men,* received the Sidney Hillman Award in 1952.

HERBERT L. BLOCK, editorial cartoonist for the Washington *Post* and *Times Herald,* has received many awards for his work. His citations include the Sidney Hillman Award and the Pulitzer Prize in 1942 and 1954. He has also published two books, *The Herblock Book* and *Herblock's Here and Now,* which have been quite successful.

MARQUIS CHILDS, one of the outstanding interpreters of the political, economic, and social climate of our time, is best known for his United Features Syndicate column originating from Washington and carried by many daily papers. He is also chief of the Washington bureau for the St. Louis *Post-Dispatch*. He has written many volumes, including *I Write From Washington; The Ragged Edge;* and *Eisenhower, Captive Hero*.

215

HENRY S. COMMAGER, professor of history and American studies at Amherst College, and member of the National Academy of Arts and Sciences has distinguished himself not only as a teacher but as a writer. He has written or edited many volumes since his first book was published in 1931; his latest publications are *Era of Reform* and *The Great Proclamation.* He is a frequent contributor to such general magazines as *The Atlantic Monthly, Harper's Magazine, The Nation,* and *The Reporter.*

ELMER DAVIS was a newspaperman, radio news analyst, and director of war information services for the government in wartime. For radio efforts he received the George Foster Peabody Award in 1940, 1947, and 1951. He served as news analyst for the American Broadcasting Company from 1945 until his death on May 18, 1958. He was author of several books including *But We Were Born Free* and *History of the New York Times, 1851–1921.*

GEORGE V. FERGUSON, editor of the Montreal *Star,* has pursued a journalistic career crossing national boundaries. He began his career with the London *Times,* then returned to Canada to serve as reporter, editorial writer, and managing editor for the Winnipeg *Free Press* before becoming editor-in-chief of the *Star.* He is author of *John W. Dafoe, a Memoir.*

JOHN FISCHER, editor and writer, has had a varied career ranging from reporter to economic intelligence work to his present positions of editor-in-chief of *Harper's Magazine* and vice-president of Harper and Row. He is also a frequent contributor to *The New Yorker* and has published several books, his latest being, *Master Plan U.S.A.*

DORIS FLEESON has been covering politics in the nation's capital for more than thirty years: her Washington column for United Features Syndicate appears in eighty newspapers. Her honors include winning the Raymond Clapper Award and on two occasions the New York Newspaperwoman's Club prize for distinguished reporting.

JAMES C. HAGERTY began his career as a newspaperman with the New York *Times.* He has always been active in political activities, serving as executive assistant to Governor Thomas E. Dewey before his appointment as press secretary to President Eisenhower. He is now vice-president in charge of news, special events, and public affairs for the American Broadcasting Company.

GERALD W. JOHNSON, presently a contributing editor of *The New Republic,* has been reporter, editorial writer, news commentator, and free-lance writer in his full and varied career as a journalist. His honors include the Sidney Hillman Award and the George Foster Peabody Award. He has published many books, including *Roosevelt, Dictator or Democrat? What Is News? An Honorable Titan,* and his most recent, *America Is Born.*

LOUIS M. LYONS, curator of the Nieman Foundation at Harvard University and editor of the *Nieman Reports,* has been concerned with the press in modern America for many years not only as an educator but as a newscaster. The George Foster Peabody Award is one of the many citations he has received for his analysis of the news.

REINHOLD NIEBUHR, professor emeritus of Christian ethics and philosophy of religion at Union Theological Seminary, has published books in such divergent fields as politics, economics, philosophy, and religion. A member of the Commission on Freedom of the Press, he now serves as editor of the biweekly *Christianity and Crisis.*

JAMES B. RESTON has won the Pulitzer Prize twice—1945 and 1957—for his outstanding national reporting; he is presently national correspondent at the Washington bureau of the New York *Times.* For his distinguished interpretation of international news, he won the Overseas Press Club Award. He has published several books, including *Prelude to Victory.*

PIERRE SALINGER, White House Press Secretary, is the youngest man ever to hold this position. He has had a varied career in journalism always being very active in political activities: he was California press officer for Adlai Stevenson's first campaign; worked as an investigator for the Senate Select Committee dealing with labor-management racketeering; and was John F. Kennedy's press officer during the 1960 campaign.

ERIC SEVAREID, chief Washington news correspondent for the Columbia Broadcasting Company and a syndicated columnist, has been a newspaper reporter and overseas correspondent as well as a radio news analyst. His news analysis for CBS won him the 1950 George Foster Peabody Award. He has also published several books including his autobiographical commentary, *Not So Wild a Dream,* and *Small Sounds in the Night.*

THOMAS L. STOKES, JR., who was an outstanding reporter, received the Pulitzer Prize in 1938. Highly esteemed by his Washington colleagues, his Washington column was carried by United Features Syndicate from 1944 until his death on May 14, 1958. He published several books, including *The Savannah.*